In Defense of
Christian Ritual

In Defense *of* Christian Ritual

THE CASE FOR A BIBLICAL PATTERN OF WORSHIP

DAVID R. ANDERSEN

In Defense of Christian Ritual

Published by:
1517 Publishing
PO Box 54032
Irvine, CA 92619-4032

Publisher's Cataloging-In-Publication Data
(Prepared by The Donohue Group, Inc.)

Names: Andersen, David, author.
Title: In defense of Christian ritual : the case for a biblical pattern of worship / by David Andersen.
Description: Irvine, CA : 1517 Publishing, [2021] | Includes bibliographical references.
Identifiers: ISBN 9781948969635 (hardcover) | ISBN 9781948969642 (paperback) | ISBN 9781948969659 (ebook)
Subjects: LCSH: Christianity—Rituals. | Worship—Biblical teaching. | Worship—Social aspects. | God—Worship and love—Biblical teaching. | Television in religion.
Classification: LCC BV176.3 .A54 2021 (print) | LCC BV176.3 (ebook) | DDC 264—dc23

Printed in the United States of America

Cover art by Brenton Clarke Little

To my beloved wife, Jeana,
who has been the inspiration of all that is best in me—
without whose constant wisdom and encouragement,
not to mention saintly patience,
this book would never have been written.

Contents

Contents

Introduction

Shortly after midnight on Sunday, April 12, 1812 William Cartwright's dog barked following several gunshots that were fired from seemingly every direction.[1] Soon after, men came through the night and beat Cartwright's watchers to the ground, breaking the windows of his mill and pounding the door with sledgehammers. In the mayhem he and his men were able to counterattack, and 20 minutes and 140 shots later the attackers retreated, carrying their wounded but unable to retrieve two men dying in the yard. The attackers called themselves "Luddites," and were English weavers who destroyed automatic looms to protect their jobs during the late eighteenth and early nineteenth centuries. They had launched several other attacks throughout northern England, but Cartwright was the first to defeat them. While in reality they weren't fighting innovation itself, they've become icons of resistance to new technology and an entrenched fear of change.

In arguing for ancient Christian ritual, this book isn't a Luddite resistance to change. The farthest thing from it, it may be relevant to note—lest my argument be dismissed as driven by an anti-technology/change bias—that I run a software firm which makes use of the latest advances, including artificial intelligence (AI) technologies. This work isn't about resisting worship innovations simply because they're new or because they're different than past traditions. Conversely, it's also not suggesting that because something is old it's therefore true. As the third century bishop of Carthage, Cyprian, once said, "custom without

---

[1] Kevin Ashton, *How To Fly A Horse* (New York 2015), 87, 140–141.

truth is but old error."[2] Age by itself is no more an argument than the contention that we need to keep our worship current with the times. Neither will we wade into the decade-old controversy about "worship style" which has become so prevalent, about whether we should use organs or praise bands. While amusing, these are merely symptoms of a more central question; namely, is there a detectable pattern of worship in scripture itself that Christians are duty bound to follow?

This question is important since, from at least the early nineteenth century, the assumption has been that the New Testament lacks any prescription for worship and that the earliest Christians had little to no ritual or institutional structure. Accordingly, early assemblies are commonly seen to have been characterized by the charismatic outpouring of the Spirit, with a sharp distinction being drawn between the primitive church of the apostles and the institutionalized church of the late second century. Thus many Christians today believe that worship is best conceived as a creative, Spirit-fueled experience that any formalized structure necessarily inhibits—a view that's only been energized by the emergence of our entertainment driven culture. Though appealing to the prevailing religious attitude that "considers every rule a symptom of the weakening of the spirit,"[3] this book will challenge the common narrative.

More specifically, we intend to demonstrate three things. First, in contrast to the anti-ritualism so prevalent in religious circles, we'll highlight ritual's indispensable role in providing context, focus, and biblically-centered content. Second, against the modern assumption that no biblically mandated worship framework exists, we'll show that a definite pattern of worship (referred to as the word/table pattern) is present in both our earliest New Testament documents and the second and third generation church fathers. Moreover, the evidence will reveal that the word/table framework was already ritually laden by the time it made its appearance in the New Testament, meaning it can be properly understood only in its ritual context. Third, in light of

---

[2] Geoffrey Wainwright, *Doxology: The Praise of God in Worship, Doctrine, and Life* (New York, 1980), 231.

[3] Alexander Schmemann, *Introduction to Liturgical Theology* (Crestwood, 1966), 33, 56.

recent research, we'll see that the assumptions about creativity lying at the heart of modern worship are fundamentally flawed.

To give our topic proper context, let's begin by examining some cultural developments that have shaped how people consume information and judge truth from error.

New Communication Media

In his classic, *Amusing Ourselves to Death*, Neil Postman describes America's trajectory from a print-based society to one now dominated by television (and its web-based descendants) as its most pervasive communication medium. What's perhaps most significant about Postman's work is his observation (following Marshall McLuhan) that, whatever the form of communication, the medium is the message. While a technology such as TV is merely a machine, a medium is the social and intellectual environment the machine creates.[4] The media of communication available to any society are a dominant influence on the formation of its intellectual and social preoccupations. Each medium, like language, creates a new orientation for thought, which is what he means in saying that the medium is the message.

At the heart of Postman's analysis is the observation that TV culture—which now includes the various web based platforms—has produced a different way of how people come to know truth that's substantially different than when culture was governed by the printing press. This is to say that the form in which ideas are expressed affects what those ideas will be. Like the brain, every technology has an inherent bias. Within its physical form it has a predisposition for being used in certain ways and not others; meaning that any major new medium changes how we discourse, which it does by encouraging certain uses of the intellect—by favoring certain definitions of intelligence and wisdom and by demanding certain kinds of content. Thus as a culture moves from print to television, its ideas of truth move with it. With print, discourse was generally coherent,

---

[4] Neil Postman, *Amusing Ourselves to Death: Public Discourse in the Age of Show Business* (New York, 1985), 8–10, 31, 84.

serious, and rational; with television, it has become shriveled and absurd.

The crucial point is that television has become a powerful and pervasive medium, which determines not just the content we learn, but more significantly the benchmark for *how* we come to know anything at all.[5] As with any medium of communication it defines and regulates our ideas of truth.

Where It Started

Postman points out that while modern discourse found its fullest expression in TV, the shift started with the telegraph. Whereas America had been a print culture in which news and ideas were dealt with in sequential propositions on a page, the telegraph began to alter how we absorb information. The most significant change was that it was now transmitted context-free; that is, the information was no longer tied to any function it might serve in social and political decision-making and action, and could be merely transmitted for its novelty, interest, and curiosity. But most of it wasn't information any person receiving it could act on, which had the effect of turning it into a commodity, something that could be bought and sold irrespective of its uses or meaning.

In both oral and print cultures, information was important because it was actionable by the person receiving it. With telegraphy the relationship between information and action was made remote and abstract. That relationship has only degraded with later technologies. For the first time in history, people were faced with the problem of information overload. To get a sense of this, how often does information delivered by TV or the internet cause you to alter your plans for the day or provide an insight into a problem you're required to solve? The reality is that for most of us the daily news is inert, giving us something to talk about but not anything we can meaningfully act on. "For the first time, we were sent information which answered no question we had asked, and . . . did not permit the right to reply."[6]

---

[5] Neil Postman, *Amusing Ourselves to Death*, 16–18, 24, 27, 84.

[6] Neil Postman, *Amusing Ourselves to Death*, 65, 68–70, 77–79.

Knowing facts took on a new meaning, as it no longer meant that a person understood implications, background, or connections. The telegraph and the discourse it produced permitted no time for historical perspective and allowed no priority for quality. Intelligence now meant knowing *of* lots of things, not knowing *about* them. Combined with the emergence of the photograph, the two created a language that denied interconnections, proceeded without context, argued the irrelevance of history, and offered fascination in place of complexity and coherence. In other words, they were more apt to amuse than to inform. Postman notes that together these new technologies brought a new world into being, in which a new event pops into view for a moment, then vanishes again. It's a "peek-a-boo" world without much coherence or sense—being entirely self-contained with no context—and endlessly entertaining. With the advent of TV and its later web based manifestations, it's not just that our knowledge of the world has been impacted, but that our knowledge of *how the world is known* has been narrow-framed. Meaning that it has created a new framework by which we know and process information about every conceivable subject, including the more lofty ones of politics and religion. Postman remarks:

> Our culture's adjustment to the epistemology [how we know the world] of television is by now all but complete; we have so thoroughly accepted its definitions of truth, knowledge, and reality that irrelevance seems to us to be filled with import, and incoherence seems eminently sane. And if some of our institutions seem not to fit the template of the times, why it is they, and not the template, that seem to us disordered and strange.[7]

Emotion-Centered

In the 1950's, television commercials made the shift from linguistic to emotional appeals. By substituting images for claims, the picture oriented commercial made emotional appeals the basis of consumer decisions rather than tests of truth. Because the distance now

---

[7] Neil Postman, *Amusing Ourselves to Death*, 80.

between rationality and advertising is so vast it's hard to imagine a time when they were connected. Today, on any given commercial, propositions are as scarce as unattractive people. It's a cliche in the marketing world that appeals need to be made to the emotional, not the rational, brain. The truth or falsity of an advertiser's claim isn't even an issue. At issue is whether they've connected to what marketers call our "lizard brain," that emotionally me-centered system common to all of us. What's important about the shift is its far-reaching consequences on once non-trivial areas like politics and religion.

As the appeal to emotion has engulfed virtually every area, some rules of thumb have become standard: short and simple messages are preferable to longer and more complex ones; drama, or storytelling, is preferred over exposition; being sold a solution is better than being confronted with questions and problems. Given that perplexity is a fast-track to low ratings, there shouldn't be anything that has to be remembered, studied, or endured. "It is assumed," says Postman, "that any information, story or idea can be made immediately accessible, since contentment, not the growth, of the learner is paramount."[8] Thus TV delivers content in the form of story-telling and fast-moving images, usually supported by emotionally-arousing music.

Certain consequences have followed, however. A person who's been raised with TV commercials may believe that political problems have fast solutions through simple measures. Also, since short messages do away with sequence and continuity, the idea that sequence and continuity have anything to do with thought has been undermined. In this environment, complex language isn't to be trusted and all problems lend themselves to theatrical expression. Argument over issues is bad taste and leads only to uncertainty, which as we'll see later, is something the human brain naturally avoids. And just as commercials use athletes, actors, and musicians to speak on a product's behalf, politicians—and too many pastors—have been freed from the limited field of their own expertise. They've gained celebrity status that rivals many movie stars. The effects are now universal. We believe that learning is a form of entertainment; or more precisely, that anything worth

---

[8] Neil Postman, *Amusing Ourselves to Death*, 127–132, 147–148, 154, 156.

learning should take the form of entertainment. Television and its off-spring have been granted sovereignty over all our institutions.

In this the politician or religious leader doesn't so much offer the audience an image of himself, as offer himself as an image of the audience—so much so that it has become common to gauge public sentiment before making policy and worship decisions. Whether deliberately or not, these once serious people have learned the lesson of all great television commercials in which a slogan is created for viewers that represents an image of themselves. In the shift from party politics to TV politics, we're not allowed to know who the best candidate is, but whose image is best in touch with part of the country's own discontent. We've seen this before when the Israelites demanded a god conforming to themselves. As Xenophanes said centuries ago, men always make gods in their own image. With the advent of the new media, those who want to be gods refashion themselves into images the viewers would have them be,[9] making crowds as inevitable as they always have been.

Finally, because the new media is speed-of-light, it's necessarily present-centered and permits no access to the past. In the age of show business, not only is ideological and theological content absent but so is any sense of history. It's not that we refuse to remember or keep things in proper context, it's that we're being rendered unfit to remember—which is becoming worse the easier it gets to access whatever facts we want with a simple search. Bottom line is that we've embraced a medium that presents information in a simplistic, non-substantive, non-historical, and non-contextual form. In other words, it's information packaged as entertainment.[10]

TV At Its Most Serious

Because TV is largely trivial, it ends up most dangerous when its aspirations are high and presents itself as a carrier of important cultural conversations, a prime example of which is our twenty-four hour news cycle. As Robert MacNeil—executive editor and

---

[9] Neil Postman, *Amusing Ourselves to Death*, 134–135.

[10] Neil Postman, *Amusing Ourselves to Death*, 136–137, 141.

co-anchor of the "MacNeil-Lehrer Newshour"—has said, the idea of news is "to keep everything brief, not to strain the attention of anyone but instead to provide constant stimulation through variety, novelty, action, and movement. You are required . . . to pay attention to no concept, no character, and no problem for more than a few seconds at a time."[11] He continues by saying that the assumptions of news shows are "that bite-sized is best, that complexity must be avoided, that nuances are disposable, that qualifications impede the simple message, that visual stimulation is a substitute for thought, and that verbal precision is an anachronism." As an illustration of how ephemeral it has become, Forbes reports (using Google's video AI) that the average news shot is only 4.8 seconds long.[12]

Because of its inherent brevity, superficiality defines even the most serious programming, meaning it requires minimal skill to comprehend and is largely aimed at emotional gratification. Unlike any other medium in history, television has perfected the idea that the sole aim is the viewer's entertainment. News producers know well that they have to strive for the largest audience possible; in fact, we hear of cable news ratings almost as much as political polling, with newscasters now having celebrity status. The result, as Postman remarks, is that Americans are the best entertained and likely the least well-informed people in the Western world. As we'll see later, we already have selective tendencies that can skew our knowledge of the world, but these are only made worse by a media that plays on our love for anecdotes and thirst for the sensational.[13]

Perhaps the problem isn't so much that television is entertaining, but that it has made entertainment itself the natural framework of all experience.[14] Thinking doesn't play well on TV as there's not

---

[11] Neil Postman, *Amusing Ourselves to Death*, 105

[12] Kalev Leetaru, "Using Google's Video AI To Estimate The Average Shot Length In Television News." https://www.forbes.com/sites/kalevleetaru/2019/06/03/using-googles-video-ai-to-estimate-the-average-shot-length-in-television-news/#7f1e2de98e3a.

[13] Nassim Nicholas Taleb, *Antifragile: Things That Gain From Disorder* (New York, 2014), 89.

[14] Neil Postman, *Amusing Ourselves to Death*, 86–87, 90–93, 106.

much to see when people think. It's not a performing art and television is a medium that requires performances rather than ideas. A good program always aims to achieve applause, not reflection. This is because it's the nature of the medium to suppress ideas to accommodate the requirements of visual interest. In other words, to accommodate the values of show business. And in keeping with the demands of show business, Americans no longer talk to each other, they entertain each other. They don't exchange ideas, they exchange images. They don't argue with propositions, they argue with good looks, celebrities, and commercials. Our pastors and presidents, surgeons and lawyers, educators and newscasters often worry less about the demands of their disciplines than those of showmanship.[15]

To make things worse, Americans are full of opinions, but they're different than eighteenth or nineteenth century opinions. It's probably more accurate to call them emotions rather than opinions, which explains how they change from week to week. Being informed unfortunately now amounts to fragmented, misplaced, and superficial information—information creating the illusion of knowing something but which in fact leads us away from knowing deeply. "My point," Postman says, "is that we are by now so thoroughly adjusted to the 'Now . . . this' world of news—a world of fragments, where events stand alone, stripped of any connection to the past, or to the future, or to other events—that all assumptions of coherence have vanished."[16]

Religious Consequences

As we've now seen, TV favors moods of appeasement and is at its best when substance of any kind is muted. When Christianity is conformed to television standards it's presented as entertainment, which for the most part goes without apology. However, the trade-off required for amusement over substance has stripped away everything that makes worship an historic, profound, and sacred activity.[17]

---

[15] Neil Postman, *Amusing Ourselves to Death*, 98, 107.

[16] Neil Postman, *Amusing Ourselves to Death*, 110.

[17] Neil Postman, *Amusing Ourselves to Death*, 116–119.

There's no longer any ritual, no dogma, no tradition, no theology, and no sense of spiritual transcendence. In place of the centrality and mystery of the altar stands the celebrity pastor and rock band. In place of well-defined doctrines and preaching of the Gospel stand practical messages in ethics on how to improve a marriage or be a better Christian.

The problem is that preachers have assumed that what's been done in ages past can be transferred without loss of meaning, which is doubtless driven by the allure of the large numbers to which a TV framework gives them access. But this is naive, the new medium has changed the message. With dazzling back-lit wall props, jumbo screens, and equipment fit for a rock concert, the mystery so prominent throughout the Old and New Testament has no place. If people aren't immersed in an aura of mystery and symbolic otherworldliness, then it likely doesn't have the state of mind required for a nontrivial religious experience. Yet numbers have been a driving factor for modern religion since at least the early nineteenth century, which is something that comes only by giving people what they want, not what they need. Postman's comments on this are important:

> You will note, I am sure, that this is an unusual religious credo. There is no great religious leader—from the Buddha to Moses to Jesus to Mohammed to Luther—who offered people what they want. Only what they need. But television is not well suited to offering people what they need. It it "user friendly." It is too easy to turn off. It is at its most alluring when it speaks the language of dynamic visual imagery. It does not accommodate complex language or stringent demands. As a consequence, what is preached on television is not anything like the Sermon on the Mount. Religious programs are filled with good cheer. They celebrate affluence. Their featured players become celebrities. Though their messages are trivial, the shows have high ratings, or rather, *because* their messages are trivial, the shows have high ratings . . . I believe I am not mistaken in saying that Christianity is a demanding and serious religion. When it is delivered as easy and amusing, it is another kind of religion altogether.[18]

---

[18] Neil Postman, *Amusing Ourselves to Death*, 121–123.

It's true that every religion tries to make itself appealing through art, music, icons, and ritual. The aesthetic dimension has been the source of attraction to many people. We see it in Roman Catholicism, Judaism, and other religions which give its congregants awe-inspiring churches, chants, and incense. But the difference between these and the glitzy sets we see in so many churches is that they're integral parts of the history and doctrines of the religion itself. They require congregants to respond with appropriate reverence. A Jew doesn't cover his head at prayer because the cap is trendy. A Catholic doesn't light a candle to improve the look of the altar. Rabbis, priests, and pastors don't, in the midst of a service, get the testimony of movie stars to find out why they're religious. What we find in traditional religions is enchantment, not entertainment—and the distinction is critical. Enchantment is the means through which we access the sacred. Entertainment is the means through which we distance ourselves from it.

The bottom line is that most religion today is fundamentalist and disdains ritual and the deeper questions that occupied our forefathers, which it does in favor of direct (and subjective) communication with God. But the result has been that God has become a vague concept. And though his name is invoked repeatedly, it doesn't make worship Christ-centered. It merely reinforces the superficiality of the experience.

While we'll add more context as we proceed, let's take a look at what's to come in the following chapters.

What to Expect

To begin our examination, chapter one will explore the misunderstood role that ritual (an ordered sequence of words and actions that are regularly re-enacted in similar situations) plays in all of our lives. Contrary to popular religion, it will be shown that we're all ritualists, so much so that if it's suppressed in one area it pops up in others. With the book of Leviticus as the background, we'll see the large role ritual plays in both the Old and New Testaments.

In chapter two, evidence from the relatively new science of expertise will be examined as it relates to the origins of creativity.

As will be demonstrated, popular assumptions are flawed: far from having its origins in spontaneity, creativity arises rather from constraints. As G. K. Chesterton once observed, while the modern man wants creativity without limits, he can't do much of anything without imposing limits. If you draw a giraffe, you must draw him with a long neck. And if in your creativity you choose to draw him with a short neck, you'll find that you haven't drawn a giraffe at all. "The moment," Chesterton says, "you step into the world of fact, you step into a world of limits. You can free things from alien or accidental laws, but not from the laws of their own nature."[19] You can free a tiger from his bars but don't free him from his stripes. Similarly, we can't free worship from the pattern found in scripture without freeing it from the God who gives it life. In Postman's sense, we can't alter the medium without changing the message.

Next, chapter three will deal with the question of epistemology (how we know, how we judge truth from error)—a question that, because of its centrality, will surface throughout this book. Specifically, we'll explore recent research highlighting the limits of human knowledge. Due to the fact that our judgments are often error prone, we'll see how important it is to have them continually benchmarked against the real world. But if we face limits in our everyday knowledge, it's doubly so for religious knowledge; making it critical that we have continual recourse to a biblically based structure that keeps our minds focused on the truly vital (a role traditionally filled by ritual).

Having uncovered some of these challenges, chapter four will explore some intriguing research on the extent to which our environment influences our thoughts, beliefs, and behaviors. What will become clear is how important it is to place ourselves, particularly in the religious realm, into an environment that's pregnant with biblical imagery and content. Chapter five will then delve into the impact of language on our thoughts, perception, and behavior—which will reinforce the centrality of biblical language for the sustenance and growth of Christian faith.

The word/table pattern of worship found in the biblical material will occupy our attention in chapter six. Two things will be

---

[19] G. K. Chesterton, *Orthodoxy* (San Francisco, 1908), 45.

shown here: (1) not only is the word/table framework visible in the New Testament, but (2) that it's couched within an inherently ritual context, without which it becomes difficult to understand. With that important background, creeds will be the subject of chapter seven. Specifically, we'll look at the creedal and formulaic passages scholars have documented within the New Testament itself, and then explore their function in the earliest congregations and following centuries. As with the existence of the word/table framework, the existence of creedal formulae within the New Testament will challenge popular assumptions that the early Christians lacked any doctrinal/ritual and institutional structure. Finally, one of the consequences of living in an entertainment driven culture is that we're especially prone to flatten out reality to fit our preconceived—and overly abstract and simplistic—beliefs about the world. Thus chapter eight will explore the value, particularly within Christianity, of being able to hold two seemingly opposed ideas in our heads at the same time. The early christological heresies will serve as fodder for our discussion, which will highlight how the church's ritual embodied in its liturgy (its framework or order of worship) provides guardrails against our reductionist tendencies.

And as a postscript, the topic of ritual as a framework for addressing and absolving sin is explored. With that overview, let's introduce the idea of ritual.

CHAPTER 1
Ritual

We're all ritualists. Whether we recognize it or not, our lives are full of rituals that guide our behavior, limit our choices, and determining where we go next. Manifesting themselves in various forms, they can range from the more obvious customs of birthday and graduation celebrations to elaborate dinners for successes and burial of the dead. But they can also be less apparent and quietly govern much of our lives, from the time we wake up, eat, go to work, to when we turn the television on after a long day.

Whether obvious or not, researchers agree that human beings are inherently ritual creatures. Anthropologists have shown that rituals span cultures and time and can take on an extraordinary array of shapes. While they can be performed communally or privately and for civic or religious reasons, they normally involve some ordered sequence of words and actions that are regularly re-enacted in similar situations—and usually to express some core belief. As to why we're so drawn to them, there are probably a myriad of explanations. We'll propose some as we proceed, but certainly one is that we turn to ritual when facing situations that cause uncertainty and anxiety. Ritual-like activities allow us to better navigate the risks of life by offering a sense of control and a feeling of emotional and physical stability. "People engage in rituals with the intention of achieving a wide set of desired outcomes, from reducing their anxiety to boosting their confidence, alleviating their grief to performing well in a competition."[1]

---

[1] Francesca Gino and Michael I. Norton, "Why Rituals Work," https://www.scientificamerican.com/article/why-rituals-work/.

In the sports world, it's been long known that athletes use rituals before, during, and after practice and game time, often with an almost religious-like fanaticism. Michael Jordan wore his North Carolina shorts under his Chicago Bulls shorts for every game, while Curtis Martin of the New York Jets reads Ps. 91 before each game. Former third baseman for the Boston Red Sox, Wade Boggs, woke up at the same time each day, ate chicken before each game, took exactly 117 ground balls in practice, had batting practice at 5:17, and ran sprints at 7:17. Twyla Tharp, who's widely regarded as one of the greatest dancers and choreographers, interestingly describes her's as follows:

> I begin each day of my life with a ritual. I wake up at 5:30 A.M., put on my workout clothes, my leg warmers, my sweatshirt, and my hat. I walk outside my Manhattan home, hail a taxi, and tell the driver to take me to the Pumping Iron gym at 91st Street and First Avenue, where I work out for two hours. The ritual is not the stretching and weight training I put my body through each morning at the gym; the ritual is the cab. The moment I tell the driver where to go I have completed the ritual. It's a simple act, but doing it the same way each morning habitualizes it—makes it repeatable, easy to do. It reduces the chance that I would skip it or do it differently. It is one more item in my arsenal of routines, and one less thing to think about.[2]

While we might think athletes are unique, researchers estimate that 40–50 percent of our daily actions are done out of habit—which carries vast implications for how we spend our time and the conditions under which our thoughts develop. In his recent best seller, *Atomic Habits*, James Clear notes that though a habit can be completed in just a few seconds, it can shape the actions we take for minutes or hours afterward. "You check your phone for 'just a second' and soon you have spent twenty minutes staring at the screen. In this way, the habits you follow without thinking often determine the choices you make when you are thinking."[3] Our habits thus have a

[2] James Clear, *Atomic Habits: An Easy & Proven Way to Build Good Habits & Break Bad Ones* (New York, 2018), 159.

[3] James Clear, *Atomic Habits*, 160, 162.

compounding effect as they stack up and set the trajectory for how we spend the next chunk of time. As such, Clear says that habits are the entry point, not the end point. They're the cab, not the gym. Bottom line is that, depending on the quality, our rituals and the habits that follow can limit where we go in life.

With this in mind we can see how important they are, particularly—as we'll see—with respect to religion. They can either facilitate or slow our growth. They can determine whether time is well spent or wasted. As we'll see, even outside our habits much of our thinking and behavior is automatic, so considering how our religious rituals either constrain or expand our understanding seems urgent. This is what we intend to explore here. We'll do so first by looking at the part ritual plays in society and how it con-tributes to our understanding of the world. With that context, we'll spend the remaining time focusing on how our worship habits may impact how deeply we understand the Christian faith. One of the questions we'll ask is, does scripture manifest any particular ritu-als that would serve as a paradigm for worship? In other words, does it betray a divinely instituted pattern of worship that Christians would do well to consider? In order to answer this, we need to exam-ine the Old Testament ritual background necessary for understand-ing the New Testament. We'll see that as God prescribed a pattern of worship for Israel, so he does in the New Testament which sets it within a word and table framework.

With that said, let's begin with the big picture.

Ritual's Pervasive Imprint

The British anthropologist, Mary Douglas, says that we severely underestimate the impact of social rituals on our lives. She notes that across culture and time, rituals have helped shape a reality that would be virtually impossible without them. "It is not too much to say that ritual is more to society than words are to thought. For it is very possible to know something and then find words for it. But it is impossible to have social relations without symbolic acts." What the data suggest is that a large part of our ritual nature comes from our social structure, of which we're always conscious. While we'll have more to say on our environmental influences later, for now we can note that our social structure curbs actions in accordance with social norms and hierarchies. So pervasive is its influence, in fact, that within it there are no items of clothing or food we don't seize on as theatrical props to dramatize the way we want to present ourselves and the scene in which we're playing.

Thus a great deal of our social interactions are ritual. Without letters of condolence or messages of congratulations, the friendship of a separated friend isn't a social reality, meaning it has no existence without the rites of friendship. Ritual creates and consolidates communities, without which they can't survive the passage of time and resist the forces of self-interest that would tear them apart. This implies that within our social reality, everything we do is significant and nothing is without its conscious symbolic load.[4] Bottom line is that the yearning for rigidity is in all of us—it's part of the human condition to long for hard lines and clear concepts. In fact, as Douglas highlights, ritual is so much a part of our nature that if it's suppressed in one point it crops up elsewhere.[5] We'll see this in action in the chapters that follow.

A Whole Way of Life

Let's drill down on this a bit further. One of the reasons ritual creates and consolidates communities is because it offers participation in the entire cycle of human life from birth to death, which explains the universal prominence of "rites of passage" that sustain people at critical points of their lives—such as birth, adolescence, marriage, sickness, and death.[6] But over the centuries it has also harmonized people with the natural and cosmic order that surrounds and sustains them; integrating and governing their daily pattern of worship and prayer, and coordinating them with day and

---

[4] Mary Douglas, *Purity and Danger: An Analysis of the Concepts of Pollution and Taboo* (London, 1979), 100.

[5] Mary Douglas, *Purity and Danger*, 162.

[6] John W. Kleinig, "Witting or Unwitting Ritualists," *Lutheran Theological Journal* 22/1 (1988), 17–18.

night and the seasons of the year.[7] Because it's able to encompass so much, from ordinary life to religious mysteries, it caters to people of all stages of maturity and sophistication. One might say that it communicates a whole way of life to the whole person by uniquely encircling the entire person, body and soul.

John Kleinig has helped us understand how it does so in three ways. First, since rituals involve bodily action, they communicate physically. This is also true of religious rites that communicate spiritual realities physically, thus drawing one's physical life into the divine domain. As an example, Christianity has maintained that believers receive the Lord's Supper for the benefit not only of the soul but for the body as well. "What is more," says Kleinig, "this ritual element in our worship not only conveys spiritual power to us via physical means, as in the water of Baptism, but it also helps us to respond physically. It not only tells us how to react to God's grace, but actually helps us to react properly by providing us with habitual models of confession, prayer, and praise."[8]

Second, because ritual affects us physically it can also move us imaginatively and emotionally—meaning that it doesn't merely express what we feel at a given moment, which in the big picture usually isn't very significant, but makes us feel something other than what we felt previously. It can can make us rejoice when we don't feel happy and mourn in Lent when we feel no personal loss. Since our minds are so prone to focus on the most superficial aspects of reality (more on this later), ritual serves a critical function by giving us a more expansive framework. With his usual perception, C. S. Lewis comments on this aspect as follows: "It [ritual] . . . is a pattern imposed on the mere flux of our feelings by reason and will, which renders pleasures less fugitive and griefs more endurable, which hands over to the power of wise custom the task (to which the individual and his moods are so inadequate) of being festive or sober, gay or reverent, when we choose to be, and not at the bidding

---

[7] Gordon W. Lathrop, *Holy Ground: A Liturgical Cosmology* (Minneapolis, 2003), 157–63.

[8] John W. Kleinig, "Witting or Unwitting Ritualists," 18.

of chance."[9] Given our natural tendencies to lose the forest for the trees, this is perhaps one of the most important benefits to viewing reality through a ritual lens.

Third, since ritual combines words with bodily gestures, it also communicates cognitively and can even reframe our default way of thinking. Douglas has shown that it does so in several ways. As a focusing mechanism, ritual gives us a frame in which a marked-off time or place alerts a special type of expectation—just as the words "once upon a time" creates a mood for fantastic tales where even the smallest action can carry significance. Framing limits experience and allows us to select certain parts for concentrated attention. It's also creative at the level of performance, as it mysteriously helps the coordination of brain and body. Actors frequently recount times in which a material thing conveys effective power; for example when a prop is passed and the actor suddenly knows how a performance should proceed.

In this function ritual aids perception, or rather it changes perception because it alters the selection principles. This is important because research shows that perception isn't simply a passive reception of ready-made impressions from the outside, like a palette receiving a spot of paint. Recognizing and remembering aren't just about stirring up old images in our minds. Rather our impressions are schematically organized from the start, meaning we select from only those stimuli that interest us—and those interests are governed by a pattern-making tendency experts call a schema.[10] As Taleb has recently noted, even from an anatomical perspective it's impossible for our brains to see anything in raw form without some interpretation, which has been convincingly shown by a series of famous experiments on split-brain patients.[11] Bottom line is that in perceiv-

---

[9] C. S. Lewis, *A Preface to Paradise Lost* (New York, 1967), 22. I'm indebted to Kleinig for highlighting this quote.

[10] William F. Brewer, "What is Recollective Memory?" in *Remembering Our Past: Studies in Autobiographical Memory*, ed. David C. Rubin (Cambridge, 1995), 44–45, 50. Mary Douglas, *Purity and Danger*, 36. Richard Bauckham, *Jesus and the Eyewitnesses: The Gospels as Eyewitness Testimony* (Grand Rapids, 2006), 335, 337.

[11] Nassim Nicholas Taleb, *The Black Swan: The Impact of the Highly Improbable* (New York, 2010), 63–65.

ing we're building, taking some cues and rejecting others. Thus it's not just that ritual helps us experience more vividly what we would have anyway. It's not merely like the visual aid that illustrates verbal instructions for opening a can, or building a grill. It can come first in formulating experience; it can permit knowledge of what otherwise wouldn't have been known at all.[12]

Thus ritual can mediate experience, including social experience; it standardizes situations and helps us evaluate them; it creates a link between the past, present, and the future. This is also true of language. There can be thoughts which have never been put into words, but once words have framed a thought, it is changed by the very words selected. Anyone who's had to put a creative idea to paper understands this; the words create something such that a concrete idea emerges from an abstract one. Beyond this, simply having a word for something helps spread awareness of it, such as naming a shade of blue in cultures lacking the term (more on this later) or introducing the idea of iatrogenics (the damage caused by treatment in excess of its benefits) in medicine and economics.[13]

Finally, Douglas notes that some things can't be experienced without ritual. Events that happen in regular sequences acquire meaning from their relation to others in the sequence. Without the full sequence individual elements get lost. Consider the days of the week beyond just their marking off time. Each day has its own significance and comes with its own pattern of habits, the observance of which have the effect of ritual. Going through one part of the pattern is necessary for being aware of the next. No experience is too lowly to be taken up in ritual and given a lofty meaning.[14] The bridegroom carries his bride over the lintel; a man bends down on one knee as he asks a woman to marry him; flowers are given to a wife on certain ritual occasions such as an anniversary or mother's day.

In these ways ritual not only communicates intentions but conveys meaning. For Christians, meaning is created by their

[12] Mary Douglas, *Purity and Danger*, 64.

[13] Nassim Nicholas Taleb, *Antifragile: Things That Gain From Disorder* (New York, 2014), 111–13.

[14] Mary Douglas, *Purity and Danger*, 114.

engagement with central past events which then continually orient them toward God's ultimate purpose.[15] In fact, Wainwright notes that putting successive generations in touch with an archetypal story that accounts for the present order of the world is one of ritual's more critical functions. "Representation, by word and deed, of a primal event asserts the foundational value of that event and allows later-comers to participate in its benefits and commit themselves to the maintenance of the established order."[16] Thus, like the Israelites, the constant rehearsal of Christianity's central events is needed for the continuance of the believer's memory, well-being (intellectual, emotional, and spiritual), and hope for the presence and the future.

Man's Sin and God's Holiness

With these details in mind, it's time to take a brief look at how ritual functions in the Bible. At the heart of both testaments lies the concept of God's holiness and man's sin; the separation between the creator and the created and the necessity of reconciliation. Since God was holy and his people weren't his presence was a danger to them. We see this early in Exodus when God tells Moses, "Do not come near here; remove your sandals from your feet, for the place on which you are standing is holy ground" (3:5); and then later when Moses asks to see God's glory (33:20), to which he receives the emphatic reply, "You cannot see My face, for no man can see Me and live!"

To provide his people safe access to him and his blessings, it was necessary for God to establish what Kleinig refers to as the "divine service"—the sacrificial ritual (liturgical) enactments that consume the bulk of Leviticus (Lev. 9:4, 6, 23–24). Through the rite of atonement God released the Israelites from their sin, cleansed them from impurity, and assured them of a favorable reception (Lev. 1:4; 17:11).[17] When the Israelites entered the tabernacle, which is where

---

[15] Geoffrey Wainwright, *Doxology: The Praise of God in Worship, Doctrine, and Life* (New York, 1980), 121–22.

[16] Geoffrey Wainwright, *Doxology*, 119, 121.

[17] John W. Kleinig, *Leviticus* (Saint Louis, 2003), 3ff.

God "resided" with his people (Lev. 26:11), they "stood before the Lord" (Lev. 9:5). But the purpose wasn't simply to establish his presence; it was rather to deal with man's problem of being sinful and unclean. And it was against this background that Leviticus' ritual grammar of holiness was set, as it prescribed when, where, how, and why God shared it with the people of Israel.[18]

Since it makes clear that the Lord alone is holy (Lev. 10:3; 1 Sam. 2:2), God's presence with his people is what made and kept them holy (Ex. 29:43–44); which is to say that their holiness wasn't something they possessed in themselves, but only as they continually received it from God. It was an acquired state, a contingent condition, an extrinsic power, and something that was lost as soon as contact with him was lost. Because of this the Old Testament doesn't define God's holiness in the abstract, but treats it as something that's experienced by personal contact and ritual interaction with him at the sanctuary.[19] That all human beings are unclean and in need of constant purification is central throughout. The congregation of Israel with its priests and high priest all needed to be purified before entering the sanctuary and sharing in God's holiness, but this occurred only through his decrees in the daily service.

Given their Old Testament prominence, Kleinig observes that God's decrees served three functions. First, like the words of Gen. 1 they were creative—they created the tabernacle as God's residence in the midst of Israel and its services. Second, they were sanctifying in that by his word God sanctified all that is holy through them (Lev. 21:23; 22:9, 16, 32). Third, they were life-giving in that by his word God shared his life-giving blessings with Israel and protected it from evil. Thus by instituting the divine service and empowering it with his creative word, it became a sacramental (an external, visible means through which God works and preserves faith[20]) divine-human enactment. "His Word turns this human enactment in his

---

[18] John W. Kleinig, *Leviticus*, 4.

[19] John W. Kleinig, *Leviticus*, 5–7, 10.

[20] John Theodore Mueller, *Christian Dogmatics: A Handbook of Doctrinal Theology for Pastors, Teachers, and Laymen* (St. Louis, 1955), 441.

presence into a divine enactment by which he meets and interacts with his people."[21]

In the divine service, God instructed his people how their behavior and communal life were to harmonize with their involvement in the sacrificial ritual. Thus in the sharpest contrast to the modern contempt for ritual, the Israelites valued and depended on it for continued sustenance—which God made possible by giving them rituals that pleased him and which they regarded as essential to their life as his people. Kleinig notes that, "Since they were God's holy people who oriented their society around his presence with them, their existence as a holy community depended on their enactment of the sacrificial ritual that he had ordained for them. So we will not understand what they believed unless we understand how their faith was ritually enacted."[22] This is a critical point and it highlights the fact that we can't properly understand the ritually-laden New Testament without seeing the people of Israel in a ritually mediated relationship with God.

But before we discuss its importance for the early Christians, a final comment deserves attention. Geoffrey Wainwright points out that Israel's ritual brought into focus the continuing benefits of an earlier and foundational act of salvation. It gave people the opportunity to thank God for the original act and for the blessings that continued to flow as a result (Deut. 26:10–19). We see this in the constant narrative recital—"for the LORD our God is He who brought us and our fathers up out of the land of Egypt" (Josh. 24:14–28)—which recalled the inaugural saving event that seems to have had two effects. First, it made the original event present again and again in the ritual, and second, it established the continuing relationship of God with his people: the same God who brought the people out of the bonds of Egypt and into the promised land continued to bless successive generations. Wainwright remarks, "The liturgy was and remains for us, the locus in which the story of the constitutive events is retold in order to elicit an appropriate response in worship and ethics to the God who remains faithful to the purposes which his earlier acts

---

[21] John W. Kleinig, *Leviticus*, 2–5.

[22] John W. Kleinig, *Leviticus*, 21–23.

declared."[23] Gordon Lathrop similarly adds that by reading the biblical texts in the assembly as if they were ours, we who seem to be
without history are given a story, an origin, an orientation in the
world and something to remember.[24]

The annual Passover liturgy is a prime example as it allowed
succeeding generations to "re-live" in ritual form the original deliverance from the bondage in Egypt. Exodus chapters 12–13 oscillate
between the events of the first Passover night itself and the later
memorial observance of Passover and unleavened bread. By commem-
orating the exodus, the annual ritual transmitted to each generation
a belief and experience of the saving power of the God who brought
Israel out of bondage. "And when your children say to you, 'What
does this rite mean to you?' you shall say, 'It is a Passover sacrifice to
the LORD who passed over the houses of the sons of Israel in Egypt
when He smote the Egyptians, but spared our homes'" (Ex. 12:26–27)
was Israel's constant refrain.

In ending we should also note that much of the Old Testament
material had its origins in the Israelite liturgy. The hymnic forms of
Isaiah may have liturgical origins and the minor prophetic books
of Joel, Obadiah, Nahum, Habakkuk, and Zephaniah are probably
the liturgies of Israel (or at least strongly influenced by their liturgical forms).[25] On top of that, it's likely that many of the Psalms had
liturgical origins. What's certain is that the message of judgment and
hope was preserved through the liturgical readings in the worship of
the synagogue.

Fulfillment by Christ

The advent of Jesus Christ altered the way the Old Testament speaks
to God's people. Because we're not looking forward to the coming
of the Messiah, as Israel was, we don't worship God with animal sacrifices at the Jerusalem temple. As we now have access to God through

---

[23] Geoffrey Wainwright, *Doxology*, 152–3.

[24] Gordon Lathrop, *Holy Things: A Liturgical Theology* (Minneapolis, 1998), 17.

[25] Geoffrey Wainwright, *Doxology*, 155.

Christ's own sacrificial death, the new covenant has superseded the old. Even so, there are some important and often overlooked continuities between the Old and New Testaments we need to recognize. First is that our faith is mediated through God's word just as it was for Israel; and second, like Israel, the Christian enactments include physical (sacramental) elements. It was partly because of this seamless connection that the early church used Leviticus to preach the Gospel, believing it to be a critical frame of reference for the concepts of sin, sacrifice, and forgiveness through the shedding of blood. Because these concepts are so central to Jesus' understanding of his own high priestly work, the New Testament can be interpreted only in light of the Leviticus material.

Specifically, we rely on it for understanding Christ's death for sinners and his vicarious atonement, which is the heart of the Gospel.[26] Fundamental is the Leviticus data on the sin offering and the rite of atonement, as God used these to do two things. First, with them he cleansed the sanctuary (Lev. 4:6, 17), the altar for incense (Lev. 4:7, 18), and the altar for burnt offering from impurity (Lev. 4:7, 25, 30, 34; 5:9). Second, he forgave those who'd sinned inadvertently (Lev. 4:20, 26, 31, 35; 5:10)—all so God's holiness wasn't desecrated by sin and so that sinners weren't threatened by his wrath. It was this that created a state of ritual purity and allowed Israel to approach God without fear.

Importantly, the sin offering provided blood that atoned only for unintentional sins (Lev. 4:2, 13, 22, 27), with no rite of atonement being established to pay for deliberate sins (Num. 15:27–31). Against this background we can better understand how profound the idea was that as our great High Priest, Jesus brought his own sin offering into the Father's presence (Heb. 9:12)[27] as atonement for both intentional and unintentional sins (Heb. 3:1–6; 9:14; 10:21–22; 12:24; 13:12). By his sacrifice, he removed sin so completely that there's no longer any consciousness of sin and condemnation in God's presence. Thus as the ultimate sin offering, Jesus cleanses us so that we can perform the divine service with him in the heavenly sanctuary (Heb. 9:11–14).

---

[26] John W. Kleinig, *Leviticus*, 121–124.

[27] *Theological Dictionary of the New Testament*, Vol. IV, ed. Gerhard Kittel and trans. Geoffrey W. Bromiley (Grand Rapids, 1964–1976), 226.

We can see this in the parable of the tax collector and Pharisee (Luke 18:9–14). Coming into the temple, the tax collector seeks atonement for himself as a *deliberate sinner*, an unclean person that's excluded from God's presence. During the performance of the daily burnt offering he prayed, "God, be merciful to me, the sinner!" Speaking directly to sin of all kinds, unintentional and intentional, Jesus points to the fact that he's the sin offering of atonement for the justification of all overt sinners. This is why Paul asserts that Christ is the "sin offering" for sinful humanity, and uses the same Greek phrase that the Septuagint (the Greek translation of the Hebrew Old Testament) uses for the sin offering in Leviticus (4:3, 14, 28, 35; 5:6–11). Jesus bore the sins of men so that he could give them his purity, and because of that they're guiltless and free from condemnation (Rom. 8:1).

Thus while the Old Testament ritual legislation of purification was superseded by Christ's work as our High Priest, we continue to be as dependent on God in Christ as Israel was on the sanctuary. Holiness is still extrinsic to us and given only by his sacrificial death, and only as we appropriate it in word and sacrament. Kleinig remarks that, "All the ritual statutes in the Pentateuch foreshadow Christ and his gifts to his baptized believers in the Divine Service (Col 2:16–17; Heb 10:1). Thus the divine service that God established through the law of Moses reaches its perfection, its consummation and fulfillment in and through Christ."[28] What's important here is that, as in Leviticus, our holiness comes only via those means that God established as pleasing to him and which the church understood as being mediated through word (the scripture reading portion of the service) and table (the Lord's Supper, or eucharist).

No Communal Worship Without Ritual

In all we've said so far, it's important to understand the ancient distinction between type and antitype. The former refers to the whole sacrificial system, which was meant "typologically" to foreshadow the work of Christ as High Priest. In line with how the New Testament

---

[28] John W. Kleinig, *Leviticus*, 25–27.

understands the Old Testament (for example, Heb. 8–9) the tabernacle, priesthood, and sacrificial system should all be seen as pointing to Christ. Thus the sanctuary at Mount Sinai and the Jerusalem temple were types: imperfect copies of the perfect "antitype," which is the heavenly temple built by God through Christ for his permanent residence with his people (Ex. 25:40; Heb. 8:5).[29] In other words, while each type resembles the antitype, each type is inferior to and surpassed by the greater and perfect antitype in Christ. The liturgical ministry of Christ far surpasses the ministry of Arron and his successors.

Guarding the distinction between the two is important for a couple of reasons, the first of which is because it's rooted in the text itself. But secondly, it prevents us from doing away with the concrete ritual realties and indulging in a hyper-spiritualism that suppresses the physical nature of the rites. Because Christ himself takes the place of the temple and sacrifice, the early church confessed his presence as our great High Priest in the ritual enactment of the liturgy; and it thereby connected Christ's work on the cross with his ongoing service through the sacraments (Baptism and the Lord's Supper). The liturgical use of typology therefore correlated the temple and its services with Christ's continuing work as High Priest and mediator through the divine service. Further, as Moses and Aaron are types of Christ and Israel a type of the church, so also the sacrifices and offerings are ordained by God as types for the sacramental aspects of the divine service. Thus, everything God offered to his people through the daily service at the tabernacle resembles what he now offers through Christ in the ministry of word and sacrament. Kleinig remarks:

> So too everything that God required—and still requires—of his people is accomplished perfectly by his Son together with the faithful in the Divine Service. The offices and ritual enactments in Leviticus therefore prefigure the celebration of the Lord's Supper in the church. There the triune God interacts with the saints through the physical means and involves them bodily in the life and fellowship of the Son with the Father. There the triune God engages them physically and

---

[29] John W. Kleinig, *Leviticus*, 28–30.

produces the bodily sacrifices that are holy and acceptable to him by animating them with his Holy Spirit (Rom 12:1; 1 Pet 2:4–5).[30]

From this two things follow: (1) without ritual there's no communal worship, and (2) although we'll have more to say on this later, the history of Christian worship didn't arise from an empty tablet, as though there were no history that shaped the earliest assemblies. The material on the tablet was always there, and it was the old material out of which the early Christian liturgy was formed—and it corresponds exactly to the "old things" we still do.[31] That being said, we need to distinguish between those rituals Christ instituted from humanly devised rituals without scriptural warrant. And we need to distinguish proper use of ritual on the one hand and its abuse in ritualism and superstition on the other. While ritual order gives us the vocabulary for the proclamation of the Gospel, it always stands under the reforming criticism of the cross. As the Reformers rightly insisted, any time it deviates from the declaration that Christ died for the wicked, the outcast, and the lost, it has to be brought back to the radical implications of the cross.

Beyond that it can't be overemphasized that like the Israelites, we're embodied beings and require a ritual system that encompasses our whole selves, physical and spiritual. Given that God instituted Old Testament rituals including both, it should come as no surprise that the same God who created and redeemed mankind bonded together Christian people in the liturgy of word and table (Acts 2:42)—therefore involving both body and soul.

This is why we find from the very beginning of the Christian movement a liturgy in which God communicates his holiness physically with believers through holy things, which would have been expected from Israel's God. It was he who made the altar and the sanctuary holy (Lev. 8:10–16; 21:23), and then through the altar made the food from the offerings holy (Ex. 29:37; Lev. 22:14–16); it was he who consecrated the priests by their consumption of the holy food at the sanctuary (Lev. 6:7–11, 17–22; 7:1–10; 8:31–36;

---

[30] John W. Kleinig, *Leviticus*, 30.

[31] Gordon Lathrop, *Holy Things*, 22, 26.

21:15; 22:9), and then consecrated the Israelites through their participation in the divine service and their consumption of the holy food from the offerings (Lev. 1:4; 4:14–15; 7:11–36; 20:8; 21:8; 22:31–33).

Given this prehistory it shouldn't surprise us that John (1 John 1:9), in continuity with the ritual legislation in Leviticus, emphasized the need for Christians to confess their sins to God the Father to receive cleansing and forgiveness. And it was because of this that early Christians began their divine service with confession and absolution so the people could serve God with a good conscience (Didache 4:14[32]). At the service's culmination, early believers celebrated the sacrificial banquet of Christ in which they ate his body and blood for the remission of sins. "Since they served as priests in the heavenly sanctuary together with Christ the great High Priest, they, like the priests of the old covenant, ate the most holy flesh of his sin offering."[33] Thus we can see from this that God continues to communicate his holiness physically with his people through holy things.[34]

Jesus Our Liturgical Minister

Some of the most vivid glimpses of heaven we have in the New Testament occur in Hebrews and Revelation. Portraying heavenly worship with the same imagery found in Leviticus (Rev. 11:19; 15:3–8), the scenes bear an unmistakable stamp of liturgical, ritual practice (Rev. 4:8–11; 7:9–12). In Rev. 15:3 the hosts of heaven sing "the song of Moses, the bond-servant of God, and the song of the Lamb," linking the ministry of Moses to Christ.

Hebrews also drips in its ritual descriptions of the angels as "liturgizing spirits" beginning at 1:7, in which the author uses the Greek word for "liturgists" or "ministers." While the term "liturgy" was originally used in classical Greek for a service performed by a person or group on behalf of a community, the Septuagint used it for

---

[32] J. B. Lightfoot, *The Apostolic Fathers* (Grand Rapids, 1986), 123–129.

[33] John W. Kleinig, *Leviticus*, 124.

[34] John W. Kleinig, *Leviticus*, 11, 21–22.

the tasks performed by the priests and Levites in and at the sanctuary, especially for the ministry of the priests at the altar. "The LXX
[Septuagint] translators obviously felt a need to try to fix a regular
and exclusive term for priestly ministry, and thereby to show that
the cultic relation to God is something special as compared with all the
other relations of service in which men might stand."[35] The author
of Hebrews makes frequent use of it and is deeply rooted in the Old
Testament ritual terminology.[36] Kleinig's remarks deserve attention:

> Just as the priests served before the Lord by "liturgizing" with the high
> priest on behalf of the congregation at the tabernacle and the tem
> ple (10:11; see also 9:21), so the angels are also "liturgizing spirits"
> (1:14) who serve together with Jesus, "the liturgical minister of the
> holy things" in the heavenly sanctuary (8:2). The "liturgy" that he
> performs there is far superior to that instituted by Moses in the old
> covenant (8:6). The angels therefore work together with Jesus as his
> holy courtiers in the performance of the Divine Service in the heav
> enly sanctuary.[37]

We should note that Heb. 8:2 in particular can be translated
that Christ is "priest of the sanctuary."[38] This, along with the fact that
scholars generally agree that Hebrews was a sermon intended for
worship, gives us a better understanding of what the author means
that Jesus as the High Priest is the liturgical minister of "the good
things to come" (10:1). While the sermon doesn't list the good things,
it does single out Jesus' "body" (10:10) and "blood" (10:29; 13:12) as
the thing that sanctifies the people. Thus like the earthly high priests
who handled the holy things that sanctified the people, Jesus is our
liturgical minister who brings God's sanctifying gifts in the divine
service through his body and blood.

---

[35] *Theological Dictionary of the New Testament*, 221, 226.

[36] William F. Arndt and F. Wilbur Gingrich, *A Greek-English Lexicon of the New Testament and Other Early Christian Literature*, Second Edition (Chicago, 1979), 471.

[37] John W. Kleinig, *Hebrews* (Saint Louis, 2017), 71-2, 85, 390-3, 396.

[38] *Theological Dictionary of the New Testament*, 230.

But unlike the earthly high priests who ministered in an earthly tent, Jesus is the liturgical minister of the holy places in the heavenly tent (9:12, 24; 10:19). An image drawn from the Old Testament, the "tent" pictures heaven (Ps. 104:2; Is. 40:22), God's holy temple and the place he sits enthroned as King (Pss. 11:4; 103:19; Is. 66:1). This is the "true" tent (Heb. 8:2), as the earthly tent Moses constructed as Israel's place of worship was a copy (8:5), an imperfect counterpart. By his appointment as High Priest in the heavenly realm, Jesus "has obtained a liturgical ministry that is more excellent," (Heb. 8:6) just as he has inherited a name that's more excellent than the angels (1:4). Given its significance in both Testaments it's no surprise that the term "liturgy," with all its ritual connotations, was also applied by succeeding generations to the actions within the divine service—especially those surrounding the eucharist.[39]

As we close, we can mention that the church's confession of faith in Jesus its High Priest in 8:1–2 has also influenced the Gloria in Excelsis, the angelic song of praise that's so prominent in the historic liturgy. In it believers confess their faith and approach the risen Jesus, the Lamb of God who's "seated at the right hand of the Father," and beseech him to "have mercy" on them. It's easy to see in the Gloria's language the influence of the Old Testament insistence that God alone is holy, and the church's continuing dependence on him, in Christ, for its sustenance. In so acknowledging Jesus as the mediator between the church and the Father, it approaches the Father only through him. It also explicitly directs its confession to Father, Son, and Holy Spirit, thus ritually expressing its worship within a trinitarian framework.

Conclusion

From what we've now seen, both the Old and New Testament are saturated with ritual, liturgical imagery and language. While not any surprise to the first Christians who were reared in a first century Jewish context, it might seem so to Christians sitting in the twenty-first century. As Douglas has pointed out, the evangelical movement

---

[39] *Theological Dictionary of the New Testament*, 229.

has long given us the tendency to believe that ritual is empty form—that any codifying of conduct is alien to natural sympathy, and that any external religion is devoid of true interior religion.[40]

Given that, we've been brought up to suspect formality and seek rather spontaneous expressions. "Home-made prayers are always best" has been the motto. As a result, even though much of our lives are governed by unconscious rituals and habits, we have little appreciation for the function and significance of ritual.[41] We think it robs us of freedom and the creativity of a spirit-fueled worship experience. Perhaps at the core, we imagine that ritual robs us of our subjectivity and individuality. Rather than a warm and subjective object of the heart's devotion, ritual makes God something "out there" and remote.

But Douglas reminds us that it's a mistake to think there can be religion which is all interior or subjective, with no rules, no liturgy, and no external signs of inward states. As with society, so with religion—external form is the condition of its existence. Even more than that our anti-ritualism misses the fact that "As a social animal, man is a ritual animal."[42] There's no getting away from the fact that we're all ritualists. And since every kind of public meeting has its "liturgy," the question for Christians is whether or not their ritual accords with the biblical pattern.[43] Unfortunately, not all rituals are created equal. Some are better than others. As we proceed we'll see why this is so.

For now, however, we need to examine our common modern assumption that ritual stifles creativity. We need to ask, what exactly is the relation between structure and creative performance? In order to answer this we'll look next at the relatively new science of expertise to see what it says about how humans are wired, and how human beings best achieve depth. Does our best come from spontaneous expression, or is it a result of something as counter-intuitive as constraints? To that we now turn.

---

[40] Mary Douglas, *Purity and Danger*, 61–69.

[41] John W. Kleinig, *Leviticus*, 20–21.

[42] Mary Douglas, *Purity and Danger*, 62.

[43] Gordon W. Lathrop, *Holy Ground*, 136.

CHAPTER 2

Creativity, Depth, and Frameworks

Beginning at Cane Ridge, Kentucky, in 1801 with the American frontier revivalists, the framework of Christian liturgy started to disappear from churches across the country.[1] Referred to as the Second Great Awakening, revivalist camp meetings spread up and down the western side of the mountains from Georgia to New York. Among its key leaders was Charles Grandison Finney, who systematized the new evangelical movement and held that no order of worship was set down in the New Testament.[2] Given this perceived scriptural silence (which we'll challenge in this book), Finney believed that we're free to use whatever measures we deem necessary to save souls. Its effects were far reaching, both in terms of how people saw themselves in relation to God and the way they understood their role in salvation. Practically it manifested itself in the changes made to the traditional order of worship—which historically included the singing of hymns, lectionary reading of scripture, celebration of the eucharist, and the prayers of the church.

In place of the traditional order, revivalists pared down the service to three basic elements: warmup singing, preaching, and conversion. After warmup singing, parishioners typically heard preaching that emphasized practical Christian living (thus its ethical focus) which was based on just a few verses of scripture mentioned

---

[1] Gordon W. Lathrop, *Holy Ground: A Liturgical Cosmology* (Minneapolis, 2003), 140.

[2] Frank C. Senn, *Introduction to Christian Liturgy* (Minneapolis, 2012), 22.

during the sermon. These two were intended to lead to the final element of the service, the conversion of hearers, which effectively eliminated the traditional centrality of the reading of scripture and Communion.

In North America and places around the world influenced by American evangelicalism, this pared down order of service is still the norm—particularly prevalent in the large non-denominational churches (the one exception being that the older "conversion" part of the service has been transformed to an invitation to participate in need-based small groups). Rooted in the revivalist movement, modern evangelicalism has retained the belief that liturgy alienates people from the spontaneous movement of the Spirit. In place of the reading of scripture, table (or altar), corporate confession and absolution, the creed, and prayers of the church, praise bands have become the central focus. Traditional hymns have been replaced with a new genre of praise music, which tends to focus not so much on the story of man's justification through Christ's death, but on more individually and ethically-centered content.

Reasons for the new practices vary, but it's alleged that the liturgy feels too formal and lacks the warmth of personal relationships. In place of a one-to-one personal touch, the liturgy separates the individual from God and creates a wall between worshippers and the spontaneous movement of the Spirit. Thus it's believed that it restricts the freedom of the Spirit to move man and the spontaneity that precedes the creative act of worship. The assumption is that man's relationship with God shouldn't be mediated by specific content, or by any framework that might dim the direct interaction of the Spirit with his people. Longevity and depth, it seems, should have no such traditional constraints.

Part of this, as we've seen, is driven by our consumerist culture. In one sense, modern evangelicalism understands that people want to be entertained, and they don't want to be forced to deal with complex topics. And they've done a spectacular job of presenting religious beliefs in a non-offensive, amusing way. The ideas of spontaneity, creativity, and the free movement of the Spirit have much in the way of popular appeal. Because of this, one can understand the sincere desire to satisfy the cultural demand for entertainment, even in worship. But while the push toward creative worship sounds compelling, we may have good reasons for hesitation. Depth may have been the price paid for circumventing a formal worship framework.

Evidence of this is multiplying in most other fields. In his careful study on business strategy, Richard Rumelt points out that bad strategy flourishes because it floats above analysis and is "held aloft by the hot hope that one can avoid dealing with these tricky fundamentals and the difficulty of mastering them."[3] Good strategy, he notes, can't materialize without dealing with brutal realities and obstacles in the path; this despite the widespread fad that all you need is to think positively and visualize the results you want. Along with other strategy experts like Harvard's Michael Porter,[4] Rumelt contends that content and how our thinking is framed makes all the difference between organizations that sustain performance and those that don't. Frameworks matter; specific content and processes produce depth in the minds of decision makers. But what's more interesting is that they matter as much for creative output, which at first seems counterintuitive. Don't creative individuals like Thomas Edison and organizations like Pixar come up with brilliant ideas in eureka moments when their minds are *free* from constraints? Fortunately, we now have the data to test how creativity and innovation arise and under what circumstances they tend to be sustained over time.

What we'll see in this chapter is that, far from restricting creativity, frameworks create the space for it to flourish. They do so by providing ritualized processes and specific content, which in turn creates depth. After Lakers coach, Pat Riley, led his team to back-to-back NBA championships in 1986–7 he commented that, "Sustaining an effort is the most important thing for any enterprise. The way to be successful is to learn how to do things right, then do them the same way every time."[5] It will be clear from the evidence that depth doesn't come from spontaneity, nor does creativity. Creativity rather comes

---

[3] Richard P. Rumelt, *Good Strategy—Bad Strategy: The Difference and Why It Matters* (New York, 2011), 58.

[4] Michael E. Porter, *Competitive Strategy: Techniques for Analyzing Industries and Competitors* (New York, 1980).

[5] James Clear, *Atomic Habits: An Easy & Proven Way to Build Good Habits & Break Bad Ones* (New York, 2018), 244.

from depth, and depth comes from specific structure. In the end, we'll
see that nothing of much value actually comes from spontaneity and
the freedom so often connected with lack of formal structure.

Creativity and Spontaneity

There are a lot of pervasive myths surrounding creative individuals.
One of the more popular ones is that highly creative people seem
to have something the rest of us don't, something they were born
with that transcends the limitations of ordinary people. One immediately thinks of geniuses like Thomas Edison, Steve Jobs, or Mozart.
If you read popular literature on the subject, you'd get the impression
we have good reasons for thinking that inborn genius plays a crucial role. Perhaps the most repeated evidence in favor of this comes
from a letter written in 1815 in Germany's General Music Journal, in
which Mozart described his creative process. So you have the context, here's what it said:

> When I am, as it were, completely myself, entirely alone, and of good
> cheer; say traveling in a carriage, or walking after a good meal, or
> during the night when I cannot sleep; it is on such occasions that
> my ideas flow best and most abundantly. All this fires my soul, and
> provided I am not disturbed, my subject enlarges itself, becomes
> methodized and defined, and the whole, though it be long, stands
> almost finished and complete in my mind, so that I can survey it,
> like a fine picture or a beautiful statue, at a glance. Nor do I hear in
> my imagination the parts successively, but I hear them, as it were,
> all at once. When I proceed to write down my ideas the committing
> to paper is done quickly enough, for everything is, as I said before,
> already finished; and it rarely differs on paper from what it was in my
> imagination.[6]

This letter implies that Mozart's greatest works came to him
complete and when he was alone and in a good mood. No framework
or process was needed, as they were produced with a spontaneity

---

[6] Kevin Ashton, *How To Fly A Horse* (New York 2015), xiii–xv.

that many argue lies at the heart of creative work. He simply had to imagine and then write them down. While romantic and appealing to common prejudices about how invention occurs, Kevin Ashton points out that there's a problem: Mozart didn't write the letter. It's a forgery that was first shown in 1856 by Mozart's biographer, Otto Jahn, and subsequently confirmed by other scholars. Despite that, it's been used by many writers to explain the spontaneous nature of creativity in books as late at 2012. Why does the myth persist? Because, as Ashton suggests, it appeals to our romantic prejudices.

There's a common narrative surrounding how new things come to be. Geniuses have dramatic moments of insight in which symphonies are created, businesses built, and scientific breakthroughs are accomplished with eureka moments and a magic touch. The problem with such myths is that we don't see the long road from nothing to something new. Perhaps, says Ashton, we don't even want to. Rather than seeing artistic masterpieces as gained by sweat and grind, we prefer to see them as misty magic. "It is seductive to conclude that great innovation is delivered to us by miracle via genius. And so the myth."[7] It dulls the luster to think that great inventions involved a lot of trial and error and good processes that, over long periods of time and inch by inch, made progress.

Unfortunately, experts tell us there are no shortcuts to creation. It isn't a moment of inspiration but a lifetime of endurance, and more monotony than adventure. It's all about having a framework that focuses attention and a process that allows you to endure through the long hours and the endless failures. The fact is that most turns end up being wrong, which means that creative people are the ones that aren't prone to quit. The rest of us don't see what they go through and the endless failures they overcome. We didn't see James Dyson develop and test five thousand prototypes over five years when he created the cyclone-based vacuum cleaner. Innovation is more accurately seen as a series of repetitive failures, and it applies to every field and innovator. Pulse News founder, Ankit Gupta, says that creativity is always in hindsight. "It's not about just coming up with the one genius idea that solves the problem, but trying and failing at a hundred other

_____
[7] Kevin Ashton, *How To Fly A Horse*, xv, 69.

solutions before arriving at the best one."[8] In other words, there are no big leaps, only developments that look that way from the outside. This is true even of Nobel Prize winners, with one study showing that they generally published scientific papers earlier in their career than most peers, and significantly more papers throughout their career. They simply worked harder than anyone else.[9]

The Real Gift

Leading scholars on expertise note that research since the 1990s reveals that the human brain—even in adults—is far more adaptable than anyone realized.[10] It responds to the right sort of triggers by rewiring itself in various ways. This adaptability explains how people like Mozart develop talents such as perfect pitch (the ability to identity which note was played on a musical instrument). As they respond to training, their brains develop particular circuitry enabling perfect pitch. Bottom line is that we now know these "gifts" are the product of intensive training and not some inborn genetic gift. Experiments in perfect pitch by Ayako Sakakibara (reported in the *Psychology of Music*) demonstrated that children who were properly trained developed perfect pitch.

Based on extensive research, Anders Ericsson and Robert Pool conclude that the gift these people have is the same one we all have: the adaptability of the brain and body, which some have taken advantage of more than the rest of us. This is true across disciplines. In response to a commentator who claimed he was born with shooting talent, Ray Allen—ten-time NBA All-Star and the greatest three-point shooter in history—strongly disagreed: "I've argued this with a lot of people in my life. When people say God blessed me with a beautiful jump shot, it really pisses me off. I tell those people, 'Don't undermine the work I've put in every day'. Not some days. Every

---

[8] Tom Kelley and David Kelley, *Creative Confidence: Unleashing the Creative Potential Within Us All* (New York, 2013), 114.

[9] Anders Ericsson and Robert Pool, *Peak: Secrets From the New Science of Expertise* (Boston, 2016), 205.

[10] Anders Ericsson and Robert Pool, *Peak*, xii–xix.

day. Ask anyone who has been on a team with me who shoots the most. Go back to Seattle and Milwaukee and ask them. The answer is me." The truth is that Allen's jump shot in high school was poor. But he practiced, worked hard at it and, over time, transformed it from mediocre to exceptional. In all cases of mastery, memory is critical, whether it's body or intellectual memory. Each chunk that's memorized opens up the mental space for more effortful thinking or movement.[11] When you know the physical routine (as in Ray Allen's case) or the basic concepts (as in other endeavors) without thinking, you're free to pay attention to more advanced details—which becomes the backbone of excellence in any discipline.

Having said this, not all practice techniques are created equal. Making random shots, indiscriminately lifting weights, or being repeatedly exposed to surface information won't yield improvements of the sort required for expertise. To achieve that level, we need to consider what works and what doesn't and adopt the method conducive to how the human mind and body best process information.[12] And that involves a framework with specific content and processes. Ericsson and Pool call it "purposeful practice." This means that to achieve any higher aim we need to set particular goals and use specific methods to achieve mastery.

How long does it take, and how much effort is typically involved? Malcolm Gladwell makes the case that it takes upwards of ten thousand hours to gain the expertise needed for original work.[13] Whether it's exactly ten thousand hours, he's right that it takes a lot. Authors and poets normally write for more than a decade before they produce their best work, and it's usually a decade or more between a scientist's first publication and his most important contribution. All of this is in addition to the years of study before the first work is published.[14] Psychologist John Hayes discovered that it takes an average of twenty years from the time a person starts studying music until he

---

[11] James Clear, *Atomic Habits*, 239.

[12] Anders Ericsson and Robert Pool, *Peak*, 9, 15, 153.

[13] Malcolm Gladwell, *Outliers: The Story of Success* (New York, 2008), pp. 35ff.

[14] Anders Ericsson and Robert Pool, *Peak*, 112–113.

or she composes an excellent piece of music, and it's generally never less than ten years.

This might suggest an answer to why mastery isn't more common. With how often we're bombarded with phrases like "it all comes down to passion," that we need to get "amped up" to achieve our goals, it's no wonder why so many lose steam. Motivational speakers abound with the message that all we need is to think about our desires, refrain from negative thoughts, and we're guaranteed to succeed. But the reality is that it can be depressing when we lose focus or motivation because we assume that successful people must have a bottomless reserve of passion. Feeling a lack of motivation brings on boredom, which becomes the greatest obstacles to success. The ugly truth is that the more you practice something, the more boring and routine it is. And most of us get bored with habits because they stop delighting; as our habits become ordinary, we derail our progress in the search for novelty. "Perhaps," says James Clear, "this is why we get caught up in a never-ending cycle, jumping from one workout to the next, one diet to the next, one business idea to the next. As soon as we experience the slightest dip in motivation, we begin seeking a new strategy—even if the old one was still working."[15] Modern society is, in many ways, slave to a consumerist mentality. More than any other time in history we want to *feel* entertained, and when we don't—even when it's in our best interest to continue the course—we abandon something for the next new thing. Rarely do we think about the fact that what we want is often not what we need. But it's those who focus on routine, pay attention to process, that can push through boredom and achieve remarkable depth.

Which brings us back to Wolfgang Mozart. Was he an exception to the thousands of hours and deliberate practice rule? The answer is no. While talented, he had a father—Leopold Mozart—who was dedicated to raising a musical prodigy. Not only had Leopold written a book on teaching music to children that he tested on Wolfgang's older sister, but Leopold was one of the first music teachers to start children at a young age. It's likely that Wolfgang started his training before the age of four, which included the push to develop his

---

[15] James Clear, *Atomic Habits*, 234.

own composing skills (unlike music training today). Still, the claims that he started composing at six to eight are overstated. We know that the first compositions he supposedly wrote were in Leopold's handwriting, who himself was a frustrated composer who'd hitched his success to his son's. Much like parents today who do their children's science fair projects or push their kids to excel at sports they love, it's not hard to imagine something similar.

This is all the more likely given what we know of Wolfgang's piano concertos written at age eleven. Though for many years they were considered original, musicologists now know they were based on relatively unknown sonatas by others. In other words, they were reworkings of the works of others. The first serious compositions of Wolfgang we can be certain were written by him arose when he was fifteen or sixteen—after more than a decade of serious practice under his father. In short, "there is no evidence for—and plenty of evidence against—the claim that he was a prodigy whose accomplishments cannot be understood as the result of practice and must therefore be attributed to innate talent."[16]

Deliberate Cultivation

In his study on Charles Darwin, Howard Gruber concludes that each of us makes a different set of decisions about how we make use of our personal resources, thereby setting the scene for the fortunate thoughts that occur and choosing among them. Darwin could notice behavioral variations in pigeons and use them in a theory of evolution because he was at once the pigeon fancier, evolutionist, and materialist. The fact he was all these things at once meant that a unique intersection of many things could occur in his mind. And that, the existence of such an ensemble, shouldn't be regarded as an accident, but rather the deliberately cultivated fruit of his effort. He organized his life to construct a new point of view.[17] The same could be said of Steve Jobs or Thomas Edison, or any innovator with sustained performance.

---

[16] Anders Ericsson and Robert Pool, *Peak*, 211–214.

[17] Howard E. Gruber, *Darwin on Man: A Psychological Study of Scientific Creativity* (Chicago, 1981), 257.

Along these lines, innovation researchers note that creative CEOs spend 50 percent more time on discovery activities (questioning, observing, experimenting, and networking) than CEOs with no innovation track record. Innovators intentionally maneuver themselves into the intersection where their diverse experiences foster the discovery of new insights, which is where associations occur between seemingly unconnected things.[18]

As we'll see, many companies deliberately adopt processes that mimic the act of cross pollination. David and Tom Kelley—founder and partner of the leading design firm, IDEO—say that you can create an "epiphany-friendly" environment within yourself and your organization, but it requires the right processes. To achieve this, IDEO brings people with different backgrounds and perspectives to the team, mixing engineers, anthropologists, and business designers on project teams with surgeons, food scientists, and behavioral economists. "Bringing together a variety of life experiences and contrasting perspectives results in a creative tension that often leads to more innovative and interesting ideas."[19]

Part of IDEO's success lies in its ritualistic practice of questioning, as their teams understand that it cultivates deep insights. Einstein highlighted this part of the scientific method when he stated that formulating the problem is often more important than its solution.[20] Knowing the right answer to the wrong question is useless. In what way, however, are questions formalized in a business context? Innovative companies like IDEO start by exploring what currently is and then ask what might be. "Collectively, these questions help describe the territory (physically, intellectually, and emotionally) and provide a launching pad for the next line of inquiry."[21] With that

---

[18] Jeff Dyer, Hal Gregersen, and Clayton M. Christensen, *The Innovator's DNA: Mastering the Five Skills of Disruptive Innovators* (Boston, 2011), 25–26, 45–46, 59.

[19] Tom Kelley and David Kelley, *Creative Confidence: Unleashing the Creative Potential Within Us All* (New York, 2013), 105, 186.

[20] Tom Kelley and David Kelley, *Creative Confidence*, 101.

[21] Jeff Dyer, Hal Gregersen, and Clayton M. Christensen, *The Innovator's DNA*, 68, 71.

knowledge, innovators treat the world as a question mark and constantly challenge the accuracy of their mental maps. Comfortably suspended between faith in and doubt of their maps, they remember that their views of the world are never the actual territory. In other words, through questioning they constantly realign their mental maps to reality.

Thus, far from the idea that creativity springs from unconstrained freedom, experts are showing just the opposite. Google's Marissa Mayer commented that, "Creativity loves constraint. People often think of it in terms of artistic work—unbridled, unguided effort that leads to beautiful effect. If you look deeper, however, you'll find that some of the most inspiring art forms—haikus, sonatas, religious paintings—are fraught with constraints . . . Creativity, in fact, thrives best when constrained."[22] Because of this, some of the most innovative ideas come from questions that artificially impose constraints.

Observation and Experimentation

One of the most ritualized forms of innovation surrounds observation and experimentation, which are well defined steps teams go through for idea creation.[23] Rather than engaging in passive surveillance, innovators deliberately inspect what people do, what works and what doesn't, and which work-arounds are used to get jobs done. This observation framework is critical because surprises are typically lost as our minds force what we see to fit preexisting beliefs. As David and Tom Kelley insist, "Don't wait for the proverbial apple to fall on your head. Go out in the world and proactively seek experiences that will spark creative thinking. Interact with experts, immerse yourself in unfamiliar situations, and role-play customer scenarios. Inspiration is fueled by a deliberate, planned course of action."[24] This is also why purposefully seeking data from completely different fields

---

[22] Jeff Dyer, Hal Gregersen, and Clayton M. Christensen, *The Innovator's DNA*, 78.

[23] Jeff Dyer, Hal Gregersen, and Clayton M. Christensen, *The Innovator's DNA*, 92–102, 166, 168–169, 202.

[24] Tom Kelley and David Kelley, *Creative Confidence*, 22.

is a skill innovators have to develop. The Japanese company, Keyence Corporation, requires its salespeople to spend hours observing customer manufacturing lines to gain insights into their problems. Very structured, deliberate, and far from spontaneous, but the practice has teeth and produces depth in its salesforce. A. G. Lafley, CEO of Procter & Gamble, similarly comments that P&G devotes hundreds of hours to observing customers, just as anthropologists observe tribes, and has specific processes around the practice.

With observation expanding the mental horizon, experimentation enables quick feedback on what works and what doesn't. Specific frameworks guide most experimentation. Jeff Bezos of Amazon remarks on this as follows: "You need to do as many experiments per unit of time as possible. Innovation is part and parcel with going down blind alleys. You can't have one without the other. But every once in a while, you go down an alley and it opens up into this huge, broad avenue . . . it makes all the blind alleys worthwhile."[25] Amazon keeps its experimenting cadence up by keeping teams small enough to be fed by two pizzas (six to ten people), which allows it to work on a large number of projects and go down more blind alleys in search for new ideas. Google uses beta labels to release products early and often for public trials, which allows the company to get instant feedback. Hundreds of teams pursue and pilot new projects simultaneously. With its 20 percent rule, in which engineers spend up to 20 percent of their time working on pet projects, Google has been able to launch half of its new products. Other companies such as 3M and P&G have similar processes.

Central to the experimentation process is prototyping, which generates a minimum viable product used to test and get early feedback.[26] About 90 percent of initial product proposals don't get the answer right, so starting with a basic prototype and iterating on feedback is critical. Having a ritual-like feel, it's a prerequisite of success and cements commitment to continuous improvement. Not unlike the methods of the natural sciences, the frameworks used in modern

---

[25] Jeff Dyer, Hal Gregersen, and Clayton M. Christensen, *The Innovator's DNA*, 208–209, 221–222, 228.

[26] Tom Kelley and David Kelley, *Creative Confidence*, 114.

companies keep their feet on the ground and in contact with the real world. They serve as a safeguard against imaginations taking flight without proper anchors to reality. As managers know, what we *think* customers need and want is often very different from what they *actually* need and want. Tom Kelley notes that a chief characteristic of innovative teams is that they connect to the outside world and "know that answers don't lie within."[27]

One final point. Frameworks are effective because they provide a common language and set of practices everyone in the organization understands, which facilitates rapid movement from one part of the process to another. Further, they force discipline and reduce the human tendency to act based on whether things feel or don't feel right. As in the sciences, they facilitate the testing of hypotheses and eschew premature optimism or pessimism about feedback. Thus, frameworks matter because they put a check on human impulsiveness and force us to look at the data, not our fleeting impressions and feelings.[28]

IDEO

One of the world's most admired design and development companies is IDEO, whose creativity brought us the Apple mouse, Polaroid's I Zone instant camera, and the Palm handheld. Because of its sustained performance, it—along with Pixar below—deserves special mention. Though on the surface things might appear a bit haphazard, the company achieves impressive results by following a five-step framework for understanding problems and developing innovative solutions.[29] Let's take a quick look.

The first step is gaining a deep understanding of the market, client, technology, and the perceived constraints of the problem to be solved. Second, IDEO teams take the time to observe people in

---

[27] Tom Kelley and Jonathan Littman, *The Art of Innovation: Lessons in Creativity from IDEO, America's Leading Design Firm* (New York, 2001), 71.

[28] Nathan Furr and Jeff Dyer, *The Innovator's Method: Bringing the Lean Startup Into Your Organization* (Boston, 2014), 173.

[29] Tom Kelley and Jonathan Littman, *The Art of Innovation*, 6–7.

real-life situations.[30] Having a deep knowledge of what makes people tick, what confuses them, what they like, what they hate, and where they have latent needs not addressed by current products are all considered prerequisites for solving issues. Third, teams visualize new-to-the-world concepts and customers, which can take the forms of computer renderings and simulations, physical prototypes (thousands per year), storyboarding scenarios, making a video portraying life with a future product, and even portraying the experience with a series of comic-book-like frames showing action and dialogue (often on simple post-it notes).[31]

The fourth step is evaluating and refining prototypes in a series of quick iterations,[32] which happens through feedback from the team, from outside knowledgeable people, and prospective customers. Incremental improvement occurs in each of the iterations based on what confuses people, what works and what doesn't, and what they like or dislike. For IDEO, prototyping is problem solving, and it's a culture and language of its own.[33] The last step is often the longest and involves implementing the new concept for commercialization. "We've demonstrated that this deceptively simple methodology works for everything from creating simple children's toys to launching e-commerce businesses. It's a process that has helped create products that have already saved scores of lives, from portable defibrillators and better insulin-delivery systems to devices that help grow sheets of new skin for burn victims."[34]

The company believes that you have to go beyond putting yourself in your customer's shoes, and it's not even enough to ask people what they think about a product or idea. The act of observing people in their natural environment, of observing the lion in the jungle, ensures that easily missed details don't go unnoticed. It's not enough to see or hear what people say—oftentimes they can't articulate their

---

[30] Tim Brown, "Design Thinking" in *Harvard Business Review* (June, 2008), 86.

[31] Tom Kelley and David Kelley, *Creative Confidence*, 138.

[32] Tim Brown, "Design Thinking," 87.

[33] Tom Kelley and Jonathan Littman, *The Art of Innovation*, 104.

[34] Tom Kelley and Jonathan Littman, *The Art of Innovation*, 7–8.

concerns—so you have to interpret shades of meaning to uncover their underlying motivations or needs.[35]

Central to IDEO's process is what they refer to as brainstorming. In these sessions, well-articulated problems serve as the idea engine of IDEO's culture. So important is the practice that many of IDEO's conference rooms have brainstorming rules stenciled on the walls, such as "Go for quantity," "Encourage wild ideas," or "Be visual."[36] But the sessions are highly structured, not free-for-alls. Every idea is numbered to encourage quantity. Because visibility is critical, they cover every wall and flat surface with paper before the session starts, which locates each idea in a space and helps people remember what spawned it when they return to that part of the room. They've also learned that good brainstormers are extremely visual and physical, so they include sketching, mind mapping, diagrams, stick figures, physical objects like blocks, foam core, and duct tape. Since the framework and practice is core, the company regularly warns against things that tend to kill brainstorming sessions.

Finally, IDEO recognizes that myths around creation are persistent and have to be continually dispelled for its culture to flourish. One of them is the myth of the lone genius. Tim Brown, IDEO's CEO, says that we "believe that great ideas pop fully formed out of brilliant minds, in feats of imagination well beyond the abilities of mere mortals."[37] As a prime example, Thomas Edison is generally regarded as one of the most creative geniuses in history. He created the lightbulb and then wrapped an entire industry around it. While the lightbulb itself is thought to be his best achievement, Edison understood that a system of electric power generation and transmission was needed to make it useful. So he created that as well. But the myth that his creative genius was solitary is resilient. The truth is more subtle.

In a six year period, Edison generated an astonishing four hundred patents, producing innovations in the telegraph, telephone. phonograph, and lightbulb; however, he did it with the help of a

---

[35] Tom Kelley and Jonathan Littman, *The Art of Innovation*, 26, 39.

[36] Tom Kelley and Jonathan Littman, *The Art of Innovation*, 57–66.

[37] Tim Brown, "Design Thinking," 85, 88.

fourteen-man team.[38] His longtime assistant, Francis Jehl, commented that "Edison is in reality a collective noun and means the work of many men." Like other innovators, his work was the result of many people and hard work which was augmented by a creative human-centered discovery process, and followed by iterative cycles of prototyping, testing, and refinement.[39] At IDEO, no one imagines that a dozen people from within the company has the answers.

Pixar

One of the most fascinating companies to watch in recent years has been Pixar, creators of the blockbuster movies Toy Story, Monsters Inc., Finding Nemo, and The Incredibles (among many others). The company has won fifteen Academy Awards and grossed over $600 million per film—and out of the fourteen features it has produced, all but one have made the list of the top fifty highest grossing animated movies.[40] As to how they've done it, Pixar founder, Ed Catmull, has a ready answer. He explains that candor—a deliberate framework of truth-telling that's treated as sacred and non-negotiable—has sat at the core of the company's success from the beginning. Fundamental to its process, candor is regularly practiced in what the company calls the Braintrust, which meets every few months to assess each movie. Catmull explains that it's the primary way Pixar pushes itself toward excellence and roots out mediocrity. "Its premise is simple: Put smart, passionate people in a room together, charge them with identifying and solving problems, and encourage them to be candid with one another."[41] The process is guarded with almost religious fervor, because you can't eliminate blocks to truth-telling once and for all and think you're safe. The fear of saying something stupid and looking

---

[38] Tom Kelley and Jonathan Littman, The Art of Innovation, 69–71.

[39] Tim Brown, "Design Thinking," 88.

[40] Greg Satell, "The Little Known Secret to Pixar's Creative Success." https://www.forbes.com/sites/gregsatell/2015/05/29/the-little-known-secret-to-pixars-creative-success/#7146f6938b28.

[41] Ed Catmull with Amy Wallace, Creativity Inc.: Overcoming the Unseen Forces That Stand in the Way of True Inspiration (New York, 2014), 86–87.

bad, of offending someone or being intimidated, all reassert themselves even after you think they've been eliminated. Candor's central role is attested by the fact that critical feedback about early storylines has transformed many potentially bad projects into blockbuster hits.

Catmull frankly admits that "early on, *all* of our movies suck . . . Creativity has to start somewhere, and we are true believers in the power of bracing, candid feedback and the iterative process—reworking, reworking, and reworking again, until a flawed story finds its through line or a hollow character finds its soul."[42] To make the process work, Pixar teams use storyboards, which provide crude mock-ups where the script is drawn and edited with temporary voices and music. From that, the Braintrust discusses what doesn't ring true and what could be better, with a new version of the film generated every three to six months. The process then repeats itself. In fact, it takes about twelve thousand storyboard drawings to make a ninety minute reel. But because of its iterative nature, story teams commonly create ten times that number by the time their work is done.

We should also mention another important reason the Braintrust is central. People who take on creative projects often get lost at some point in the process. Where a writer or director once had perspective, he can lose the forest for the trees. With details overwhelming and obscuring the whole, it's difficult to move forward in any one direction. No matter how talented the director, it can be hard to get him to address a problem he can't see, and it may be that what he *thinks* is visible on the screen isn't to others. Like the rest of us, he needs feedback to reality check his thoughts.

Lastly we should mention that, like IDEO, Pixar institutionalizes the importance of learning from failure. "Fail early and fail fast" and "be wrong as fast as you can" express recognition that progress happens only at the intersection of doing and failing.[43] Failure is a manifestation of learning and exploration, and it's best to acknowledge it rather than pretend it doesn't occur. In fear-based cultures, people avoid risk and seek to repeat safe practices that worked in

---

[42] Ed Catmull with Amy Wallace, *Creativity Inc.*, 90–91.

[43] Ed Catmull with Amy Wallace, *Creativity Inc.*, 108–109.

the past. However, their work is always derivative, not innovative. Catmull says that "If we as leaders can talk about our mistakes and our part in them, then we make it safe for others. You don't run from it or pretend it doesn't exist. That is why I make a point of being open about our meltdowns inside Pixar, because I believe they teach us something important: Being open about problems is the first step toward learning from them."[44]

Ray Dalio, founder of one of the largest investment firms, Bridgewater, agrees. Everyone makes mistakes, says Dalio, but the successful people learn from them. While they cause pain, you shouldn't shield yourself or others from it. Pain indicates that something is wrong. To deal with weaknesses well you have to acknowledge them frankly and openly, and work to find ways of preventing them from hurting you in the future. We'll conclude this section with Dalio's comments because they're instructive:

> If you want to evolve, you need to go where the problems and the pain are. By confronting the pain, you will see more clearly the paradoxes and problems you face. Reflecting on them and resolving them will give you wisdom. The harder the pain and the challenge, the better . . . Because these moments of pain are so important, you shouldn't rush through them. Stay in them and explore them so you can build a foundation for improvement. Embracing your failures—and confronting the pain they cause you and others—is the first step toward genuine improvement; it is why confession precedes forgiveness in many societies.[45]

Not Outliers

Lest we think that IDEO and Pixar are outliers, we should note the strong trend toward more ritualistic business environments. Examples abound, but many competing systems exist for setting a cadence and keeping work flowing through an organization. A few of the more prominent ones will suffice here as illustrations.

---

[44] Ed Catmull with Amy Wallace, *Creativity Inc.*, 111.

[45] Ray Dalio, *Principles* (New York, 2017), 349–353.

Although formerly confined to software development and manu-facturing, the principles of Agile, Lean, and Kanban have combined as a mainstream and effective way companies sustain innovation and efficiency. So that we have the context, I'll give a brief descrip-tion of each.

Agile began in software development and promotes adap-tive planning (meaning that plans are only made when the project is about to start), evolutionary development (progress happens in short time periods and step-by-step), continuous improvement, and early delivery. As the name implies, it facilitates quick response to changes in a company's goals or business environment. Kanban, which was developed by Taiichi Ohno of Toyota, focuses on limiting the buildup of excessive inventory in a production line. The reason it's important is that excessive buildups create waste and indicate inefficiencies requiring correction. One of the main things Kanban does is establish upper limits to work in process (WIP) inventory in order to avoid overcapacity. Closely related is Lean, which seeks to minimize waste in the process of delivering value. By reducing things down to the minimal number of steps, Lean tries to make it obvious what does and doesn't add to value delivery.

Many frameworks, such as the Scaled Agile Framework, com-bine these concepts into a single system designed to create and deliver ever-increasing value. They do so through highly structured meetings that are governed by the same questions, in the same order, and on the same days of the week. Often referred to as "ceremo-nies," the ritual nature of the gatherings are further emphasized and communicate accountability up and down the organization. While strange from the outside, these ceremonies accomplish some key things: (1) they enforce a common language (2) guarantee rapid feedback and faster value delivery (3) institutionalize continuous improvement, and (4) embed retrospectives on the quality of work and efficiency of the process.

Part of what's driving ceremonial approaches is the pivot to a more systematic, or holistic, view of business. Important in this evolu-tion was the work of W. Edward Deming, who was a pioneer of systems thinking and influenced an entire generation of top management. He described a system as a "series of functions or activities . . . within an organization that work together for the aim of the organization.

The mechanical and electrical parts that work together to make an automobile or a vacuum cleaner form a system."[46] In any system, he argued, there's interdependence between the parts, and the greater the interdependence the greater the need for communication and cooperation. It was an important insight because many organizations fail to understand that it's the system, and not simply parts of it, that ultimately delivers value. Waste in one area produces waste in the whole and reduces overall quality. Seeing the big picture forces managers to think differently about how each part interacts with the others for maximum output.

More recently, James Clear has argued something similar. To improve over time, he says that "What we really need to change are the systems that cause those results. When you solve problems at the results level, you only solve them temporarily. In order to improve for good, you need to solve problems at the systems level. Fix the inputs and the outputs will fix themselves. . . . You do not rise to the level of your goals. You fall to the level of your systems."[47] The purpose of setting goals is to win the game, but the purpose of building systems is to continue playing the game. It's the commitment to the *process* that determines progress.

What's important for our purposes is how the pivot to systems thinking, and more specifically the adoption of highly structured frameworks, impacts the people using them. They do so in a few key ways. First, a good framework provides a common language everyone understands and uses on a daily basis. Though elementary, one of the chief problems of any organization is that teams understand similar terms differently—which causes confusion across functions and introduces waste and delays into the system. Second, frameworks help people understand how they fit in the organization by instituting specific practices and processes around a common goal of delivering value. In other words, they provide context. Third, they recognize how humans perceive the world—through sight, sound, smell, touch, and taste. Of the eleven million sensory receptors the

---

[46] W. Edwards Deming, *The Essential Deming: Leadership Principles from the Father of Quality*, ed. Joyce Nilsson Orsini (New York, 2013), 72, 154–155.

[47] James Clear, *Atomic Habits*, 25, 27.

body has, about ten million of them are dedicated to sight.[48] Making work visible with things like Kanban boards—a visible representation of the work being done and where it is in the process—allows people to see (literally) progress and spot bottlenecks in the workflow. Fifth, by forcing teams to explore the brutal truth through retrospectives, they continuously improve by asking the tough questions. The result: teams are constantly compelled to go deep and thus spared from the superficiality that comes all too naturally.

Conclusion

We noted earlier that as a social animal, man is a ritual animal. "If a ritual is suppressed in one form," noted Mary Douglas, "it crops up in others, the more strongly the more intense the social interaction."[49] We're witnessing that in action. As Christians moved away from liturgical, ritual, worship, other areas—from sports, to creators, all the way to large organizations—they adopted ritualized frameworks to improve results and embed continuous improvement. Though they've implemented them in different ways, here are a few of the benefits we've observed.

First, frameworks provide people, whether individuals or teams, with the mental furniture necessary for sustained creativity. This shows that structure doesn't constrain creativity, it spawns it. As counterintuitive as it may be, creativity loves constraints and takes its cue from being bound in common practice and language. Second, frameworks push us beyond the superficial to a deeper understanding of ourselves and the world. They do so by spotlighting ugly truths, blocks, and dependencies. Third, as a bulwark against the common illusion that truth lies within, frameworks challenge our mental maps and force realignment to reality.

Fourth, as it's easy to get lost in the weeds, frameworks keep our eyes on the big picture and force us back to what's most vital. Fifth, frameworks don't let us annex one truth for the sake of another.

---

[48] James Clear, *Atomic Habits*, 84.

[49] Mary Douglas, *Purity and Danger: An Analysis of the Concepts of Pollution and Taboo* (London, 1979), 62.

Reality is complex, and our tendency is to make things easier by flattening the tensions between seemingly conflicting truths. Things like freedom and constraints, law and Gospel, bread and body, wine and blood, earthly and spiritual, are much easier if one idea annexes the other. Good frameworks maintain tensions and keep them front and center.

Bottom line is this: remove the structure provided by a good framework and we lose depth; and with it, creativity and freedom. This being true, should Christian worship be carved out as an exception? Should we expect believers to grow in Christian faith and develop depth absent a liturgical, ritual framework? I believe the answer is no. As we'll see in the next chapter, the odds are against us as we navigate what's right in front of our noses. We're prone to skew what we see and hear, form irrational biases in the blink of an eye, and develop elaborate stories with little connection to reality. That being true of things to which we have immediate access, it's exponentially so with theological and spiritual realities. Thus worship, which should define the Christian life, can't be viewed as an exception to the rule. Whether it's business, musical mastery, or Christian belief, depth is best achieved with purposeful ritual; or more specifically for our purposes, ritual drenched in biblical content and consistent with the patterns we see in the New Testament and the historic church. More on this later.

For now, let's turn our attention to some additional problems with the idea that worship shouldn't come with the constraints imposed by the church's historic liturgy.

CHAPTER 3

What We Know

Mark Twain once said that it's "not what you don't know that gets you into trouble, it's what you know for sure that ain't so."[1] Nothing hampers the progress of knowledge as much as knowing for certain what's true and what's not. For centuries, everyone knew that doctors were gentlemen, and that a gentlemen's hands are clean and can't transmit disease.[2] Thus washing hands between the dissection of cadavers and delivering babies was considered unnecessary. And for centuries, everyone knew that bacteria can't grow in the stomach, so Robin Warren's evidence to the contrary couldn't possibly be right. We now know how wrong both beliefs were despite how coherent they seemed at the time.

If we've learned anything from the history of science, it's that truth is often counterintuitive—a fact that hasn't gone unnoticed in most fields, including even business. Example after example could be cited—ranging from the denial of mountains on the moon because Aristotle never mentioned them to Kodak's denial of the digital revolution. Our knowledge has limits, despite the fact that we're certain about so many things. The question we'll attempt to answer in this chapter is, how limited is it? What do we understand about how humans think, how they make judgments and conclusions? Most importantly, what are the underlying biological,

---

[1] Tom Kelley and David Kelley, *Creative Confidence: Unleashing the Creative Potential Within Us All* (New York, 2013), 94.

[2] Kevin Ashton, *How To Fly A Horse* (New York, 2015), 72–75, 91–95.

neurological, and social constraints preventing us from breaking out of those limits?

If maintaining a biblically based faith matters, these questions merit attention. Just as with scientific and medical blunders of the past, it's important we aren't fooled by what we "know for sure" about the world, ourselves, and God. What we'll see is that we're not perfectly equipped to deal with complex questions about which we have plenty of information; which means that when we come to questions about God and how he wills to bless his people, we're even less equipped.

Having said this, a caveat is in order before proceeding. My purpose won't be to suggest a postmodern despair of knowledge—which falls on its own axe and has been generally destructive—because we can and do come to know things of all sorts. What follows operates under the assumption, in direct opposition to the postmodernist contention, that we can truly know the world outside of our own mind. Yet with that we need to acknowledge two things: (1) the active role we take in our judgments—what we bring to the knowing process that often inhibits our recognition of truth, and (2) the traditional medium of communication that existed in oral and print based cultures has more and more disappeared in favor of a soundbite, decontextualized, emotionally driven society.[3] Given this, it will be easier to see in the research below why the odds are stacked against many of our beliefs; which should make clear why we need to check our views of the world—and of God—against a standard that can correct our natural and learned biases against truth.

With that said, let's talk about what we're up against.

Our Penchant for Story

Our minds are in constant motion, scanning our environment, other people, and situations in search for a story that puts everything in

---

[3] For more on the dual insight that there exists a world independent of the observer and the acknowledgement that the knower is involved in the knowing process, see Alister E. McGrath, *A Scientific Theology: Volume 2—Reality* (Grand Rapids, 2002), 195ff., and Andrew Collier, *Critical Realism: An Introduction to Roy Bhaskar's Philosophy* (New York, 1994).

WHAT WE KNOW   45

its place. They're sense-making machines, and in an important way they can be myth factories—and by that I don't mean the great myths of ancient culture, but the type of myths that cause unwarranted judgments and poor decisions. As to the underlying reasons, Daniel Kahneman notes that the stories people find compelling have a few basic qualities: they're simple; concrete rather than abstract; assign a larger role to talent, stupidity, and intention than to luck; focus on a few notable events rather than on the countless ones that didn't happen, and are usually biased toward more recent events.[4] Overconfidence is often the result, with people drawing more confidence from a small data set than from a much larger set of less consistent data.[5]

We're always ready to interpret people's behavior as a manifestation of personality traits, and good stories give us a simple and coherent account of their actions and intentions. If someone cuts us off in traffic, we're prone to think the person is a jerk rather than rushing his wife to the hospital or having a bad day. Similarly, if a political candidate is good looking, we're likely to rate him as competent and smart; if he's not, we're likely to rate him as more incompetent and less intelligent (called the halo effect). Halos keep explanatory narratives simple and coherent by exaggerating our evaluations of people, such that good people only do good things and bad people only bad things. Thus our minds crave simple and consistent explanations, with inconsistencies reducing the ease of our thoughts and the clarity of our feelings.

One of the things we seem to love about compelling narratives is their seeming inevitability. They foster the illusion that we know the true causes of an event or behavior, which is reinforced constantly in media narratives about every subject under the sun. In a typical business column, for instance, it's not uncommon to read about the latest tech start-up that went from nothing to billions at

---

[4] Daniel Kahneman, *Thinking, Fast and Slow* (New York, 2011), 199–204.

[5] Daniel Kahneman and Amos Tversky, "Intuitive Prediction: Biases and Corrective Procedures." Technical Report PTR-1042-77-6, Sponsored by Defense Advanced Research Project Agency, June 1977, 4–5. https://apps.dtic.mil/dtic/tr/fulltext/u2/a047747.pdf

lighting speed. The trouble is that they're rarely the whole truth. While success is usually attributed to the founder's brilliance, little is said about the role of luck, the countless things that didn't occur, and the hapless competitors who failed to respond to the new threat until it was too late. Google has such a story. Stanford graduate students came up with a better way to search for information and raised initial funding. While things went relatively well, the founders were willing to sell the company for less than $1 million dollars early on, which the buyer rejected because he thought the price was too high. Due to that bit of luck and the many poor decisions of competitors, Google's founders are now some of the richest individuals in the world.

But even with a more fleshed out story of Google's success, there's reason to believe that our understanding is largely illusory. That's because the ultimate test of an explanation of why the company (or any other company) succeeded is whether it would have made the event predictable in advance. Kahneman explains:

> No story of Google's unlikely success will meet that test, because no story can include the myriad of events that would have caused a different outcome. The human mind does not deal well with nonevents. The fact that many of the important events that did occur involve choices further tempts you to exaggerate the role of skill and underestimate the part that luck played in the outcome. Because every critical decision turned out well, the record suggests almost flawless prescience—but bad luck could have disrupted any one of the successful steps. The halo effect adds the final touches, lending an aura of invincibility to the heroes of the story.[6]

Adding to this, experts have established our tendency to assess the quality of a decision not by whether the process used to make it was sound, but by whether its outcome was good or bad (called outcome bias). Think about a low-risk surgical procedure where an unpredictable event occurred causing the patient's death. After the fact, juries will be prone to believe the operation was risky and

---

[6] Daniel Kahneman, *Thinking, Fast and Slow*, 200.

that the doctor should have known better. This bias makes it difficult to evaluate a decision in the present that was reasonable when it was made. With outcome bias in mind, imagine the criticism of the buyer who rejected Google's purchase, which at the time may have had reasonable concerns. One area we see outcome bias being especially harsh is on decision makers. The Swedish-Swiss industrial company ABB serves as an example. While the company was successful, people said that CEO Percy Barnevik had a clear vision, excellent communication skills, impressive, charm, and self-confidence. When ABB's fortunes turned, Percy was demonized as arrogant, too controlling, and abrasive.[7] Interestingly, no one argued Percy had changed. Assessments of him were completely biased on outcomes.

How We Think

Kahneman points to evidence that we have two distinct thinking systems.[8] System 1 operates automatically and quickly and requires little to no effort. It's gullible, biased to believe, forms causal connections that aren't backed by evidence,[9] and isn't prone to doubt its quick conclusions. Not only does it fail to keep track of alternatives it rejects, it doesn't acknowledge that there were alternatives. Because of its tendency to create causal connections, it constructs coherent stories (even when there are none) and suppresses ambiguity—meaning that it jumps to conclusions from little evidence. Philip Tetlock calls this system 1 feature the "tip-of-your-nose perspective."[10] On top of that, our subjective confidence in our stories correlates with their coherence, and unless they're immediately challenged the stories can spread as if they were true. "Where this propensity can go

---

[7] Phil Rosenzweig, *The Halo Effect . . . and the Eight Other Business Delusions That Deceive Managers* (New York, 2007), 57–58.

[8] Daniel Kahneman, *Thinking, Fast and Slow* (New York, 2011), 19–49, 208.

[9] Daniel Kahneman and Amos Tversky, "Intuitive Prediction," 4–5.

[10] Philip E. Tetlock and Dan Gardner, *Superforecasting: The Art and Science of Prediction* (New York, 2015), 137.

wrong," observes Nassim Taleb, "is when it increases our *impression* of understanding."[11]

System 2 involves all that effortful mental activity that includes complex calculations. While in charge of doubt, it's often lazy and avoids the investment required to check the automatic suggestions of System 1. Because of this, people tend to be overconfident and place too much faith in their intuitions—which is spurred on by the fact that cognitive effort feels unpleasant and we avoid it as much as possible. Further, when people believe something is true, they're likely to believe arguments that appear to support it, even when they're unsound. Annie Duke reports similar research, noting that we form our beliefs rather haphazardly, accepting all sorts of things based on what we hear but haven't verified.[12] She puts the problem as follows:

This is how *we think* we form beliefs:

1. We hear something;
2. We think about it and vet it, determining whether it's true or false, and only after that
3. We form our belief.

But this is how we *actually* form beliefs:

1. We hear something;
2. We believe it to be true;
3. Only sometimes, and later, if we have time or the desire, we think about it and vet it, determining whether it's true or false.

Citing Harvard professor Daniel Gilbert, she points out that people naturally find it easy to believe and very difficult to doubt.

---

[11] Nassim Nicholas Taleb, *The Black Swan: The Impact of the Highly Improbable* (New York, 2010), 64.

[12] Annie Duke, *Thinking in Bets: Making Smarter Decisions When You Don't Have All the Facts* (New York, 2018), 50–51.

Believing is so easy it's more like involuntary comprehension than rational assessment, meaning that our default setting is to believe as true what we hear and read. And even when the information is clearly presented as false, we're still likely to process it as true.

This was demonstrated in a 1994 study in which subjects read messages about a warehouse fire. Some of them read that the fire started near a closet containing paint cans and pressurized gas cylinders, which predictably caused them to infer a connection. Five messages later, however, the same subjects received a correction that the closet was actually empty, yet they still blamed burning paint for toxic fumes and cited negligence for keeping flammable objects nearby. Thus while we think we're capable of easily updating our beliefs based on new information, numerous studies like this prove otherwise. Duke puts it best: "Instead of altering our beliefs to fit new information, we do the opposite, altering our interpretation of that information to fit our beliefs."[13]

Making matters more precarious is that human rationality inclines dangerously to pride, in the sense that what I know is all that needs to be known. Jordan Peterson observes that pride falls in love with its own creations and tries to make them absolute.[14] Rationality is therefore subject to the single worst temptation: to raise what it knows now to the status of an absolute. This doesn't mean that rationality is doomed because it can and does produce clarity, but it shows that it has the capacity to deceive, falsify, mislead, deny, omit, rationalize, bias, and exaggerate.

Peterson also drives home another rarely recognized point: namely, reason falls in love with itself—something Luther highlighted centuries ago. It falls in love with its own productions, elevates them, and worships them as absolutes. Peterson puts it this way: "To say it again: it is the greatest temptation of the rational faculty to glorify its own capacity and its own productions and to claim that in the face of its theories nothing transcendent or outside its domain need exist. This means that all important facts

---

[13] Annie Duke, *Thinking in Bets*, 55–56.

[14] Jordan B. Peterson, *12 Rules for Life: An Antidote to Chaos* (Canada, 2018), 210, 217–218.

have been discovered. This means that nothing important remains unknown."

Why does it all matter? First, because it shows that we're wired for gullibility and for preferring nicely stated conclusions over reasoning based on probabilities and facts. Second, we seem to be stubbornly attached to the first things we read and hear, which serve as anchors for future beliefs. Third, it shows that we have the dangerous tendency to fall in love with our own ideas, and in an almost idolatrous way, to worship them. The point isn't that we can't have evidence-based reasoning, but that in light of our natural tendencies it has to be carefully cultivated. The short of it is that it takes discipline to get at truth, and this is as true in academics and business as it is in religious matters.

Jumping to Conclusions

In a fascinating study that measured how people jump to conclusions from limited information, participants were given one-sided evidence of a disagreement between a union representative and a manager that led to the representative's arrest. Not only was the evidence one-sided, but participants were fully aware of it. The conclusions they jumped to were telling because based on how the information was presented, the participants could have easily generated the arguments for the other side. Despite that, the one-sided information skewed their judgments in favor of the side presented. Further, the evidence made the participants more confident in their judgments than another group exposed to both sides. Kahneman, who reports the study, says that this is what you'd expect if the confidence people have is determined by the coherence of the story they construct from available information. "It is the consistency of the information that matters for a good story, not its completeness. Indeed, you will often find that knowing little makes it easier to fit everything you know into a coherent pattern."[15]

He calls this tendency "what you see is all there is." Information that isn't retrieved or present might as well not exist. Recall that this is a symptom of System 1, which excels at constructing the best story

---

[15] Daniel Kahneman, *Thinking, Fast and Slow*, 85–88.

from currently activated ideas—without allowing for information it doesn't have. System 1 measures success by a story's coherence, with the amount and quality of the data it's based on having little importance. Despite the fact that information is often scarce, System 1 operates as a machine for jumping to conclusions. But the lack of information doesn't affect our confidence in our judgments, as that depends mostly on the quality of the story we can tell about what we see, even if what we see is very little. In other words, we often settle on a coherent pattern and suppress doubt and ambiguity.

The human preference for cognitive ease explains much of this. Ease is a sign that things are going well, meaning no threats, no major news, and no need to mobilize our logical mind which is the purview of System 2. You might recall that System 2 is lazy, however, and that mental effort is aversive. The bottom line is that predictable illusions occur if a judgment is based on cognitive ease or strain. Anything that makes it easier for our brain's machinery to run smoothly tends to bias beliefs. In fact, something politicians know well, a reliable way to make people believe in falsehoods is frequent repetition because familiarity isn't easily distinguished from truth. Many studies have demonstrated this. In one of them, people who were repeatedly exposed to the phrase "the body temperature of a chicken" were more likely to accept the statement "the body temperature of a chicken is 144 degrees" as true (or any other arbitrary number). The familiarity of one phrase made the whole statement feel familiar, and therefore true in the person's mind. "If you cannot remember the source of a statement, and have no way to relate it to other things you know, you have no option but to go with the sense of cognitive ease."[16]

Moreover, if a statement is linked to other beliefs or preferences you hold, or comes from a source you trust and like, you'll feel a sense of cognitive ease. Here's the trouble, though. There may be other causes for your feeling of ease but you have no simple way of tracing the feelings to their source. Kahneman notes that people can with some difficulty overcome some of these problems when motivated, but on most occasions System 2 is lazy and will adopt the suggestions of System 1, and march on.

---

[16] Daniel Kahneman, *Thinking, Fast and Slow*, 59, 62, 64.

Along the same lines, Brené Brown cites her own research that we naturally form stories about people and situations which tend to be untrue.[17] She points out that our brains are wired to love tight stories with simple conclusions, which our bodies encourage through dopamine hits.[18] Acting on our stories, we not only fail to engage with what's real and what's not, but our behavior often damages those involved, including ourselves. Because of this she talks about the need to "rumble" with the stories we tell ourselves and ask the tough questions about truth. Seeing the delta (or difference) between our stories and the truth allows us to develop a more healthy outlook.[19] Because jumping to false conclusions is so natural, you can see why we'd want to check our thinking against the facts; forming half-baked judgments and then acting on them isn't something any of us would be proud of.

From Judgments to Theories

Kahneman and Brown both talk about our tendency to create stories from limited information, and then act on them as though we had all the facts. For our purposes, we can view our stories loosely as theories (though not of course in the technical scientific sense) of how the world works and our relationship to it. What's clear from the research is that our theories about the world have a huge impact on how we think and behave. We all form loose theories about the world; about ourselves, other people, and a vast array of circumstances. Yet time and again we fail to hold them up to reality to see if they're actually true.

At least one problem with our theory-making appetite—our "theorizing disease" as Taleb puts it[20]—is that we're rarely stumped. We have intuitions and feelings about almost everything. We like or dislike people way before getting to know them; we trust or

---

[17] Brené Brown, *Rising Strong: How the Ability to Reset Transforms the Way We Live, Love, Parent, and Lead* (New York, 2017), 77–82.

[18] R. A. Burton, *On Being Certain: Believing You Are Right Even When You're Not* (New York, 2008), 98–99.

[19] Brené Brown, *Rising Strong*, 94–97.

[20] Nassim Nicholas Taleb, *The Black Swan*, 64ff.

distrust strangers without knowing why; we feel that an organization will succeed without analyzing it.[21] Bottom line is that we
often have answers to questions we don't completely understand
and rely on evidence we can't explain or defend. Kahneman suggests that we generate intuitive opinions on complex matters by
substituting an easier question for a harder one. In other words,
if an answer to a hard question isn't found quickly, then System
1 finds an easier related question and answers that instead. For
instance in place of the more difficult question, "How happy are
you with your life?" we answer instead the easier "What is my
mood right now?" Or for the hard question, "How popular will
the president be six months from now?" we substitute the easier "How popular is the president right now?" Because System 2
often follows the path of least effort, it quickly endorses the answer
without much scrutiny. "You will not be stumped, you will not
have to work very hard, and you may not even notice that you did
not answer the question you were asked."[22]

Up to this point, we've only dealt with how our reason operates,
but what happens when you throw emotions in the mix? Some interesting research throws light on this.

Emotions: Ups and Downs

Professor of neuroscience, Antonio Damasio, says that emotions are
enmeshed with the proper function of reason, for good and bad.[23]
On the positive side, emotions are a critical tool for people with
normal brain function. For example, when we're presented with a
choice, emotions spare us an endless cost/benefit analysis of the
vast array of options when a bad outcome comes to mind and we
experience an unpleasant gut feeling (a somatic marker, *soma* being
the Greek word for body). Sounding the alarm, the marker puts an
image in our mind and we reject the option immediately, thereby

---

[21] Daniel Kahneman, *Thinking, Fast and Slow*, 97–98.

[22] Daniel Kahneman, *Thinking, Fast and Slow*, 99.

[23] Antonio Damasio, *Descartes' Error: Emotion, Reason, and the Human
Brain* (New York, 1994), xvi–xix, 172–174, 179, 185, 193–194.

narrowing down the possibilities. Markers operate whether we're aware of them or not, and they're indispensable for our ability to choose among what might be an otherwise overwhelming number of possibilities.

Yet while emotions can be positive, they can derail decision quality by creating a bias against objective facts, something that happens too quickly to be recognized. In addition, they can steer us into irrational behavior and impair sound decision making by (1) causing us to skew the probabilities of things outside our control (2) causing us to think our actions are more effective than they are (3) creating the tendency to jump to conclusions and act immediately, even if we have nothing to lose by waiting to find out more.[24] In sum, emotions can subvert rationality by their disregard for consequences and concern for more information.

The question is, why? One finding provides a clue. Brain research reveals that the connections from the cortical areas (higher level thinking) to the amygdala (the emotional center) are far weaker than the connections from the amygdala to the cortex, which is why it's so easy for emotions to invade our conscious thoughts but so hard for us to gain control of our emotions.[25] Connections from the emotional systems to the cognitive systems are much stronger than the connections from the cognitive systems to the emotional systems. Emotions can easily bump mundane things out of our awareness, but nonemotional events (like thoughts) don't easily displace emotions from the mental spotlight; simply telling yourself you shouldn't feel depressed or anxious isn't helpful. The takeaway? We have little direct control over our emotional reactions, which means that emotional arousal can easily dominate and control our thinking.

---

[24] Jon Elster, *Alchemies of the Mind: Rationality and the Emotions* (Cambridge, 1999), 285–87, 298.

[25] Joseph LeDoux, *The Emotional Brain: The Mysterious Underpinnings of Emotional Life* (New York, 1996), 265.

All In The Way We're Built

Consider another point. Emotions are regulated by the lower levels of our brain. The lower levels in turn maintain a direct connection with our bodily organs and are constantly scanning the landscape of the body. Because there's a direct connection between the lower levels and the highest reaches of our brain, emotions and biological regulation all play a role in human reason—they all work together. Nature has built the apparatus of rationality not just on top of our biological regulation, but also *from* it and *with* it such that rationality results from their joint activity.[26] But because emotions are tied to body states, much of emotion occurs without our awareness. The background sensing of our body is continuous, although we hardly even notice it since it represents everything rather than just a specific part of anything in the body. Emotions offer a glimpse of what goes on in our flesh and modify our understanding of situations. Damasio tells us that feelings thus have a privileged status, and they retain a primacy that subtly pervades our mental life. Feelings are winners among equals because of they way we're built.[27]

Here's the point in all this. While this body-based mechanism is advantageous in many ways, it can also impair the quality of our reasoning. One example concerns the fear most people have of flying compared to driving, despite the fact that statistically we're far more likely to survive a flight from one city to another than a car ride between the same cities. Perhaps the most dangerous part of the journey is the car ride to the airport. Yet still most people feel safer driving than flying. Why? Because the image we have of a plane crash, with all of its emotional drama, dominates our reasoning and generates a negative bias against the correct choice.

The same problem afflicts how we evaluate many other decisions, such as investment and business decisions where probabilistic reasoning delivers better outcomes. Studies abound showing how our emotions and attitudes are activated automatically, but the real kicker is that their influence isn't even questioned by our conscious mind. Bottom line is that we're often mistaken about the

[26] Antonio Damasio, *Descartes' Error*, 147, 192.

[27] Antonio Damasio, *Descartes' Error*, 159–60.

internal causes of our actions and beliefs; meaning that our own understanding of why we do what we do isn't knowable to our conscious self.[28] Much of our mental life occurs outside of conscious awareness.

The Hidden Layer

Stanford professor of social psychology, Leon Festinger, pointed out that the more committed we are to a belief, the harder it is to give up—even in the face of overwhelming contradictory evidence. Instead of acknowledging our error, we tend to develop a new attitude or belief that will justify keeping it. The question is, why? How could even the supposedly most rational among us be prone to justify beliefs that fly in the face of the evidence? Neuroscientist, Robert Burton, suggests that it's because we all have *feelings of knowing*, which is a primary mental state not dependent on any underlying actual knowledge.[29] It's a sense that we know something to be true, and that we know it based on our thoughts and the facts. But while the feeling of knowing may seem like it's occurring in response to a thought, it actually *precedes* the thought and is responsible for bringing the thought into awareness. Thus the feelings of knowing, correctness, conviction, and certainty aren't necessarily deliberate conclusions and conscious choices. They're mental states that *happen* to us.

To describe what's happening under the covers, Burton uses the artificial intelligence (AI) phrase, hidden layer, as a way to picture how the brain processes information—and how we come to have a feeling of knowing about things *before* we really do. Technically, the hidden layer consists of the connections between all the neurons involved in any neural network. In the human brain, a typical neuron receives incoming information from about ten thousand other neurons. Each bit of information either stimulates or inhibits cell firing, and the neuron acts like a small calculator. Despite its complexity, the

---

[28] Joseph LeDoux, *The Emotional Brain*, 32–3. Jon Elster, *Alchemies of the Mind*, 269–70.

[29] Robert A. Burton, *On Being Certain*, 12, 41, 217–218.

neuron has two options; it either fires or it doesn't, making it appear like a massive compilation of on-and-off switches.

But what makes it so complex is that the connections between neurons aren't fixed. They're rather in constant flux, being strengthened or weakened by ongoing stimuli. Connections are enhanced with use and weakened with neglect, and are themselves affected by other connections to the same neurons. "Once we leave the individual synapse between two neurons, the complexity skyrockets—from individual neurons to a hundred billion brain cells each with thousands of connections. Although unraveling how individual neurons collectively create thought remains the Holy Grail of neuroscience, the artificial intelligence (AI) community has given us some intriguing clues to how this might occur."[30] It's in the hidden layer that all the elements of our biology (genetic predispositions to neurotransmitter variations) and all our past experience affect the processing of incoming information. In other words, it's the interface between incoming sensory data and final perception, or the anatomic crossroad where nature and nurture intersect. It's why your blue isn't my blue, why your idea of beauty isn't the same as mine, and why we don't all put our money on the same roulette number.

As an example of a neural network in action, Burton asks us to imagine a bright light that's briefly flashed into our eyes. The retina turns the light into electrical data that travels along the optic nerves and into the brain (this is the input). But instead of taking a direct route to our conscious mind, it first goes to a subconscious holding station where it's scrutinized, evaluated, and discussed by a screening committee representing all of our biological tendencies and past experiences. Trouble is that the committee meets behind closed doors, operating outside of consciousness in the hidden layer. Yet it's out of this complex hidden layer, and outside of conscious thinking, that the feeling of knowing arises.

So that we understand the magnitude, imagine billions of committee members, each with at least ten thousand hands reaching out to shake hands, seduce, or fend off the other members. Incredibly, this seemingly massive chaos is transformed into a seamless stream

---

[30] Robert A. Burton, *On Being Certain*, 43–45, 49.

of consciousness. "Such neural networks are the brain's real power brokers, the influence peddlers and decision makers hard at work behind closed doors of darkened white matter. How consciousness occurs remains an utter mystery, but conceptually, it must arise out of these hidden layers."[31] This explains why our habits, beliefs, and judgments are so difficult to change, and it's somewhat comparable to how a riverbed is formed. An initial flow of water randomly moves downstream, but once a creek has been formed, water follows this new path of least resistance—and as the water continues, the creek deepens and a river develops. The brain too relies on established ways. As interneuronal connections increase, they become more difficult to overcome. And once established, a neural network that links a thought and the feeling of knowing isn't easily undone. Even an idea known to be wrong continues to feel correct.

Having said all this, here's where the rubber meets the road. Burton notes that there's no isolated circuitry within the brain that can engage itself in thought free from involuntary and undetectable influences. Without this ability, certainty isn't a biologically justifiable state of mind.[32] In other words, we can't see the hidden layer in action and any attempt at self-awareness has to accept this limitation. The trouble is that we have all kinds of ideas, good and bad, true and untrue, bubbling up constantly. Some of them, maybe even most, feel like truths.

Adding to the problem is that we tend to accept our own thoughts without critical reflection. The hidden layer makes calculations that produce a feeling of knowing about the world, but it doesn't have any ability to justify the truth or falsehood of what it comes up with. We don't have a mechanism for establishing the accuracy of our thoughts until they've produced testable ideas. But as we've seen, we rarely want to test our ideas for correctness. Our mental limitations prevent us from accepting our mental limitations. This is partly due to the fact that if we have a gut feeling—which is an unconscious thought plus a strong feeling of its correctness—then this feeling influences how we assess the thought. Unfortunately, a feeling that

[31] Robert A. Burton, *On Being Certain*, 51–52, 59, 97–98.
[32] Robert A. Burton, *On Being Certain*, 141, 146, 151–152, 154, 159, 167.

a decision is right isn't the same as providing evidence that it's right. This means that good science has to distinguish between "felt knowledge" and knowledge arising out of testable observations.

Conclusion

We've now seen some important limitations on what and how we know. Our addiction to a coherent story often prevents us from truth. Because our minds superimpose simplicity and coherence onto much of what we observe, critical distinctions and contradictions are ignored in the aim of easy plot lines and intentions. Further, our biases blind us to underlying causes and dupe us into believing falsehoods about our leaders, organizations, and ourselves. Beginning with conclusions already fixed, we then justify our beliefs even in the face of overwhelming evidence to the contrary—made all the worse by pride in our story creations.

Because so much of our thinking happens under the covers, in the hidden layer, we're often automatically biased against objective facts. Emotions become a major driver of what we believe, which happens outside our awareness and usually without our recognition. Feelings end up winners among equals, so much so that they determine our judgments more than we'd like to admit. Because of this, we're overconfident about the accuracy of our intuitions—all of which is supported by an anatomical structure that makes the limits themselves hard to see.

Finally, compounding the issue is something Luther recognized long ago: namely, that we're inherently religious and can't help but to worship—even if the object is ourselves. Religious feelings of faith give us the strong impression of genuine knowledge about God, ourselves, and the world. But that's the trouble. If we face limits in our everyday knowledge, it's doubly so for theological knowledge; making it critical that we have continual recourse to a biblically based structure that keeps our minds focused on the truly vital. As we proceed, we'll argue that the church's historic ritual must continue to play an important role in keeping us grounded in the language and practice of scripture.

To do so, let's turn our attention to research showing the profound role our environment plays in how and what we think.

CHAPTER 4

Context, Bias, and Purpose

Think about how much of our life is automated by habit. We routinely go through it and rarely stop to consider how little we actually have to think about what comes next. Most of us get up every morning and do the exact same thing over and over. We eat the same thing, go through the same steps to get ready, take the same roads to work or school, and then come home and do the same thing before going to bed. This isn't necessarily bad, but like so much else in life habits have their pros and cons. One of their benefits is that they give us shortcuts and allow us to operate on autopilot. But they also have a weakness: they allow us to operate on autopilot. If I come home and automatically sit on a couch with potato chips and ignore my family, then it's clear I've succumbed to some bad habits. If, like a growing number of Americans, I obsessively check social media every hour then I'm at risk of alienating the only people that really matter. Psychologists are only beginning to understand the negative implications such habits are having on social development and relationships.

One of the interesting things that research has made clear is that habits are context dependent, meaning that we slip into different automatic behaviors in different environments. We often default to different thinking and behavior depending on where we are, whether it's home, work, a family gathering, or church. To say this isn't to make the all-too obvious point that we're more quiet, for example, when entering a church out of respect. It's rather to say that our environment has a profound yet subtle influence on our thinking and behavior, but one that often eludes our conscious minds. It is to say that context matters, which we implicitly acknowledge when we don't invite a recovering alcoholic to the bar where the very environment can trigger a relapse. But context is important for all human beings, not just those struggling with addiction. We're all similarly impacted by where we are, who we're with, and the cues that trigger automatic responses.

Because of its importance, in this chapter we'll explore the research on how environment can affect us in surprising ways, from how we choose products, to leaders of companies and our country. We'll discover that we behave in particular ways *in relation* to other people and situations, which is to say that we're highly susceptible to what goes on outside and around us, and in ways we still don't fully understand. With that data in mind we'll then ask the important question, what happens when we're placed in a more purposeful/directed context? In other words, is there any demonstrable benefit to being in an environment built around a particular framework of ideas and actions?

To begin, let's start with something we can all relate to: how our environment affects our purchasing habits.

Environment and How We Shop

Over the years, researchers in marketing have shown that people often choose products because of *where* they are, not *what* they are. If you walk into work and find free donuts prominently displayed on the table, it's hard to resist taking one (or two) even though you weren't thinking about it before. Studies show that customers tend to buy things not because they want them but because of how they're presented. Walk into a retail store and consider how the impeccably dressed mannequin subtly influences your desire to look fashionable. Further, consider product placement in your local grocery store. The most purchased items are usually at eye level, with the ones at the bottom driving the least sales. End caps, which are at the end of the aisle, are hugely profitable because of their prominent location. In fact, a full 45 percent of Coca-Cola sales comes from end-of-aisle racks. Thus, many of our purchases come not from simple choices but from how visible and available they are. As James Clear points out in his best-selling book, "Environment is the invisible hand that shapes human behavior."[1]

Clear says that certain behaviors arise over and over in particular environments. When we're in a church we talk quietly, when on a dark street we acted warily. We're constantly adapting to the world around us, which means that every habit we have is context dependent. So much so that human behavior has been described formulaically as a function of the person in their environment.

It makes sense given that of all our sensory abilities, the most powerful is vision. Humans have about eleven million sensory receptors, of which around ten million are dedicated to sight. Since we're more dependent on vision than any other sense, it's not surprising that visual cues are the greatest catalyst of behavior. Clear notes that it's the reason "a small change in what you *see* can lead to a big shift in what you *do*."[2] This is because certain cues trigger habits. Many people drink more, for instance, in social situations or workout harder at a gym when others are present. For much of human behavior, the context is the cue and we mentally assign habits to the locations in which they occur.

Social Influences

In the first century the famous Stoic Roman philosopher, Seneca, wrote to a friend and observed that people in large numbers are harmful, and as much as possible should be avoided. "There is not one of them," he said, "that will not make some vice or other attractive to us." The larger the crowd the greater the danger because we so easily cave to majority opinion. As the letter closes he asks, "what then do you imagine the effect on a person's character is when the assault comes from the world at large? Lay these up in your heart . . . that you may scorn the pleasure that comes from the majority's approval. The many speak highly of you, but have you really any grounds for satisfaction with yourself if you are the kind of person

---

[1] James Clear, *Atomic Habits: An Easy & Proven Way to Build Good Habits & Break Bad Ones* (New York, 2018), 82–84.

[2] James Clear, *Atomic Habits*, 84, 87.

the many understand?"[3] While Seneca's observations have the ring of truth—we've all seen this happen—can they be demonstrated apart from mere anecdotes? Modern research says yes.

For social psychology, the power of group influence is one of the most durable lessons of human behavior and largely confirms Seneca's suspicions. Evidence shows that we interpret things in light of the emotional expressions of others as early as twelve months old. Because social groups are a primary source of personal values, people safely assume that members of their group have values similar to their own. What's interesting is that although people deny it individually, they vastly underestimate the influence a group has over their thinking.

The extent to which this is true was demonstrated in well-known experiments in which participants, both politically conservative and liberal, were asked about welfare policy.[4] They were randomly assigned to one of two versions of a policy report. Naturally appealing to liberals was the "generous policy" with its lavish welfare spending, while the "stringent policy" appealed to conservatives with its strict spending limits. No existing program was more generous than the generous one in the study, and no existing program was more stringent than the stringent one. Participants were asked to comment on the randomly assigned policy.

Naively we'd expect their reactions to be based solely on content, as in fact they were when party opinions weren't mentioned. Here's what happened, though, when party preferences *were* mentioned. For both liberal and conservative participants, information from political parties completely overrode policy content. If they were told their party endorsed the plan, then liberals supported even a harsh welfare policy and conservatives supported even a lavish one. Once a policy was defined as liberal or conservative, its objective content was reduced to nothing.

---

[3] Seneca, *Letters from a Stoic*, trans. Robin Campbell (New York, 1969), 41–44.

[4] Geoffrey L. Cohen, "Party Over Policy: The Dominating Impact of Group Influence on Political Beliefs" in *Journal of Personality and Social Psychology*, 2003, Vol. 85, No. 5, 808–810.

In other words, participants assumed the position of their group as their own and gave no weight to policy content. Further, they denied being influenced by the stated party positions, and instead claimed that their opinions were based on policy content (as well as by personal government philosophy).[5] Even more interesting is that participants understood the power of group influence in a general sense: they could accurately estimate its impact on the attitude of others. However, they believed that they themselves were exempt from its effect.[6] Self-deception, it turns out, arises from the failure to apply a valid social theory to oneself.

Neural Basis of Conformity

The need for conformity is pre-wired in the human brain. It takes less than 200 milliseconds for the brain to register that the group has picked a different answer from yours, meaning that our brains are biased to get along by going along in less than a second. It's not hard to see why our concept of who we are is heavily shaped by social context. Numerous studies have shown that when subjects in a group are asked to answer a question, the probability of changing their minds is greatly increased if everyone else disagrees.

Not surprisingly, finding that your answer is out of step with others activates the amygdala and insular cortex—which is what drives the desire to remain in lock-step with the group. People are more likely to change their answer if shown a picture of others who disagree with them. Neurobiologically, conforming comes from the anxiety created by dissonance with the group where we equate differentness with wrongness, which is followed by the changing of our opinion. Robert Sapolsky comments as follows:

> When you get the news that everyone else disagrees with you, there is also activation of the (emotional) vmPFC, the anterior cingulate cortex, and the nucleus accumbens. This is a network mobilized during reinforcement learning, where you learn to modify your behavior

---

[5] Geoffrey L. Cohen, "Party Over Policy," 811–812.

[6] Geoffrey L. Cohen, "Party Over Policy," 820.

when there is a mismatch between what you expected to happen and what actually did. Find out that everyone disagrees with you and this network activates. What is it basically telling you? Not just that you're *different* from everyone else. That you're *wrong*. Being different = being wrong. The greater the activation of this circuit, the greater the likelihood of changing answers to conform.[7]

Thus we're wired (1) to compare ourselves to others, and (2) with the need to fit in. No doubt it's the neurological basis of the old proverb, "The nail that sticks out gets hammered down." No one wants to be the contrarian in a group as the feeling of dissonance from one's peers feels uncomfortable.

With this in mind, let's explore a few of the more publicized examples demonstrating the extent to which humans will fall in line, even when they know better.

Three Famous Experiments

The capacity for humans to conform, even at times to degrading behavior, was given prominence in three famous experiments: the conformity experiments of Solomon Asch, the obedience and shock studies of Stanley Milgram, and the Stanford prison experiment of Philip Zimbardo.[8] Let's look at each in turn.

In Asch's study, a volunteer—who thought it was a study of perception—was given a pair of cards. One had a line on it while the other had a trio of different-length lines, one of which matched the length of the single line. They were asked which line on the card with the trio is the same length as the line on the card with the single line. The task was easy enough, demonstrated by the fact that when sitting alone volunteers had about a 1 percent error rate. However, an experimental group was taking the same test but with seven other people, and designed so that each would say his choice out loud. Unbeknownst to the volunteer, the other seven worked as part of the

[7] Robert M. Sapolsky, *Behave: The Biology of Humans at Our Best and Worst* (New York, 2017), 458–460.

[8] Robert M. Sapolsky, *Behave*, 461–469.

project and had orchestrated it so that the volunteer went last. The first seven answers by the group unanimously picked a glaringly wrong answer. Contrary to what happened when volunteers were alone, about a third of the time when the volunteer was part of the group he agreed and picked the incorrect answer. And it wasn't just this one experiment. It's been replicated in other studies and serves as a startling demonstration of the human desire to conform.

The second experiment by Milgram took a pair of volunteers for a psychology "study of memory," in which one person would be designated the "teacher" and the other the "learner." They were placed in separate rooms and could hear but not see the other. Along with the teacher was the lab-coated scientist supervising the study. As the teacher recited pairs of words, the learner's job was to remember the pairing. After a series was given the learner's memory was tested, and each time a mistake was made the teacher was supposed to shock them. Each mistake caused an increase in intensity up to a life-threatening 450 volts. Though no shocks were actually given (they were prerecorded with increasing levels of painful groanings), the teacher thought they were real. As the intensity of the supposed shocks increased, the teacher would hear the learner responding in pain and begging for him to stop.

Interestingly, amid the screams of pain teachers became hesitant, but they'd be urged by the scientist to continue: "Please continue;" "The experiment requires that you continue;" "It is absolutely essential that you continue;" "You have no other choice. You must go on." Teachers were assured that the learner had been informed of the risks. "And the famed result was that most volunteers complied, shocking the learner repeatedly. Teachers would typically try to stop, argue with the scientist, would even weep in distress—but would obey. In the original study, horrifically, 65 percent of them administered the maximum shock of 450 volts."[9]

The third study is the Stanford prison experiment that's become the subject of movies and documentaries. In the experiment, twenty-four young male volunteers were split into a group of twelve "prisoners" and twelve "guards." The prisoners were to spend seven to

---

[9]   Robert M. Sapolsky, *Behave*, 462.

fourteen days in a pseudoprison in the basement of the Stanford psychology department, and the guards were to keep order. In an attempt to make it as realistic as possible, the prisoners were picked up by the Palo Alto police, arrested and taken to the police station for booking. Afterwards, they were taken to the "prison" and dumped as trios in cells. The results were shocking. With pointless and humiliating rituals of obedience, the guards deprived prisoners of sleep and food, forced them to relieve themselves in unemptied buckets in the cells, put people in solitary, and addressed them by number rather than by name. Some of the prisoners revolted on the second day by barricading the entrance of their cell, but the guards subdued them with fire extinguishers. Most of them sank into passivity and despair. Tragically, some of the guards—and some of the teachers in the Milgram study—were psychological wrecks after it was evident what they were proven capable of.

What do experiments like this show? That, as Sapolsky points out, "average people will go along with absurdly incorrect assertions in the name of conformity," and that "average people will do stunningly bad things in the name of obedience and conformity."[10] There were also some larger implications of the experiments. Milgram's study was prompted by the war-crimes trial of Adolf Eichmann who'd been an architect of the mass deportation and extermination of Jews in Nazi-occupied Eastern Europe. Many at the time were trying to make sense of Germans "just following orders." The implications of the experiments, however, were clear: given the right situation, humans—even the most normal—are capable of far more than they might want to believe. As Aleksandr Solzhenitsyn said in *The Gulag Archipelago*, "The line between good and evil cuts through the heart of every human being. And who is willing to destroy a piece of his own heart?"[11]

Having said this, we should note that the experiments, especially the second and third, have been criticized for various reasons. Milgram, for instance, seems to have exaggerated some of his work in that there might have been more teachers than reported who refused to shock. However, the finding of roughly 60 percent compliance

[10] Robert M. Sapolsky, *Behave*, 464.
[11] Robert M. Sapolsky, *Behave*, 465.

rates has been replicated in other studies. Even more criticized was the prison experiment. Zimbardo might have influenced the outcome, and it's possible that the volunteers were distinctive and not necessarily representative of the general population. Replication was an issue as well.

The only study like the one at Stanford was the 2001 "BBC Prison Study," which ended with the prisoners organizing to resist abuse from the guards. So it replicated more of what happened in the French Revolution than what Zimbardo found. However, Sapolsky concludes that two vital things are indisputable from these and other studies. First, there are always people who resist the pull of groups, which explains why some Germans risked everything to save people from the Nazis. Second, and more disturbingly, when "pressured to conform and obey, a far higher percentage of perfectly normal people than most would predict succumb and do awful things. Contemporary work using a variant on the Milgram paradigm shows 'just following orders' in action, where the pattern of neurobiological activation differs when the same act is carried out volitionally versus obediently."[12]

How We Pick Leaders

If anything has become clear so far, it's that we don't form judgments or make decisions in a vacuum. We're never context free. Different behaviors and biases manifest themselves in different situations and groups, and how we choose our leaders is no exception. While most people believe they pick politicians, CEOs, and job candidates with deliberation that's context-free, the evidence suggests otherwise. Consider this. It's been shown that of candidates with identical positions, people are more likely to vote for the better-looking one. Given the prevalence of male candidates, votes tend to go for masculine traits—tall, healthy-looking, symmetrical features, high forehead, prominent brow ridges, and and a jutting jaw.[13]

A prime example is the presidential election of Warren Harding, who was (as many historians agree) one of the worst presidents in

---

[12] Robert M. Sapolsky, *Behave*, 468–469.

[13] Robert M. Sapolsky, *Behave*, 443.

American history.[14] People looked at Harding and saw how extraor-
dinarily handsome and distinguished-looking he was and jumped to
the immediate—and unwarranted—conclusion that he was a man of
courage, intelligence, and integrity. No further need to dig below the
surface. The way he looked was so powerful that it short-circuited
the normal thinking process. As unbelievable as it sounds, it correlates
with other findings. For instance, attractive people are typically rated
as having better personalities and higher moral standards—and as
being kinder, more honest, more friendly, and more trustworthy.
Because of this they're treated better. They're more likely to be hired
for the same resume, they get higher salaries for the same job, and
are less likely to be convicted for the same crime.

Malcolm Gladwell reports a similar bias in how we respond to
tall men. After polling half of the companies on the Fortune 500 list,
he found that male CEOs were just a shade under six feet tall. With the
average height of American males at five foot nine, CEOs have about
three inches on the rest of their sex. "But this statistic actually under-
states the matter. In the U.S. population, about 14.5 percent of all men
are six feet or taller. Among CEOs of Fortune 500 companies, that
number is 58 percent. Even more striking, in the general American
population, 3.0 percent of adult men are six foot two or taller. Among
my CEO sample, almost a third were six foot two or taller."[15] Relatively
few short people make it to the executive suite. Of the tens of millions of American men below five foot six, only ten in Gladwell's sample reached the level of CEO, meaning that being short is probably
as much of a handicap to corporate success as being a woman or an
African American. Most of us, says Gladwell, automatically associate
leadership ability with imposing physical stature. We have a sense of
what leaders are supposed to look like, which is so powerful that when
someone fits it we become blind to more rational considerations.
This is borne out by numerous studies, one of which found that faces
judged to look more competent won elections 68 percent of the time.[16]

---

[14] Malcolm Gladwell, *Blink: The Power of Thinking Without Thinking* (New
York, 2005), 72–76.

[15] Malcolm Gladwell, *Blink*, 86–87.

[16] Robert M. Sapolsky, *Behave*, 442.

There are also what experts call contingent automatic responses. When considering war, for example, Westerns and East Asians prefer candidates with older, more masculine faces. During peacetime, they prefer younger, more feminine faces. Further, when fostering cooperation between groups is important, people prefer intelligent-looking faces; at other times, more intelligent faces are viewed as less masculine and desirable. And our biases fall into place early. One study showed kids (ages five to thirteen) pairs of faces of candidates from obscure elections and asked who they'd prefer as captain on a hypothetical boat trip. Incredibly, they picked the winner 71 percent of the time. This demonstrates that these are very generalized and entrenched biases, which means that the decisions happen in an instant and then our conscious cognitions play catch-up to make them seem careful and wise.[17]

What About Genes?

Before moving into the idea of purposeful context, let's talk briefly about the role of genetics in behavior. After all, popular literature can overly stress the role of genes over environment with human behavior and preferences. The idea of genetic determinism, which states that behavior is determined by genes, has been as resilient as the myths surrounding creativity and genius. But researchers such as Robert Sapolsky have shown how much influence environment actually has.[18]

In an important experiment, three behavioral geneticists studied mouse strains known to have genetic variants relevant to particular behaviors (specifically, addiction and anxiety). To ensure the mice were put in exactly the same environments, the scientists did cartwheels to make sure each one was as identical as possible. Every detail was standardized. Because some of the mice were born in the lab and others from breeders, the homegrown mice were transported in bouncy vans during shipping just in case this was important. Further, they were tested at the same age, on the same

---

[17] Robert M. Sapolsky, *Behave*, 443–444.
[18] Robert M. Sapolsky, *Behave*, 246–248.

date, at the same local time; they had the same brand of cage with the same brand of sawdust bedding, which was changed on the same day of the week; they were handled the same number of times by people wearing the same brand of surgical gloves; they had the same food and were kept in the same lighting environment and temperature. It's hard to imagine how they could have made things more exact.

The outcome was telling. Some of the gene variants showed huge gene/environment interactions, and had radically different effects in different labs. Sapolsky sums the findings up this way: "What does this mean? That most of the gene variants were so sensitive to environment that gene/environment interactions occurred even in these obsessively similar lab settings, where incredibly subtle (and still unidentified) environmental differences made huge differences in what the gene did . . . This suggests a radical conclusion: *it's not meaningful to ask what a gene does, just what it does in a particular environment.*"[19] Thus even at the genetic level, evidence shows how important the contribution of environment is in preferences and behavior.

With the foregoing in mind, let's conclude by talking about the possible benefits of being more deliberate with the context in which we place ourselves.

Purposeful Context

Thus far the research is eye opening. Context influences our thought processes and decisions far more than we might think, and in ways we still don't understand. Wherever and with whomever, we manifest biases and develop habits that are automatically triggered when we step into a particular environment. The question is, given its profound influence, can we be more purposeful about the context in which we place ourselves with a view to developing different thought processes and habits? The answer seems to be a resounding yes. Many examples exist but a case in point will help.

---

[19] Robert M. Sapolsky, *Behave*, 248. See also Carol S. Dweck, *Mindset: The New Psychology of Success* (New York, 2006), 5ff.

Charles Duhigg reports that in October of 1987, Wall Street investors and analysts of the Aluminum Company of America (or Alcoa as it's known) met in Manhattan to hear from its new CEO.[20] A large and bureaucratic company, Alcoa's management had made a series of mistakes and was losing customers to competitors at an alarming rate. To right the ship, the board named a man by the name of Paul O'Neill as CEO, formerly—of all things—a government bureaucrat. Much to everyone's disbelief, he informed the crowd that his top priority was safety. As you might imagine, an audience like that expects the standard language of profit and shareholder value, so not only did it shock but many stormed out of the room to inform their largest clients to sell their stocks. Not a pretty scene.

What most people didn't realize was that O'Neill's plan to reduce injuries required a radical realignment of the way Alcoa conducted operations. To understand why injuries happen, you have to explore how the manufacturing process is going wrong. To understand that, you have to educate workers on quality control and the most efficient work processes; and once that's all in place, it becomes easier to do everything right, since correct work is safer work. Thus to protect workers, the company needed to become the most streamlined aluminum company in the world. O'Neill would need to fundamentally change the environment for this to happen.

To implement his plan, he made an employee injury the trigger for action in which the unit president had to report the incident to him within twenty-four hours, along with a plan for ensuring it wouldn't happen again. The only people who got promoted were the ones who embraced the new system. But to really understand the foundational change it required we need to consider the reality of the plan. In order to contact O'Neill within twenty-four hours, presidents needed to hear about the accident from their vice presidents as soon as it happened. Thus vice presidents needed to be in constant contact with floor managers, and floor mangers needed to get workers to raise warnings as soon as possible. Further, floor managers needed to keep a list of suggestions close so that when the VP asked

<hr>

[20] Charles Duhigg, *The Power of Habit: Why We Do What We Do in Life and Business* (New York, 2014), 97–122.

for a plan they were already prepared. To make all that happen, every unit had to create new communication systems making it easier for the lowest worker to get an idea to the highest executive. Virtually everything about the company's rigid hierarchy had to change for the program to work. O'Neill essentially built a new corporate environment that created new habits, and the results speak for themselves. By 1996, his leadership had been studied by top business schools and he was regularly mentioned as a potential for Secretary of Defense. Under his almost ten year watch, Alcoa's stock price rose more than 200 percent.

This is a prime example of the rule that by changing the context, you change the habits, thoughts, and behavior of the people affected. While we'll see more examples of this later when we examine the impact of language, we'll end our review here by exploring an unexpected contributor to the topic: the surgeon Atul Gawande.

The Checklist Manifesto

Gawande relates the tragic crash of the Boeing Model 299 test plane that almost bankrupted the company in 1935. With a small crowd of army brass gathered to witness the flight, the sleek and impressive plane taxied onto the runway for takeoff.[21] It had a 103-foot wingspan and four engines rather than the usual two. The plane roared down the tarmac, lifted off the ground and climbed to three hundred feet. It then stalled, turned on one wing, and crashed in a fiery explosion. Two of the five onboard died, including the pilot. After an investigation showed that nothing mechanical had gone wrong, it was determined that the crash was caused by pilot error. However, it also revealed something else: how complicated the new aircraft was to operate compared to any other airplane. In fact, so much so that a prominent newspaper said it was too much airplane for one man to fly.

Despite the disaster, the army pressed for a solution to the problem because of the plane's potential to impact the war efforts. Clearly more training wasn't the answer—the killed pilot had an abundance.

---

[21] Atul Gawande, *The Checklist Manifesto: How To Get Things Right* (New York, 2009), 32ff.

So an army team came up with another more innovative approach: they developed the first pilot's checklist. Why a checklist? Because the new plane was far too complicated for every important detail to be left to a pilot's memory, no matter how experienced. The brilliance of the checklist is that it was simple and could fit on an index card, with step-by-step checks for takeoff, flight, landing, and taxiing. With these in place, the Model 299—which was dubbed the B-17—went on to fly a total of 1.8 million miles without a single accident. As you might guess, checklists are still used today.

Given their effectiveness, can they be applied in other areas? Guwande makes the point that, like flying a modern aircraft, much of our work today is too complex to carry out from memory alone. Whether you're a software engineer, financial manager, firefighter, police officer, or lawyer, something akin to a checklist can guard against human forgetfulness and sloppiness. In complex environments, even the experts are up against two main problems. Number one is the fallibility of human memory and attention, especially in mundane, routine matters easily overlooked under any type of stress. A surgeon himself, Guwande says that it's easy to forget you haven't checked a patient's pulse when they're throwing up and the family is asking what's happening.[22] Faulty memory and distraction can be particularly problematic, whether you're at the store for ingredients for a cake, preparing to take off in a plane, or evaluating a sick person in the hospital. Number two is that people can lull themselves into skipping steps even when they remember. Checklists can protect against such failures as they remind us of the minimum necessary steps by making them explicit. They not only verify but instill discipline, and with it higher performance.

Examples of their impact are growing exponentially. In 2001, a critical care specialist at Johns Hopkins Hospital named Peter Pronovost developed a checklist to prevent central line infections. On it he reminded doctors of the following: (1) wash hands with soap (2) clean patient's skin with chlorhexidine antiseptic (3) put sterile drapes over the entire patient (4) wear a mask, hat, sterile gown, and gloves and (5) put sterile dressing over the insertion site once the line

---

[22] Atul Gawande, *The Checklist Manifesto*, 35–36.

is in. Even though every doctor knew the steps, more than a third of the time they skipped at least one. To give the new procedure some teeth, Johns Hopkins authorized nurses to stop doctors when a step was missed, and the results were dramatic. The ten day line-infection rate went from 11 percent to zero, and after another fifteen months only two line infections occurred during the whole period. That means that in this one hospital, the checklist prevented forty-three infections and eight deaths, and saved two million dollars in costs.

In 2003, the Michigan Health and Hospital Association asked Pronovost to test his central line checklist throughout the state's ICUs. It was a huge undertaking, but the results provided the most compelling evidence yet of its effectiveness in preventing infections and deaths. They were published three years later in the *New England Journal of Medicine*. Within the first three months, the central line infection rate in the ICUs decreased by 66 percent, with most cutting their quarterly infections rates to zero. Gawande comments as follows: "Michigan's infection rates fell so low that its average ICU outperformed 90 percent of ICUs nationwide. In the . . . first eighteen months, the hospitals saved an estimated $175 million in costs and more than fifteen hundred lives. The successes have been sustained for several years now—all because of a stupid little checklist."[23] As Pronovost discovered, checklists established a higher standard of baseline performance.

Gawande says that he has yet to go through a week in surgery without a checklist, which prompts the team to catch anything they've missed. No matter how routine the operation, checklists have caught unrecognized drug allergies, equipment problems, confusion about medications, and mistakes on labels for biopsy specimens going to pathology. To illustrate, he relates a story in which he removed a rare tumor where there was a small chance that the vena cava (the main vessel returning blood to the heart) could be injured and cause life-threatening bleeding. Unfortunately, that's exactly what happened. The patient lost almost his entire blood supply into his abdomen in about sixty seconds and went into cardiac arrest. However, because the team had gone through the checklist prior to the surgery—which

---

[23] Atul Gawande, *The Checklist Manifesto*, 37–39, 44.

included introducing all the team members to one another and discussing potential risks—the nurse had enough blood available for the worst case scenario. Gawande adds that the checklist impacted how the team worked together, of which he'd previously worked with only two. Here's how he describes it:

> But as we went around the room introducing ourselves—"Atul Gawande, surgeon." "Rich Bafford, surgery resident." "Sue Marchand, nurse"—you could feel the room snapping to attention. We confirmed the patient's name on his ID bracelet and that we all agreed which adrenal gland was supposed to come out. The anesthesiologist confirmed that he had no critical issues to mention before starting, and so did the nurses. We made sure that the antibiotics were in the patient, a warming blanket was on his body, the inflating boots were on his legs to keep blood clots from developing. We came into the room as strangers. But when the knife hit the skin, we were a team . . . As a result, when I made the tear and put disaster upon us, everyone kept their head.[24]

As unimpressive as they seem, checklists are a staple in environments ranging from aviation, software, engineering, all the way to medicine. Functioning as reminders of the most vital factors and the steps that can't be cut short, checklists serve to correct human weakness, including some of the cognitive biases we've seen. Thus they become the de facto framework within which people's thinking and behavior are directed. And they often do so in moments of crisis and high risk, which they're able to do by modifying the context with their focusing effect—thereby keeping one's attention on core elements that, without which, huge blunders can occur.

Conclusion

We've now seen how important environment is for the development of thought and behavior, down even to the level of how genes manifest themselves in the real world. Having implications on everything we think and do, our contexts can influence how we shop,

---

[24] Atul Gawande, *The Checklist Manifesto*, 191–192.

the positions we take, and the shape of our beliefs. Add to this our neurobiological need to conform and we have the perfect recipe for superficiality and obscuring of the truly vital. And not to be forgotten are the habits that form around context specific situations which serve to automate how we spend the limited time we have.

Considering their impact, Duhigg sees habits as creating new values, in that what we spend our time on is de facto what we value—no matter how we might protest to the contrary. With that insight in mind, it's imperative we consider the environments in which we place ourselves, as habits naturally arise and reflect the quality of the surroundings, language, and shared beliefs of others. "Keystone habits," he says, "transform us by creating cultures that make clear the values that, in the heat of a difficult decision or a moment of uncertainty, we might otherwise forget."[25]

But it's not just everyday habits that should concern us; we have religious habits as well that place us on theological autopilot. That's why attentiveness to context is all the more critical, because it helps to shape our thoughts about the nature of God, the cross, and the Christian life. To sustain and grow Christian faith, we need keystone habits created and reinforced by a purposeful environment to help navigate life's complexities. We need a framework steeped in biblical language and practice so our minds are focused on what's vital, the things on which scripture itself focuses. We don't do that naturally: not in life, and definitely not in religion. We're much more apt, as the Old Testament makes painfully clear in the often tragic history of Israel, to run after the golden calf—after the things and ideas that tantalize our sinful nature and give it fuel.

Thus a deliberateness about Christian worship needs to occupy our attention, and it needs to reflect what we see in the Old and New Testaments. Human sin, with the biases and weaknesses that follow, require consistent remedies—remedies that, like checklists, have a focusing effect on how God chooses to be with his people and remedy their sin. It's in this way that the liturgical framework evident in our earliest materials provides a corrective to the human condition. Not only does it act as a guardrail against idolatry, it embeds the

---

[25] Charles Duhigg, *The Power of Habit*, 123–125.

Gospel through the pattern of word and table. Like a checklist, the liturgy steps us through an acknowledgment of sin and reception of God's grace in Christ—jarring us to attention, refocusing our memory, and establishing the proper benchmark of who God is and who we are. Just how important this is will become clear as we talk about the nature and extent of sin. For now, it's enough to say that our weaknesses and biases, our sin and demand to be entertained, need to be held at bay. Ritual, as embodied in the church's historic liturgy, serves as that reorienting framework.

Having considered the importance of context, we now turn to the effects of the language we internalize.

CHAPTER 5
Language

The emergence of language is one of the most remarkable features of creation. While it's been argued, perhaps correctly, that man's reason separates him from the beasts of the field, it's notable that reason would be of little practical value without the ability to express thoughts and emotions in language. What would these be if not capable of being expressed and understood? Given this, one could argue that language is the linchpin binding humans to other humans, and therefore of society itself. Yet as important as this is, language has two additional functions: namely, it shapes and focuses thought. Insofar as language speaks, man's thoughts continue to form and deepen—meaning that there's a connection between what he *thinks* and what he's *told* by his language.[1] Martin Heidegger made this point by saying that man speaks to the extent that he listens. Insofar as language forces us to think about the thing we're saying, and in this sense makes it present, it also has the ability to create focus. As Heidegger put it, language speaks by bidding that which has been bidden.

What's clear is that, however we slice its various functions, language plays a central role in our lives—allowing us to express thoughts and emotions, make distinctions and convey relationships, while simultaneously shaping our thoughts and focusing us on what is said. Because of its contribution to our development, this chapter will look more closely at its ability to influence what we think,

---

[1] Martin Heidegger, *Poetry, Language, Thought* (New York, 1971), 191–2, 195–6, 203, 206–7.

believe, and how we behave. To do so, we'll cast a rather wide net. We'll begin with a mini case study on how one organization was impacted by the language it used and reinforced, particularly how its common lingo drove toxic behavior. Next, we'll look at some intriguing new research on how the use of certain language can create a focusing effect on a person's thinking and perception. We'll then conclude by considering language's impact on how we think about our faith—zeroing in on how the words we use influence the content of our beliefs in ways not generally appreciated or understood.

Before forging ahead however we should point out that, despite the recent interest in the topic, we won't say anything particularly new. Already in the fifth century we find the idea that the language we use, particularly in prayer, impacts the formation of a person's faith. During the heart of the Semi-Pelagian controversy, Prosper of Aquitaine (a disciple of the church father, St. Augustine) wrote "let the law of prayer establish the law of belief," in which he argued that prayers should reflect our dependence on God's grace. Pelagians disagreed, contending that our works play a central role in salvation. Though Prosper's statement has since launched a debate between the priority of liturgy on theology or theology on liturgy, we'll focus only on the more benign axiom that "praying shapes believing;"[2] meaning that those who pray routinely in a certain way will be formed in the faith according to the language they use.

This shouldn't be terribly controversial. Even the nineteenth century German philosopher, Ludwig Feuerbach, once commented that "man is what he eats" along similar lines. While it's been said in various ways over the centuries, the observation that the language we use influences our thinking should come as no surprise. In light of the data we'll explore, it should be easier to understand why many of the great thinkers in church history insisted that the beliefs of Christians are deeply affected by their religious diet.[3] What will become clear is that the nature and quality of the inputs matter.

Let's begin by what we're seeing in modern organizations.

---

[2] Frank C. Senn, *Introduction to Christian Liturgy* (Minneapolis, 2012), 13.

[3] Geoffrey Wainwright, *Doxology: The Praise of God in Worship, Doctrine, and Life* (New York, 1980), 18.

Consistency, For Good or Bad

In business, we've known for many years how our language impacts the thinking and behavior of people in an organization. CEOs spend hundreds of thousands of dollars per year in corporate training and offsite events aimed at directing company culture and getting everyone on the same page. "Alignment" is a common buzzword for the recognition that companies need to operate as one from top to bottom. As Jim Collins remarks, it's important that core beliefs are explicitly built into an organization and that they're preserved over time.[4]

Though correct, Collins' advice is often ignored, which makes the money spent ineffective because of corporate inconsistency. Messages get defused and momentary crises derail what are usually well-intentioned top level initiatives. However, there are notable exceptions in which executives constantly reinforce the values and behaviors they're looking for and end up achieving remarkable results—results, incidentally, that can be either productive or corrosive. Zappos is an example of the former, which CEO Tony Hsieh details in his best-selling book *Delivering Happiness*.[5] With remarkable precision, Zappos' core values have been reinforced over time and with a persistence any CEO would find enviable, such that its $1.2 billion acquisition by Amazon would have come as no surprise to anyone who understood its culture.

A particularly interesting example of the latter comes from Ben Horowitz' recent best-seller, in which he details Uber's company culture that was set down by its then CEO Travis Kalanick. Kalanick designed the organization with care and programmed it with language intended to create a hyper-competitive environment. He stressed over and over certain values and qualities he sought from employees; for instance, Meritocracy and Toe-Stepping, Winning, Champions Mindset, Always Be Hustlin', Fierceness, and Super Pumpedness. Taken as a whole, these elevated one value above all: competitiveness. It worked. By 2016 the company was valued at $66 billion.

---

[4] Jim Collins, *Good To Great: Why Some Companies Make the Leap . . . and Others Don't* (New York, 2001), 195.

[5] Tony Hsieh, *Delivering Happiness: A Path to Profits, Passion, and Purpose* (New York, 2010).

As with any well articulated culture, the language used in the company's value system was reinforced in training. In one of the training scenarios, a hypothetical rival company was launching a carpool service in four weeks. It's not possible (in the scenario) for Uber to beat them to market with a reliable carpool service, so the question is, what should the company do? Answer: "Rig up a makeshift solution that we pretend is totally ready to go so we can beat the competition to market."[6] The underlying message was clear. If the choice is between integrity or winning, at Uber it has to be whatever it takes to win.

The message got through. When Uber challenged Didi Chuxing, the Chinese market leader in ride-sharing, its response to Didi's counterattacks were telling. After Didi hacked Uber's app to send it fake drivers, Uber responded by doing the exact same thing. What's more telling is that Uber brought the arguably illegal practices back to the United States, hacking Lyft with a program known as Hell which inserted fake riders into Lyft's system while funneling Uber the information it needed to recruit Lyft drivers. Though Kalanick may or may not have instructed his team to use such measures, he didn't have to. It was baked into Uber's culture. Its language had created and reinforced it for a long time. As Horowitz notes, "Cultural design is a way to program the actions of an organization, but, like computer programs, every culture has bugs. And cultures are significantly more difficult to debug than programs."[7] It's unlikely that Kalanick intended on building an unethical organization, but people digest the words that are reinforced and act accordingly. Though Uber's culture had to be altered by Kalanick's successor, our aim is to point out how effective and sticky consistent messaging is.

Why does it work so well? Because when a conflict or crisis occurs, our brains have an automatic way of reverting to the ideas and beliefs we've internalized.[8] This is true of our bodies as well,

[6] Ben Horowitz, *What You Do Is Who You Are: How to Create Your Business Culture* (New York, 2019), 78–80.

[7] Ben Horowitz, *What You Do Is Who You Are*, 81–85.

[8] Chet Holmes, *The Ultimate Sales Machine: Turbocharge Your Business with Relentless Focus on 12 Key Strategies* (New York, 2007), 24–5, 28.

as any karate teacher would tell us, implying that repetition is a key component of being able to address challenges. Applied to an organization, we can see that when people all speak the same language and follow the same practices, communication improves because everyone shares a knowledge base. Chet Holmes puts it this way: "When your employees confront any situation, they're in one of two categories. Either you've addressed it and trained them and they have the information they need to deal with it, or you haven't . . . and they're going to be guessing. Which category would you rather your staff be in?"[9]

While examples could be multiplied, this is sufficient to show how effective consistent use of language is to people and organizations. Not only does it work, it's necessary for people to know how to deal with challenges; because in times of crisis, we instinctively fall back on what *has* been consistently messaged. And the one thing we don't want is to default to the wrong one.

Thinking and Our Mother Tongue

Some intriguing new research highlights how a culture's mother tongue (its language) can influence the thinking of its people. While there's no evidence that language imposes limits on intellectual abilities or constrains our capacity to understand concepts of other languages, there's growing evidence that our language fosters certain habits of mind that can affect how we think.[10] Specifically, the frequent use of certain ways of expression creates habits of mind that can have a focusing effect on a person's thinking and perception—making the individual more attune to recognizing things associated with the frequently used words. In other words, language creates habits of speech which, in turn, shapes habits of mind that affect more than just the knowledge of the language itself.

What does this mean? Simply that a person's perception can be influenced by the distinctions the mother tongue imposes on his or

---

[9] Chet Holmes, *The Ultimate Sales Machine*, 26.

[10] Guy Deutscher, *Through the Language Glass: Why the World Looks Different in Other Languages* (New York, 2010), 234.

her speech. It does so by highlighting those things corresponding to the distinctions the language imposes. We can see something analogous to this in a simple example. Think about the last time you were in the market for a new car, say a Ford Mustang. You probably did your research online, talked to people who own one, and test drove the car at your local dealership. Yet even before you made the purchase, recall how many of them you suddenly started seeing on the road. This is because your mind had been trained to focus on that particular model and it started seeing them in places it didn't before. In that sense the focusing altered your perception. The language we use over and over can have the same effect.

In his study on the subject, Guy Deutscher cites three fascinating examples. The first involves how different languages can impact a person's thinking about simple directions. Speakers of Guugu Yimithirr (spoken by Aborigines off the northeastern coast of Australia), for instance, need to know where the cardinal directions are at every moment of their waking life.[11] The language, as spoken by the older generation, doesn't have words for "left" or "right" as directions, nor does it use terms such as "in front of" or "behind" to describe an object's position. Because of that its speakers need to know exactly where north, south, west, and east are—since otherwise they wouldn't be able to convey the most basic information. To speak such a language you have to have a compass in your mind, and one that operates all the time. This means that memories of things you want to report will have to be stored in your brain with cardinal directions as part of the picture. So instead of saying "the window to the left of the girl," you'd have to remember if it was north of her or east or south or west.

As strange as that may sound, it was documented and filmed in 1980 by John Haviland when he recorded a Guugu Yimithirr member tell an old friend how, in his youth, he capsized in shark-infested waters but managed to swim safely ashore. What's interesting is that it was remembered throughout in cardinal directions. He recalled that he jumped into the water on the western side of the boat, his companion jumped to the east of the boat, and they

---

[11] Guy Deutscher, *Through the Language Glass*, 165, 172, 174–175, 184.

saw a giant shark swimming north. Even more telling was that, by chance, Stephen Levinson filmed the same person two years later telling the same story. The cardinal directions matched exactly in both tellings, with even his hand gestures matching how he was facing in both. It showed that the Guugu Yimithirr had a perfect pitch for directions. Many such experiments have been done with speakers of different languages, demonstrating that the preferred coordinate system in the language corresponds strongly with the solutions people pick. Speakers of different languages perceive and remember space differently.

Deutscher suggests that a language like Guugu Yimithirr indirectly brings about a geographical memory because its speech is confined to geographic coordinates, which compels speakers to be aware of directions at all time—forcing them to pay constant attention to environmental cues and develop an accurate memory of their own changing orientation. As many as one in ten words in a normal Guugu Yimithirr conversation is north, south, east, or west, often accompanied by precise hand gestures.[12] This makes sense, because if you have to know your bearings to understand the simplest things people say, you'll develop the habit of calculating and remembering cardinal directions at every moment of your life. Interestingly, now that Guugu Yimithirr children are dominated by English the older geographical thinking is being displaced by an English-centric orientation.

Deutscher's second example shows how various languages grammatically deal with gender.[13] Male human beings almost always have masculine gender, but women are often denied the privilege of belonging to the feminine gender and are relegated instead to the neuter. In German, there's a range of words for women that are treated as "it." Greeks are a little better, but if one speaks about a pretty buxom girl the resulting noun belongs to the masculine gender. Long ago, English was no more generous when it assigned the word "woman" to the masculine gender. However, where things get interesting is in the realm of inanimate objects. In French, German, Russian, and most other European languages, the masculine and

---

[12] Guy Deutscher, *Through the Language Glass*, 187.

[13] Guy Deutscher, *Through the Language Glass*, 201–202, 209, 211.

feminine genders extend to thousands of objects that aren't in any way male or female. A Frenchman's beard is feminine, Russian water is a "she" until you dip a tea bag in it, at which point she becomes a "he." The German sun lights up the masculine day and the masculine moon shines in the feminine night.

With this in mind, researchers have conducted experiments to answer whether the grammatical gender of inanimate objects influences speakers' associations. In one of them, psychologist Maria Sera and her colleagues compared how French and Spanish speakers attached voices to inanimate objects that were going to speak in a movie. French and Spanish mostly agree on gender, but there are still many nouns that diverge. For instance, French beds are masculine but Spanish ones are feminine, and the same goes for clouds and butterflies. The participants were asked to help bring everyday objects to life and choose the appropriate voice for the movie. To do so they were shown a series of pictures, and for each they chose a man's or a woman's voice. While the names of the objects were never mentioned, when French speakers saw the picture of a fork most of them had her speak in a woman's voice, whereas the Spanish speakers tended to choose a male voice. The situation was reversed with the picture of a bed.

Another experiment asked a group of Spanish and German speakers to participate in a memory game (which was conducted wholly in English to avoid leading participants). They were given a list of two dozen inanimate objects, and for each they had to memorize a person's name. "Apple," for example had the name of Patrick and "bridge" had the name Claudia. Given a fixed period of time to memorize the names, they were then tested on how well they did. The results showed that they were better at remembering the assigned names when the gender of the object matched the sex of the person; and they found it more difficult to remember the names when the gender of the object clashed with the sex of the person. Spanish speakers found it easier to remember the name associated with "apple" if it was Patricia rather than Patrick, and they found it easier to remember the name for a bridge if it was Claudio rather than Claudia.

As Deutscher notes, we can conclude that when inanimate objects have a masculine or feminine gender, the male or female association with them are present in the speaker's mind even when they're not actively solicited, and even when they're speaking English.[14] The bottom line is that the constant drilling of gender affects the associations speakers develop about inanimate objects and can clothe their ideas of them in womanly or manly traits.

Deutscher's third example concerns how the habits of mind that are instilled by our color vocabulary can make us more sensitive to fine color distinctions from language to language. In a 2008 experiment by a team from Stanford, MIT, and UCLA, participants were measured on their reaction time when selecting two of three colors that were exact matches. The Russian language has two distinct color names for the range that English subsumes under the name "blue."[15] The aim of the experiment was to see whether these distinct "blues" would affect Russians' perception of blue shades. Participants were seated in front of a computer screen and shown sets of three blue squares at a time. One square was at the top and a pair was below. One of the two bottom squares was always exactly the same color as the upper square, with the other a different shade of blue. The task was to choose which of the two bottom squares was the same color as the one on top by pressing one of two buttons, right or left, as quickly as they could. What's interesting is that the average speed with which the Russians pressed the button was shorter if the colors had different names. The results showed that there's something objectively different between Russian and English speakers in the way their visual processing systems react to blue shades.

Even more remarkable was a 2006 experiment by four researchers from Berkeley and Chicago.[16] At its basis were two well established facts about the human brain: first that the left hemisphere is the seat of language, and second that each hemisphere of the brain is responsible for processing visual signals from the opposite half of the field of vision. This means that signals from our left side are sent to the right hemisphere for processing, while signals from our right side are processed in the same half of the brain as language.

---

[14] Guy Deutscher, *Through the Language Glass*, 213–214.

[15] Guy Deutscher, *Through the Language Glass*, 222, 224.

[16] Guy Deutscher, *Through the Language Glass*, 226–230.

Their questions were simple. Do people perceive colors differently depending on which side they see them on? Would, for instance, English speakers be more sensitive to shades near the green-blue border when they see them on their right side rather than the left? The results mirrored those in the Russian experiment, with the left half of the English speakers' brains showing the same response toward the green-blue border that the Russians had toward light-dark blue border. Deutscher notes that this—along with subsequent studies, one of which used an MRI to show activity in the cerebral cortex—leave little room for doubt that the color concepts of our language interfere directly in the processing of color. Though subtle, it appears that language affects perception to some degree.

Formation of Faith

Given the influence of language on thought, perception, and action, it's time to ask if there's a particular parlance best suited to sustain and deepen Christian faith. To answer that we need to keep in mind that words can as easily mislead as inform, which combined with our cultural preference for abstract language (perhaps especially in popular religion), gives our question some urgency. Though we'll argue the affirmative for the remainder of this work, we can encapsulate our position in Paul's insistence that "I determined to know nothing among you except Jesus Christ, and Him crucified" (1 Cor. 2:2). Throughout scripture, the mystery of the cross (and the triune nature of God it entails) surfaces as the foundational event of the Christian faith. Since this is so, the assembly's language needs to be steeped in the biblical imagery of the sacrificial death of the Son of God. Considering human limits and the fact that knowledge of God comes only in his self-revelation on a criminal's cross—which is foolishness to natural man (1 Cor. 1:18)—a faithful adherence to the grammar and language of scripture is more vital than often appreciated.

But in what way does the Bible provide such language for the Christian assembly? It does so in the pattern of worship we see in Acts 2:42, beginning with baptism as the community-forming event in Acts 2:41. From this early text, we can see believers gathered for the regular reading of scripture ("the apostles' teaching") and the breaking of bread at the table and prayer (we'll refer to this as the word/table pattern). Significantly, the same pattern is shared by all four Gospels as they move from the baptism of Jesus, to the collected stories and sayings of Jesus that "lean forward" toward the passion, to the meal that shows the passion's meaning, to the passion itself, and then to the resurrection and sending of the disciples out into the world.[17] In short, they all have the framework of baptism, narratives, meal and passion, resurrection and sending. It's thus no coincidence that in our earliest records we find baptism and the remembrance of baptism as the community-forming event, an assembly around narratives and preaching, the meal encounter with the cross, and the resurrection-based sending.

It was in this way that the church kept—and still keeps—the biblical vocabulary and grammar before the people and transmits a vision of reality which helps them interpret life and the world. Worship is the place where that vision comes to its sharpest focus, which it achieves by mimicking the pattern of scripture itself and thereby reorienting Christians in their proper relation to the God who created, redeemed, and preserves them.[18] Though we'll discuss the word/table pattern in greater detail later, we can be content here by noting that it's the way in which the church ponders and applies scripture—and the way in which believers share with each other and with God a common history focused in Jesus Christ. As it does so it puts the assembly in first-hand contact with the foundational events and provides believers with a common language with which they're able to greet Abraham as their father in the faith.[19]

Creedal Language

Throughout history, educators have understood that memorization and rehearsal is critical for a child's ability to learn and recall essential information. Whether in mathematics, English, literature, or science children memorize basics that become part of their mental furniture

---

[17] Gordon Lathrop, *Holy Ground: A Liturgical Cosmology* (Minneapolis, 2003), 130–2.

[18] Geoffrey Wainwright, *Doxology*, 2–3, 19, 39–40.

[19] Geoffrey Wainwright, *Doxology*, 176, 178.

and form the basis for subsequent development. But memory studies on older adults also demonstrate that the more frequent the
rehearsal the more they remember significant details—to the point
that they're often preserved very much as the person first remembered or reported an event.[20] Repetition thus isn't only for children,
but can serve adults just as well and provide a much needed default
in times of crisis and instability.

With this in mind, recall our previous discussion on the limits
of human knowledge. Given that our intuitions are often wrong, that
System 2 tends to be lazy, and that we favor coherence over truth, it's
important—particularly in the religious domain where our limits are
even more acute—to repeat the biblical language of the cross and the
triune nature of God. As Chesterton correctly said, it's easy to be a
heretic,[21] which is something that even a cursory survey of Christian
history would show. Why is it easy? Because as we'll see, not only
does sin love idolatry but we naturally flatten out truths to suit our
own constricted view of the world; which was one reason the historic creeds were put together. Originally connected with the rite of
baptism, their intent was to instruct Christians in the basic content
of the faith; and in so doing, they drew a boundary around what was
and wasn't Christian. Given their vital function, it's tragic that modern churches have abandoned creedal repetition to meet the cultural
demand for more abstract language.

This is especially so because creeds express the believer's
renewed reception of the Christian message. In their baptismal focus,
the faith is being summed up and rehearsed, and in a sense re-lived.
In other words, when confessing our faith via the creed we're initiated once again into a people of God which has a historic identity
secured by the Christ who is "the same yesterday, today and forever."
As long as believers continue to repeat and re-live their Christian
confession, they can be assured of their own identity in the identity
of the crucified and resurrected Jesus.[22]

---

[20] Richard Bauckham, *Jesus and the Eyewitnesses: The Gospels as Eyewitness
Testimony* (Grand Rapids, 2006), 345–346.

[21] G. K. Chesterton, *Orthodoxy* (San Francisco, 1908), 106–7.

[22] Geoffrey Wainwright, *Doxology*, 190–1.

Thus the rehearsal of the creed is a sign that it is in fact the assembly of Jesus Christ to which we belong and not another. In this way we expresses solidarity with the universal church, while being simultaneously safeguarded from the errors that require the smallest touch to turn them into something monstrous. This is why the fourth century church father, St. Augustine, recommended the creed's daily repetition: "Say the creed daily. When you rise, when you compose yourself to sleep, repeat your creed, render it to the Lord, remind yourself of it, be not irked to say it over."[23] Augustine's phrase, "Render it to the Lord," is a reminder that saying the creed expresses praise to God. "The self-reminder is part of the shaping of a life which will bear faithful witness to the Lord before fellow human beings: the riches of the creed become, in Augustine's phrase, 'the daily clothing of your mind.'"[24] Creeds allow Christians to bring their faith to verbal expression in summary form for the purpose of witness, memory, and praise. Adding to this, they're necessary given the linguistic nature of man and Christianity's belief in revelation as Word, in addition to the fact that the New Testament itself imposes limits on the way it should be understood.[25]

Perhaps the most important take-away is that creeds keep man on firm ground and within scriptural boundaries. With explicit language around core doctrines such as the trinitarian nature of God and his self-revelation in the flesh of Jesus, they safeguard scriptural tensions and condemn the flattening out of realities that end in heresy; an example of which concerns the difficult notion of God becoming man in Jesus to redeem humanity. We have no trouble with the idea of man as the image of God, as growing into moral and spiritual likeness of our maker. But that the relationship should operate in reverse with the maker becoming man, and further going to death for his love of man—that not only evokes praise but it's also an idea that needs protection against our natural tendencies toward self-righteousness and hyper-spirituality. Paul recognized this in his rebuke of the Corinthian church, which kept veering away from the

---

[23] J. N. D. Kelly, *Early Christian Creeds*, 3rd ed. (New York, 1972), 370.

[24] Geoffrey Wainwright, *Doxology*, 184–89.

[25] Geoffrey Wainwright, *Doxology*, 243.

stigma of the cross (1 Cor. 2:2). But when confessed repeatedly in the church's creeds, worshippers won't be satisfied with a God who'd be less committed to the world in self-giving love than the God who gave himself in the incarnation and crucifixion of Jesus.[26]

We can conclude by noting that this is how the deep patterns of core Christian doctrines enter the memory and shape the faith of believers. What's confessed in the biblical language conditions what's believed in the heart and mind, and it's that which is lived each day. The word/table pattern of the liturgy, with its creedal and biblical language, then becomes the locus in which God's self-giving love promotes the interiorization of faith.

Conclusion

In an aptly titled chapter, "Limit Your Inputs," Ryan Holiday reminds his readers that there's profound truth to the old saying "garbage in, garbage out."[27] If you want good outputs, he says, you have to watch the inputs. His point is that we're so bombarded with information of various quality (much of it bad) that we've become less able to deal meaningfully with what's truly important. Annie Duke agrees, pointing out that we're "ticker watchers" (a reference to daily stock market results) ever consumed with the smallest details and no longer able to see the big picture.[28] We're thrown here and there and moved more by raw emotions than reasoning that's been tempered by a long-term perspective.

The heart of the problem, as Holiday recognizes, is that bad inputs can only lead to bad outputs. This is no less less true of our lives as Christians. Since worship is central to the life of the church, it's critical that we manage the inputs and ensure that they correspond to the language and focus of scripture itself. We've seen sufficient reason to beware of our natural impulses in even mundane matters, let alone in the spiritual arena where our sinful minds compulsively

---

[26] Geoffrey Wainwright, *Doxology*, 206, 209, 214, 217.

[27] Ryan Holiday, *Stillness Is the Key* (New York, 2019), 34–5.

[28] Annie Duke, *Thinking in Bets: Making Smarter Decisions When You Don't Have All the Facts* (New York, 2018), 191–4.

make us the center of the universe. Here, more than anywhere, the quality of the inputs matter. And since words can as easily mislead as inform, we need to avoid worship centered on the self, either through music or a concentration on Christian ethics; as self-oriented inputs can only create an idolatrous and unscriptural works orientation that revolts, if ever so subtly, against the death of the God who was crucified between two wretches.

Having said this, we can note that after a century or more of modern attempts to cast it off as a relic of bygone days, the word/table framework of the historic liturgy remains unsurpassed in its ability to make the biblical language, as Augustine rightly said centuries ago, the daily clothing of our minds.

As we turn our attention to the historical context of the old and new testament church, it is time to explore the word/table pattern of worship we've mentioned on several occasions.

CHAPTER 6

The Ordo: Word, Table, and Prayer

Since the time of the American frontier revivalists a significant number of modern Christians have assumed that there's a scriptural silence about the structure of worship, with the result that churches have patterned it in accordance with popular trends and whatever they deem necessary to save souls. Recall from our previous discussion that, in place of the traditional order, revivalists paired down the service to the three elements of warmup singing, preaching, and conversion. Most notable about this was the fact that the new pattern eliminated the traditional order of the reading of scripture (word), the eucharist (table), and common prayer.

As we noted, modern evangelicalism has generally retained the revivalist order which is particularly prevalent in the large non-denominational churches. An underlying (if not explicit) reason for this, from the nineteenth century onward, has been that a liturgical framework alienates people from the spontaneous movement of the Spirit. In place of the traditional order praise bands have become the central focus. Hymns have been replaced with a new genre of praise music, which focuses not so much on the story of man's justification through Christ's death, but on more individually and ethically centered content.

Unfortunately, the more central question of whether there exists a biblical pattern of worship that believers are duty bound to follow has been largely ignored in popular Christian circles. But given that a biblical framework—if it existed—would prove important, this chapter will focus on a few key questions: can we detect any pattern in the early biblical documents and first century environment, and do the second-generation Christians offer any clues about the practices of the primitive assemblies? Was it the spontaneous Spirit-fueled community so often assumed, or did it conform to some normative structure grounded in scripture itself? What we'll see is that the modern idea of an early community with little concern for structure is a myth, and that both scripture and our earliest Christian documents show a clear pattern of worship; a pattern consisting of word, table, and common prayer. (Note that as we proceed this pattern will often be referred to simply as word and table.)

No Blank Slate

Since we're all influenced by the spirit of our times, it's likely not a coincidence that during the same period the frontier revivalists were replacing the traditional liturgy, scholars were pushing a Spirit-fueled theory of how Christianity began. From roughly 1860 to 1914 scholars made a sharp antithesis between the Spirit-guided, spontaneous New Testament phase and the second century period of formalism and institutionalism.[1]

Regardless of its truth, the theory's stickiness in the popular mind has been remarkable. No doubt part of its persistence is the prevailing religious attitude which, as Alexander Schmemann observes, "considers every rule a symptom of the weakening of the spirit."[2] Because of this, early Christian worship has been stubbornly seen as rooted in "charismatic" free-wheeling assemblies without a fixed structure.

Though undoubtably appealing to modern sensibilities, this view has been shown to be false. Scholars have demonstrated that there's nothing more artificial or improbable than the contrast between the first century church, with its pure creative religion of the Spirit and its complete absence of organization, and the embryonic Catholic Church with all its institutional structure of the late

---

[1] J. N. D. Kelly, *Early Christian Creeds*, third ed. (New York, 1972), 6.

[2] Alexander Schmemann, *Introduction to Liturgical Theology* (Crestwood, 1966), 33, 56.

second century.[3] It's now generally agreed that the early Christian assemblies had a definite *ordo* (a shape or structure of worship) that was adopted from the Jewish roots from which it arose. "This comparative study of early Christian worship and the liturgical forms of Judaism . . . leaves no doubt about the formal dependence of the former on the latter."[4] That is, there exists a structural dependence, a similarity in the basic elements which determine the liturgical content and general pattern of the *ordo*.

We can see this in several areas: in the overall structure of the early service and in what was new to the Christian assembly, baptism and the eucharist. As for the general structure, the same pattern of the blessing in the name of God, praise, confession of sins, intercession and glorifying God for his work in history is found in both the synagogue and early Christian prayer. That is, there's an obvious dependency of order, an identity of sequence and the subordination of one part to another. Also, the Christian adoption of official church lectionaries followed the synagogue custom in which portions of the Law and Prophets were read at the divine service each sabbath. From early on, lectionaries were developed as a similar system of lessons from the New Testament to be read according to fixed Sundays and other holy days.[5] The word portion of the service (the reading of scripture) for which the lectionary was designed was critical enough, in fact, that an astounding 2,135 lectionaries of the Greek New Testament have been catalogued.

What this reveals is that the early Christian communities preserved the traditional form of synagogue worship to which the people who made up these churches were accustomed. They didn't start with an empty tablet or blank slate. The material on the tablet was rather made from the old, from the language and practices of the Old Testament and first century Jewish environment. And these determined the whole future development of what was new

---

[3] J. N. D. Kelly, *Early Christian Creeds*, 7–8. See also Aidan Kavanagh, *The Shape of Baptism: The Rite of Christian Initiation* (Collegeville, 1978), 24.

[4] Alexander Schmemann, *Introduction to Liturgical Theology*, 53–60.

[5] Bruce M. Metzger, *The Text of the New Testament: Its Transmission, Corruption, and Restoration*. 2nd ed. (New York, 1968), 30–31, 33.

in the Christian assembly: baptism and the eucharist, which became so essential that one could be part of the community only through baptismal washing, participation in the eucharist, and the common prayers of the assembly. Yet their true meaning couldn't be experienced other than in relation to the old, to that which the new was fulfilling and renewing.

In short, it was on this "liturgical dualism," a participation in the old and at the same time the presence of the new, that early Christian worship was patterned. Christians observed the week as a ritual unit that was both like and unlike the sabbath assembly. They held a gathering focused around scripture, interpretation, and prayer in line with the synagogue. But their worship was also founded on a baptismal washing in the name of the Father and of the Son and of the Holy Spirit, and a meal in observance of Jesus' command (Luke 22:17–20; 1 Cor. 11:23–27). What's important is that the new wasn't drawn from any other sources than the old, meaning that the particulars of the early assemblies weren't new inventions but rearrangements and new relationships within the old material.

The Bath

Given the church's liturgical roots, it's important to note that there's a prehistory to the baptismal washing "in the name of Jesus" or "in the name of the Father and of the Son and of the Holy Spirit" that reaches back to the beginning of the Jewish religion and beyond.

Throughout ancient history water was often considered sacred. A spring or well could be regarded as a sacred place, a mysterious source of life beyond mankind.[6] Yet for all its abundance on our planet it comes from beyond our circle, from oceans, sky, and mountains. It comes from God. And because it's a source of life—it's our first need as living beings—it has loomed large in our imagination. The psalmist, as an example, uses the image of water to describe his complete dependence on God (Ps. 42:1–2). Water also plays a vital role in the first chapters of Genesis, which compels Tertullian (second

---

[6] Gordon Lathrop, *Holy Things: A Liturgical Theology* (Minneapolis, 1998), 94–5.

century) to comment that "'the waters' were the first to receive the precept 'to bring forth living creatures.'" Water was first to produce that which had life, so he adds that it should be "no wonder in baptism if waters know how to give life."[7] As the Spirit of God hovered over the waters from the beginning, it now continues over the waters of the baptized.

For Judaism, we know there were purification rituals involving water for both people and things (insofar as they caused impurity in individuals, such as food) that were used by the prophets to internalize religious sentiment;[8] the washing of bodies went hand-in-hand with the cleansing of hearts. We also know that there was a water rite in later Judaism with a more initiatory character—in other words, a rite in which gentiles became Jews—involving proselyte (convert) baptism. Originally perhaps little more than the proselyte's first ritual purification after circumcision, the water bath began to absorb the initiatory aspects of circumcision, but then displaced it altogether as the act by which gentiles became Jews. By the Christian era proselyte baptism assumed an increasingly initiatory status. Thus, the bath—with or without circumcision—made gentiles Jews by purifying converts from their uncleanness and admitting them into the covenant life of Judaism.

Along with the bath itself we should note the prehistory of one more thing. As the Jewish proselyte stood in the water, it was common for the commandments of the Torah (which served as a foundation of the proselyte's instruction) to be recited—as it was into these commandments as a way of living that the person was baptized. And it was primarily this catechetical instruction before the washing that influenced Christian baptism in the New Testament. But of the baptismal rite itself, the prototype was John's because of what happened when it was applied to Jesus—something that, as Aidan Kavanagh puts it, at once both consummated John's baptism and rendered it obsolete. At Jesus' baptism the old covenant mutated into the new by the divine act manifesting Jesus as Messiah.

---

[7] *Ante-Nicene Fathers*, Vol. 3, eds. Alexander Roberts and James Donaldson (Peabody, 2012), 670.

[8] Aidan Kavanagh, *The Shape of Baptism*, 7–11, 29–30.

That baptism became an essential rite in the Christian assembly is seen very early, and can only be understood in light of what the apostles believed it conferred. Their confession of its meaning in light of Jesus' death is aptly conveyed in the following: "Or do you not know that all of us who have been baptized into Christ Jesus have been baptized into His death? Therefore we have been buried with Him through baptism into death, so that as Christ was raised from the dead through the glory of the Father, so we too might walk in newness of life" (Rom. 6:3–5); "For all of you who were baptized into Christ have clothed yourselves with Christ" (Gal. 3:27); "Christ also loved the church and gave Himself up for her, so that He might sanctify her, having cleansed her by the washing of water with the word" (Eph. 5:25); "He saved us . . . by the washing of regeneration and renewing by the Holy Spirit" (Titus 3:5–7, the washing being a clear baptismal reference); and "baptism now saves you—not the removal of dirt from the flesh, but an appeal to God for a good conscience" (1 Pet. 3:21).

Further, in Acts Peter exhorts his audience, "'Repent, and each of you be baptized in the name of Jesus Christ for the forgiveness of your sins; and you will receive the gift of the Holy Spirit'" (2:38). Later in 22:16, Ananias says to the young Paul, "'Now why do you delay? Get up and be baptized, and wash away your sins, calling on His name.'" Throughout the New Testament, baptism is connected with the forgiveness of sins which is a sanctifying and cleansing water by virtue of the word connected with it—meaning that it isn't merely a symbol of the cross, but the power of the cross actualized for those who believe. The bath plunges one into the name of Jesus (1 Cor. 1:13; Acts 19:5) so profoundly that it sets believers apart as circumcision did for the Jews (Col. 2:11)—burying them in Christ's death so completely (1 Cor. 12:13, 27) that they become participants with him as Israel participated in Moses' passage from Egypt through the waters of the Red Sea, and ultimately to the promised land (we see the same connection in Justin's early second century *Dialogue With Trypho*[9]).

---

[9] *Ante-Nicene Fathers*, Vol. 1, eds. Alexander Roberts and James Donaldson (Peabody, 2012), 216.

Thus, it's no surprise we find the early church fathers repeating the biblical and apostolic language. Justin, for example, reports that the baptized "are regenerated in the same manner in which we were ourselves regenerated. For, in the name of God, the Father and Lord of the universe, and of our Savior Jesus Christ, and of the Holy Spirit, they then receive the washing with water . . . and may obtain in the water the remission of sins;" and "who has been washed with the washing that is for the remission of sins, and unto regeneration . . ."[10] Tertullian asks, "Is it not wonderful, too, that death should be washed away by bathing?"[11]

As another example, The *Apostolic Tradition* (an ancient church order)—after instructing that the little ones who can't speak for themselves and require a sponsor to speak on their behalf should be baptized first—sets down the following prayer after the rite: "Lord God, you have made these worthy to deserve the remission of sins through the washing of regeneration: grant that they may be filled with the Holy Spirit, sending your grace upon them so they may serve you in accordance with your will; for to you be glory, to the Father and the Son and with the Holy Spirit in the holy church both now and to the ages of the ages. Amen."[12] The same document, as it instructs the faithful to regularly make the sign of the cross, bears witness to the early belief in the efficaciousness (the power to produce the result) of baptism. The sign of the cross is seen as a return to one's baptism:

> Always attempt reverently to sign yourself on the forehead. For this sign of the passion is displayed against the Devil, if it is made in faith and not to please people, but through the emblem, putting it before you as a shield. For if the Adversary sees the power of the Spirit (from the heart) being outwardly demonstrated in the likeness of baptism, he will flee away trembling, not because you spat on him but because you breathed on him. This is what Moses did in a type with the sheep

[10] *Ante-Nicene Fathers*, Vol. 1, 183, 185.

[11] *Ante-Nicene Fathers*, Vol. 3, 669, 671.

[12] Hippolytus, *On the Apostolic Tradition*, second edition (New York, 2015), 134–5.

which was sacrificed on the Passover. Sprinkling the blood on the lintel and anointing the two doorposts he signified that faith in the perfect sheep which is now in us. By signing forehead and eyes with the hand we shall escape the one who is seeking our destruction.[13]

Given the clear language of the New Testament it was impossible for the ancients not to recognize the connection between the bath and the forgiveness of sin. Bottom line is that when the church washed "in the name of Jesus" (Acts 2:38; 10:48; 19:2–7) and said that Jesus' death was such a washing (Mark 10:38; Luke 12:50), and that the community's washing was identified with Jesus' death (Rom. 6:3), they proposed something remarkably new out of the old language and practice.

The Table

As we've now seen, the early Christian gathering for scripture, interpretation, and prayer (the "standing prayers") is similar to what we know of the first century synagogue service.[14] Set next to this word service, however, Christians added a meal that quickly occupied center stage in worship. But as before there's an important prehistory that serves as the background for a proper understanding of the eucharistic rite. It involves the Jewish Passover meal which was the context in which Jesus celebrated the last supper with his disciples.

Perhaps the most important thing to note about it is Jesus' announcement of his pending passion that he added to the traditional words spoken over the bread and wine, which was a fixed part of the Passover ritual. Still practiced today, the custom was taken from Ex. 12:26ff. and took place after the preliminary course and the mixing of the second of the four ritual cups. It was customary that these special elements had to be mentioned: the Passover lamb, the unleavened bread, and the bitter herbs. We can see this in comments made by Gamaliel I (30 A.D.) when he said, "The Passover lamb (should be interpreted as follows): because God passed over in mercy the houses

---

[13] Hippolytus, *On the Apostolic Tradition*, 195–6.
[14] Gordon Lathrop, *Holy Things*, 43–4.

of our fathers in Egypt (Ex. 12:27); unleavened bread: because our fathers were redeemed from Egypt; the bitter herbs: because the Egyptians embittered the lives of our fathers in Egypt (Ex. 1:14)."[15] The official Passover *haggadah* (a text with the order of the Passover) cites Ex. 12:34, 39 to explain that the unleavened bread is used because the Israelites didn't have time to leaven the dough when God revealed himself and redeemed them.

While remembrance of the past played an important role, it should be pointed out that the special elements were also interpreted as related to the present—in every generation a man must regard himself as if he himself came out of Egypt. Yet by the first century there was also a looking forward to the end with regard to the unleavened bread, to the saving event of the Messianic future. Thus, it's no accident that it's similarly interpreted in the New Testament (1 Cor. 5:7–8). Evidence of this is found in Paul's interpretation of the Passover lamb, the bitter herbs, and the unleavened bread which corresponds to the Passover ritual. That he's delivering a much older tradition (which he also does elsewhere, such as 1 Cor. 11:23–27 and 15:3–8) we know from the fact that the language is un-Pauline and Semitic.

The theme in this early meditation is that the great Passover festival began on Good Friday. To be a Christian means to live in the Passover, in the deliverance from the bondage of sin. As it's developed in the 1 Corinthians text, the Passover lamb is the symbol of the Messiah who was sacrificed as the unblemished lamb. The leaven is the symbol of the evil and wickedness of the old world, and the unleavened loaves are the pure dough that represent the purity and truth which characterizes the new world—and as new dough they symbolize the redeemed community.

The Disciples' Understanding

Before leaving the last supper, some additional background will be helpful. In the first century, people believed that a meal binds diners

---

[15] Joachim Jeremias, *The Eucharistic Words of Jesus* (London, 1966), 41ff., 56, 59–61, 137.

into a "table fellowship" which was religious in nature. Its violation
was considered a troubling crime (Ps. 41:9), adding another layer
to why Jesus was so deeply grieved in Mark 14:20 at Judas' betrayal.
While the Passover table fellowship was particularly religious, its
binding nature was also true of the common meal which through the
rite of the breaking of bread constituted the table fellowship. When
the head of the family recited the blessing over the bread—which
diners made their own by the "Amen"—and broke it for each member, they were all made recipients of the blessing by the eating. The
common "Amen" and eating of the bread of benediction united
the members into a table fellowship. This was also true of the "cup of
blessing" that, by drinking, mediated a share in the blessing.[16] Thus
as Jesus blessed the bread and wine and added words connecting
the broken bread and red wine to his atoning death, the disciples
understood that by eating and drinking he gives them a share in
the atoning power of his death.

This is made all the more potent when we recall that to the
ancients the idea that divine gifts are imparted by eating and drinking
was very familiar. Within Jewish and New Testament works, there are
many variations on the idea of the bread of life that satisfies all hunger
(John 6:35, where Jesus calls himself the bread of life; Luke 6:21); the
heavenly manna that will be the food of the redeemed world to come
(John 6:31); the water of life (Is. 49:10; Rev. 7:17) which is given freely
and quenches all thirst forever (John 4:13ff.; 6:35; 7:37–39; Rev. 21:6;
22:1, 17); the wine of the world to come which is reserved for the children of heaven (Mark 14:25); the feast of salvation in the last days that
imparts salvation and life (Is. 25:6ff.; 65:13ff.; Didache 10[17]). The New
Testament is pregnant with the notion of the feast of salvation impart-
ing the gifts of redemption (Matt. 5:6; 8:11; 22:1–4; Luke 14:15–24;
22:15–18; John 4:10, 14; Rev. 3:20; 19:7, 9; 1 Cor. 10:4 where Jesus
is the giver of the water of life). In all of these, divine gifts are seen as
being imparted in eating and drinking.

What's important is that Jesus' words and actions at the last
supper belong to this circle of ideas. When at the distribution of the

---

[16] Joachim Jeremias, *The Eucharistic Words of Jesus*, 232–34, 236–7.

[17] J. B. Lightfoot, *The Apostolic Fathers* (Grand Rapids, 1986), 127.

bread and wine he gave his interpretation, the intention was to make the disciples' participation in the gift clear. The eating of the bread and the drinking from the cup that Jesus had blessed was meant to give them a share in the blessing and the redemptive work of Jesus as savior. This is Jesus' greatest gift, the forgiveness of sins. That the disciples and Paul understood it this way is demonstrated in 1 Cor. 10:16, in which Paul asks: "Is not the cup of blessing which we bless a sharing in the blood of Christ? Is not the bread which we break a sharing in the body of Christ?" To share in the atoning death of Jesus is the gift of the eucharist.

We can add to this the fact that the Passover meal closed with Ps. 118, with special liturgical emphasis on verses 21–29. Scholars note that this was the high point of the whole Passover ritual, as these verses were an anticipation of the antiphonal choir with which the Messiah would be greeted. By this we know that at the time of Jesus the Passover wasn't simply a memorial meal but primarily a representation of the hour of redemption, a fact that helps us understand the deepest meaning of the Lord's Supper: (1) that it's an anticipatory gift of the consummation and (2) that it was (and still is) meant to assure the disciples of their possession of salvation, which Jesus did by making them partakers of the atoning power of his death by their eating and drinking—and in this way including them already in the victory of God. "*As surely as they eat the bread* which Jesus breaks for them and *drink the wine* over which he spoke the word referring to his outpoured blood, *so surely the 'for many' of his dying and the 'with you' of the future eucharist fellowship on a transformed earth is valid also for them.*"[18] The bottom line is that in the eucharist, then as now, the messianic kingdom is actualized—it becomes real in the here and now—in the assembly when believers come together to partake of Christ's body and blood.[19]

Before moving on, a word needs to be said about Paul's remembrance language in 1 Cor. 11:23–26—"do this, as often as you drink it, in remembrance of Me." While the usual interpretation suggests that it's the disciples who should remember, Jeremias offers another

---

[18] Joachim Jeremias, *The Eucharistic Words of Jesus*, 260–62.
[19] Alexander Schmemann, *Introduction to Liturgical Theology*, 72–3.

perspective. He argues (1) that it would be strange if it were directed at the disciples as though Jesus was afraid they would forget him, and (2) that it doesn't fit its Palestinian context. In the New Testament we find parallel constructions (e.g., Acts 10:4), but these are in line with what we see in the Old Testament and Palestinian memorial formulae in which it's *God* who remembers. Meaning that Paul's statement may be best understood as "This do, that God may remember me." In other words, that God may remember me mercifully at the last judgment. This might make the best sense of Paul's immediately following, "For as often as you eat this bread and drink the cup, you proclaim the Lord's death until He comes." The Lord commanded its repetition and the church fulfills the command at every celebration of the Lord's Supper, by which it proclaims his death until he comes. *"As often as the death of the Lord is proclaimed at the Lord's supper, and the maranatha* ["come Lord Jesus"] *rises upwards, God is reminded of the unfulfilled climax of the work of salvation* 'until (the goal is reached, that) he comes.'"[20]

Understood in this way, Paul would be in line with other texts of the period to which we have access. The Didache, a first century church order, reads the same way in its wording of the grace after ordinary meals, which leads to a prayer for the eschatological (end of time) remembrance of God: "Remember, Lord, Thy Church to deliver it from all evil and to perfect it in Thy love; and gather it together from the four winds—even the Church which has been sanctified—into Thy kingdom which Thou has prepared for it; for Thine is the power and the glory for ever and ever."[21] Thus Jesus' command to repeat the rite of the Lord's Supper isn't a summons to the disciples to remember him, but rather an eschatologically oriented instruction; as we join ourselves together at the table, God is regularly implored to bring about the consummation of history, which is the reason why the assembly still repeats the maranatha during the eucharistic rite.

Whatever the merits of Jeremias' argument, we should point out that these two interpretations aren't necessarily exclusive. Given that Jesus' language is what linguists and philosophers call

---

[20] Joachim Jeremias, *The Eucharistic Words of Jesus*, 251–55.

[21] J. B. Lightfoot, *The Apostolic Fathers*, 127.

performative—meaning his aim isn't merely to describe or state something he's doing, but rather to do it—his utterance is the actual *performance* of the action. Thus, as he gives the disciples (and us through the pastor) the bread and wine and says the words "This is my body," "This cup . . . is my blood," and commands "Do this," actions (albeit supernatural) are carried out through the language. The point is that in any performative utterance, for it to be valid, the person invoking the words must have the same thoughts and feelings as the participants.[22] This means that, ultimately, the remembrance goes both ways. Thus, while it's necessarily the case that in the very act of the eucharist believers remember Jesus, the language suggests that Jesus too is called on to remember his promises as he gives us his body and blood for the forgiveness of sins.

Early Ritualization

Given their meaning, we're in a better position to understand why Jesus' eucharistic words were so quickly ritualized even before the New Testament was written. That is, much of what we see in those documents already reflects liturgical usage within the earliest assemblies. In 1 Cor. 11:23-26, for example, Paul echoes the words that Jesus used in the Last Supper, yet we can detect its early liturgical use. For context, here's the passage:

> For I received from the Lord that which I also delivered to you, that the Lord Jesus in the night in which He was betrayed took bread; and when He had given thanks, He broke it and said, "This is My body, which is for you; do this in remembrance of Me." In the same way He took the cup also after supper, saying, "This cup is the new covenant in My blood; do this, as often as you drink it, in remembrance of Me." For as often as you eat this bread and drink the cup, you proclaim the Lord's death until He comes.

Jeremias notes that the first words—"the Lord Jesus in the night in which He was betrayed took bread; and when He had given thanks,

---

[22] J. L. Austin, *How To Do Things With Words* (Cambridge, 1975), 14–5.

He broke it and said"—not only have a solemn ring but must already be part of the church's liturgy because the phrase "the Lord Jesus" isn't used in the Gospel accounts; it belongs rather to the early liturgical formula (1 Cor. 12:3; Rom. 10:9).[23] Further, "in the night in which He was betrayed" is also liturgical because it's not a chronological statement. The description of the grace at the table, "took bread and having given thanks broke," has the exact characteristic of a liturgical rubric (an instruction for how the liturgy should proceed).

As for the Gospels, Mark's account of the last supper shows evidence of its liturgical church use in the way he segues it into the passion narrative. In addition to the same three verbs used by Paul, Mark adds a fourth "and He gave it to them," which strengthens the impression that it was a liturgical rubric. Also, in contrast to Paul and Luke, the introduction to the word over the cup is phrased in ceremonial liturgical language. While Matthew keeps the account close to Mark, he has the addition of "Jesus" and "the disciples" (Matt. 26:26) which betrays its liturgical tone. The differences between the four aren't literary corrections by the authors, but rather reflect early liturgical development. That the eucharist was instantly enshrined in ritual is further attested in the Didache, which insists that "on the Lord's own day gather yourselves together and break bread and give thanks, first confessing your transgressions,"[24] and describes a meal that was framed by prayers over the bread and wine.

In all this it's important to emphasize why a ritual framework was the most appropriate medium for Jesus' eucharistic words: because in them lies the essence of his person and work, and in them—through the eucharistic rite—forgiveness of sin is given. Maintaining its ritual structure was the church's only choice. The last supper encompassed the meaning of Jesus' death: the vicarious death of the suffering servant that atones for the sins of the "many," the peoples of the world.[25] This is why we can see a concern early in the first century to protect the sacredness of the eucharist from

---

[23] Joachim Jeremias, *The Eucharistic Words of Jesus*, 112–13.

[24] J. B. Lightfoot, *The Apostolic Fathers*, 126, 128. Gordon Lathrop, *Holy Things*, 48.

[25] Joachim Jeremias, *The Eucharistic Words of Jesus*, 136, 231.

error. The development towards protection runs from the book of Hebrews (reservation of eucharistic teaching to the "mature"), to the Didache[26] (silence about eucharistic procedure), to Luke (limitation of the first words of the formula), to John who has only a homily on the eucharistic words (6:51, 53–58), but omits the account of the institution. The sacred text must be protected. So important was this that the early church, as seen in the Didache, dismissed the unbaptized for the eucharistic liturgy as an extra measure.[27]

This explains the position of those immediately following generations, of which we'll only cite a few. Irenaeus (120–202 A.D.), for instance, argues: "But if this [salvation of the flesh] indeed does not attain salvation, then neither did the Lord redeem us with His blood, nor is the cup of the Eucharist the communion with His blood, nor the bread which we break the communion of His body . . . And as we are His members, we are also nourished by means of the creation . . . He has acknowledged the cup (which is part of the creation) as His own blood, from which He bedews [sprinkles] our blood; and the bread (also a part of the creation) He has established as His own body, from which He gives increase to our bodies."[28]

Justin (second century), who provides one of the earliest descriptions of the Sunday eucharist in his text to the emperor Antoninus Pius, also insists:

And this food is called among us the Eucharist, of which no one is allowed to partake but the man who believes that the things which we teach are true, and who has been washed with the washing that is for the remission of sins, and unto regeneration, and who is so living as Christ has enjoined. For not as common bread and common drink do we receive these; but in like manner as Jesus Christ our Savior, having been made flesh by the Word of God, had both flesh and blood for our salvation, so likewise have we been taught that the food which is blessed by the prayer of His word, and from which

---

[26] J. B. Lightfoot, *The Apostolic Fathers*, 123–129.

[27] Arthur A. Just Jr., *Luke 1:1–9:50* (Saint Louis, 1996), 11. J. B. Lightfoot, *The Apostolic Fathers*, 126.

[28] *Ante-Nicene Fathers*, Vol. 1, 528.

our blood and flesh by transmutation are nourished, is the flesh and blood that Jesus who was made flesh. For the apostles, in the memoirs composed by them, which are called Gospels, have thus delivered unto us what was enjoined upon them; that Jesus took bread, and when He had given thanks, said, "This do ye in remembrance of Me, this is My body;" and that, after the same manner, having taken the cup and given thanks, He said, "This is My blood;" and gave it to them alone.[29]

Similarly, The *Apostolic Tradition* says that "Everybody should be concerned that one who is not of the faithful, nor a mouse nor any other animal, should eat of the Eucharist, and that none of it should fall and be altogether lost. For it is the body of Christ to be eaten by the faithful, and not to be despised." Also concerning the cup it prescribes that, "For this reason do not pour it out, that no alien spirit might lick it up because you despised it; you shall be guilty of the blood, like one who despises the price with which he has been bought."[30]

Finally, we should note that no orthodox father of the second or third century thought the presence of Christ's body and blood in the eucharist was just symbolic.[31] This view, so common in today's churches, simply didn't exist among the first generations of Christians. For these, a real presence in the bread and wine was a given, which the adoration of Christ in the eucharist through the words and actions of the liturgy presuppose. Bottom line is that their beliefs were shaped by the "memoirs" of the apostles which connected the rite with the forgiveness of sin, and because of this Jesus' eucharistic words would have been thought inseparable from their liturgical framework.

---

[29] *Ante-Nicene Fathers*, Vol. 1, 185.

[30] Hippolytus, *On the Apostolic Tradition*, 192–3.

[31] Jaroslav Pelikan, *The Christian Tradition: A History of the Development of Doctrine*, Vol. 1 The Emergence of the Catholic Tradition (100–600) (Chicago, 1971), 167–8.

Early Worship Pattern

Gordon Lathrop points out that all four Gospels share a peculiar pattern.[32] In contrast to the apocryphal (non-canonical) works that emerged in the second and third centuries, the canonical Gospels conform to the Greco-Roman genre of biography.[33] This being so, they move from the baptism of Jesus, to the collected stories and sayings of Jesus that "lean forward" toward the passion, to the meal that shows the passion's meaning, to the passion itself, and then to the resurrection and sending of the disciples out into the world. In short, they all follow exactly the same pattern: baptism, narratives, meal and passion, resurrection and sending. It's no coincidence that the liturgy has the same basic shape. There too we find baptism and the remembrance of baptism as the community-forming event, an assembly around narratives and preaching, the meal encounter with the cross, and the resurrection-based sending. In other words, the liturgy embodies the same biographical framework as the Gospels.

It's in this framework that we find a primitive *ordo* of word and meal that was widely shared in Christian circles, such that by the time the Gospels were written assemblies were gathering on Sunday for word and meal and sending, which they understood as being constituted by baptism. "Such an outline ought not to be regarded, then, as the accidental development of later Christian history. The very dynamics of the *ordo* are available to us in the canonical Gospels."[34] We can detect the word/table pattern in various places, but particularly in Acts 2:42: "They were continually devoting themselves to the apostles' teaching and to fellowship, to the breaking of bread and to prayer." Based on the verb which means "to attend worship regularly" and the four phrases that are dependent on "devoting themselves," scholars have noted that the passage describes the early Christian

---

[32] Gordon Lathrop, *Holy Ground: A Liturgical Cosmology* (Minneapolis, 2003), 130–2.

[33] Richard A. Burridge, *What Are the Gospels? A Comparison with Graeco-Roman Biography* (Grand Rapids, 2004), p. 184, 210–12, 249.

[34] Gordon Lathrop, *Holy Ground*, 134, 38.

service: first the teaching of the apostles and the table fellowship, then the breaking of bread and the prayers.[35]

Jeremias notes that this is supported by numerous observations. First, that the early services began with the word/teaching is shown directly in Acts 20:7 and Justin's early remarks which we'll discuss below, and also indirectly by the reference to the holy kiss (Rom. 16:16; 1 Cor. 16:20; 2 Cor. 13:12; 1 Thess. 5:26; 1 Pet. 5:14). What this shows is that the celebration of the meal, introduced by the holy kiss, followed the teaching of the apostles or the reading of the letters (when an apostolic letter was present it took the place of the teaching). The service then concluded with psalms and prayers (Eph. 5:19), all of which is supported by the eucharistic liturgies of the whole ancient church (Rome, Egypt, and Africa).

Second, it's no coincidence that after the three thousand are baptized in Acts 2:41, that the very next verse has those newly initiated believers "continually devoting themselves to the apostles' teaching and to fellowship, to the breaking of bread and to prayer." The Spirit begins to be lived in baptism which serves as the believer's initiation into the fellowship of the church, yet it's to be lived in the Spirit-filled community animated by apostolic teaching and centered around the eucharistic meal.[36] Thus baptism was seen as initiating a full engagement with the church and a whole new way of life. Justin bears witness to this pattern, reporting that after the new believer is "thus washed" he or she is brought "to the place where those who are called brethren are assembled," where prayers and the meal take place.[37] Paul too makes the connection between bath and meal (1 Cor. 10:1–4; 12:13). Third, the Acts 2:42 description of the early service helps us understand how the Lord's Supper came to be known as the "breaking of bread" (Acts 2:42, 46; 20:7, 11). In Judaism, the "breaking of bread" never referred to the whole meal, but only to the action of tearing the bread and the rite with which the meal opened. As believers devoted themselves to the teaching and the fellowship, we can see already in Acts the separation of the

[35] Joachim Jeremias, *The Eucharistic Words of Jesus*, 118–20.

[36] Aidan Kavanagh, *The Shape of Baptism*, 16, 22.

[37] *Ante-Nicene Fathers*, Vol. 1, 185.

eucharist itself as a distinct rite, which explains why the "breaking of bread" came to be synonymous with the eucharist.[38]

In addition, the word/table framework appears in the Emmaus account (Luke 24:13–35) and the first day meeting at Troas (Acts 20:7–12). As Lathrop shows, the Emmaus and Troas accounts make the connection between word and table and the observance of Sunday clear. "We may isolate Sunday," he remarks, "and its word-table event, giving them a certain priority, because of their presence in at least some New Testament communities, near the origins of the tradition."[39] Its presence in those early assemblies corresponds to a pattern we see throughout scripture.

Outside the New Testament, Justin provides an important witness to the early worship pattern.[40] Immediately following a description of baptism, he gives the following report:

> And on the day called Sunday, all who live in cities or in the country gather together to one place, and the memoirs of the apostles or the writings of the prophets are read, as long as time permits; then, when the reader had ceased, the president verbally instructs, and exhorts to the imitation of these good things. Then we all rise together and pray, and, as we before said, when our prayer is ended, bread and wine and water are brought, and the president in like manner offers prayers and thanksgivings, according to his ability, and the people assent, saying Amen; and there is a distribution to each, and a participation of that over which thanks have been given, and to those who are absent a portion is sent by the deacons. And they who are well to do, and willing, give what each thinks fit; and what is collected is deposited with the president, who succours the orphans and widows, and those who, through sickness or any other cause, are in want, and those who are in bonds, and the strangers sojourning among us, and in a word takes care of all who are in need. But Sunday is the day on which we all hold our common assembly, because it is the first day on which God, having wrought a change in the darkness and matter, made the world; and Jesus Christ our Savior on the same day rose from the dead. For He

---

[38] Joachim Jeremias, *The Eucharistic Words of Jesus*, 121.

[39] Gordon Lathrop, *Holy Things: A Liturgical Theology*, 34, 53.

[40] Aidan Kavanagh, *The Shape of Baptism*, 43.

was crucified on the day before that of Saturn (Saturday); and on the day after that of Saturn, which is the day of the Sun, having appeared to His apostles and disciples, He taught them these things, which we have submitted to you also for your consideration.[41]

As with the pattern of the Gospel's themselves, Justin reports that the Christian assembly was formed by baptism, gathered around the word, celebrated the meal, and sent the community "to him who has nothing prepared" (Neh. 8:10). The *ordo*, in other words, was shared with those books Justin calls the "memoirs of the apostles," our canonical Gospels. The passage is significant not only because it reflects the New Testament pattern but also because of its early date (148 A.D.).[42] It's well established that liturgical texts are extremely conservative and resistant to change, especially before the invention of the printing press, so we can safely infer that Justin's description reflects first century practice. "For all the development of the Christian eucharist over the past two millennia, its core still centers upon bread broken and wine poured out in a context of prayerful thanksgiving for all God has wrought, just as the earliest churches would have done in obedience to the exalted Lord's command, 'Do this', at the Last Supper."[43]

We can summarize the basic pattern of worship visible in the New Testament and Justin's early remarks—which is the essential order of liturgy found in both the Eastern and Western churches—as follows:

> Word—gathering, reading of scripture, interpreting and praying as a synagogue-like gathering.
> Meal—setting out eucharistic elements, thanksgiving, distribution, sending to the absent, and concern for the poor as a communal action.[44]

---

[41] *Ante-Nicene Fathers*, 186.

[42] Arthur A. Just Jr., *Luke 1:1–9:50*, 9.

[43] Aidan Kavanagh, *The Shape of Baptism*, 35–6, 40.

[44] Gordon Lathrop, *Holy Things*, 47.

Common Prayer

We close this chapter with a note on the common prayers that played such a central part of early worship. As we mentioned above, there's been a pervasive belief within popular Christian circles that, like the worship service itself, primitive Christian prayers were fueled by the spontaneous movement of the Spirit and lacked the structure we find in the later institutionalized church. No doubt energized by the prevailing attitude that structure is a symptom of the weakening of the spirit, many Christians today believe that "home-made," extemporaneous (or unprepared) prayers, are more desirable than prepared ones. But if the antithesis between the pure creative religion of the Spirit and the institutional structure of the late second century is false, what of the popular conception of the early prayers? What do we know of the actual prayer practices of those earliest assemblies? Fortunately, we have data that points us in the right direction, of which we'll cite just a few examples.

In addition to the liturgical prayers noted throughout this book in and outside the New Testament, we have information on church practices from our earliest Christian sources—one of which is Hippolytus' *Apostolic Tradition*. As noted earlier, this early document is an example of church order literature which contains instructions and regulations for the life of the church, such as for ordinations, the offering of the eucharist, catechism, baptism, and the offering of prayer. While the document has been traditionally attributed to the third century Hippolytus of Rome, scholars now believe that Hippolytus was actually the last in a series of people who put the *Apostolic Tradition* together. Meaning that it's the product of a community that was produced over a number of years prior, making it one of the earliest liturgical sources we possess. It was probably completed by 235 A.D. Given that the church's liturgical development was extremely conservative and resistant to change, the *Apostolic Tradition's* historic value is high because of its primitive origins. With that said, what does it tell us about the assembly's prayers?

An example comes from instructions it gives for the ordination of bishops. Beginning with a familiar liturgical structure, it prescribes the following prayer:

"The Lord be with you."
And all shall say:
"And with your spirit."
"Hearts on high."
"We have them to the Lord."
"Let us give thanks."
"It is fitting and right."
And then he shall continue thus:

   We give thanks to you, God, through your beloved child Jesus
Christ, whom, in the last times, you sent to us as savior and redeemer
and angel of your will, who is your inseparable Word through whom
you made all things and who was well pleasing to you. You sent him
from heaven into the womb of a virgin, and he was conceived and
made flesh in the womb and shown to be your Son, born of the Holy
Spirit and the virgin. He fulfilled your will and won for you a holy people, opening wide his hands when he suffered that he might set free
from suffering those who believed in you. When he was handed over
to voluntary suffering, in order to dissolve death and break the chains
of the devil and harrow hell and illuminate the just and fix a boundary and manifest the resurrection, he took bread, and, giving thanks
to you, he said: take eat, this is my body which will be broken for you.
Likewise, with the cup saying: this is my blood which is poured out
for you . . .[45]

The document also prescribes that the trinitarian formula, "To you
be glory, to the Father and to the Son with the Holy Spirit in the holy
church both now and forever and to all the ages of the ages,"[46] be
added to every blessing. In another interesting example, it instructs
Christians to pray the following in the evening:

   We give you thanks, O God, through your child Jesus Christ our Lord,
   through whom you have illuminated us, revealing to us the incor-
   ruptible light. Therefore, we have completed the length of the day and
   we have arrived at the beginning of the night, being sated with the
   day's light which you created for our satisfaction. And now, having
   arrived at the light of evening through your grace, we give you praise

---

[45] Hippolytus, *On the Apostolic Tradition*, 15–6, 77–8.
[46] Hippolytus, *On the Apostolic Tradition*, 92.

and glorify you through your child Jesus Christ, our Lord, through whom to you be power and honor together with the Holy Spirit, now and always and to the ages of ages. Amen.[47]

An important note here is that the *Apostolic Tradition* bears witness to the early Christian practice of daily prayer, with prayer in the morning and evening, which is supplemented by prayer three times in the day, and prayer at midnight. This pattern likely comes from the ancient Hebrew prayer pattern, which consisted of prayer in the morning, afternoon and evening. We know from Acts that the early believers observed the fixed hours of prayer (3:1),[48] so it's not surprising that daily prayer was an integral part of the early Christian community.

A final example of early set prayers comes from the Didache. In the context of the eucharist, it prescribes the following: "We give Thee thanks, O our Father, for the holy vine of Thy son David, which Thou madest known unto us through Thy Son Jesus; Thine is the glory for ever and ever . . . We give Thee thanks, O our Father, for the life and knowledge which Thou didst make known unto us through Thy Son Jesus; Thine is the glory for ever and ever. As this broken bread was scattered upon the mountains and being gathered together became one, so may Thy Church be gathered together from the ends of the earth into Thy kingdom; for Thine is the glory and the power through Jesus Christ for ever and ever." Also, in its instructions for personal prayer, the Didache exhorts believers to pray the Lord's Prayer, "Three times in the day pray ye so."[49]

It deserves repeating that in their set prayers the assembly conforms to the biblical pattern of prayer, first by praising God and recounting his mighty deeds, which then establishes the ground on which the people beseech his faithfulness and beg him to remember his promises.[50] "It is because of what the LORD did for me when I came out of Egypt" (Ex. 13:8) was the confession generation after

---

[47] Hippolytus, *On the Apostolic Tradition*, 165, 209–10.

[48] Alexander Schmemann, *Introduction to Liturgical Theology*, 58.

[49] J. B. Lightfoot, *The Apostolic Fathers*, 126.

[50] Gordon Lathrop, *Holy Things*, 56.

generation and a constant feature in both Testaments. When scripture was read in the "great synagogue"—the gathering in Jerusalem that was the heart of book of Nehemiah and taken as a pattern of all synagogues—the people stood up, and as led by Ezra, blessed God in a prayer that recounted his deeds of creation and redemption (Neh. 9:3–37). Afterwards the present needs of the people were set next to this praise in its intercessory prayers.

Before closing we should point out that in addition to their Old Testament origin, the church's intercessory prayers would have followed directly from Paul's injunction in 1 Tim. 2:1–2, in which he urges that "entreaties and prayers, petitions and thanksgivings, be made on behalf of all men, for kings and all who are in authority, so that we may lead a tranquil and quiet life in all godliness and dignity." From this we can see that the structured prayers of the earliest assemblies had biblical and apostolic authority as their origin—a fact that shouldn't be underestimated. It was the biblical pattern of prayer that gave (and still gives) the assembly the proper framework within which it could confidently intercede for those in need, for the sick and the suffering, for leaders, and for the church itself.

Conclusion

In the first centuries of the Christian era, a heretical system of thought called gnosticism arose which denied the central doctrines of the Christian faith. While its relevance will be clear shortly, we can note that gnostics taught the cosmic redemption of man's spirit through secret knowledge (gnosis).[51] In opposition to Christianity, they believed that the body—and matter generally—was evil and the creation of the Old Testament God who was the enemy of the Supreme God. Because for them matter was incapable of being saved, knowledge leading to redemption wasn't of a corporeal nature. Not surprisingly they denied that Jesus was composed of a material, fleshly body, believing that at baptism Christ descended upon Jesus (who before that was an ordinary man) and then departed from him

---

[51] Jaroslav Pelikan, *The Christian Tradition: A History of the Development of Doctrine*, Vol., 82–91.

again before his crucifixion (a position known as docetism). Given that God was thought to be impassable—unable to feel pain or pleasure—the Spirit of Christ had to depart before Jesus' suffering.

Why then his passion? To reveal the hidden mystery of human origins and destiny. As one gnostic teacher exhorted, "Abandon the search for God and the creation and other matters of a similar sort. Look for him by taking yourself as the starting point . . . If you carefully investigate these matters, you will find him in yourself."[52] Salvation thus was attained by looking inward and pertained only to the soul, not the body. What's important for our purposes is that these themes run through many apocryphal (non-canonical) "gospels" of the second and third centuries. The Gospel of Thomas, for instance, spoke repeatedly of the "liberation from matter and reunion with the light-world," and we can see docetist tendencies running through the Gospel of Peter.

These are sometimes referred to as "discourse gospels" and have no stories of Jesus and display no interest in the Jesus of history.[53] They're rather full of postresurrection sayings purporting to be revelations to certain individuals. In sharp contrast to our canonical Gospels, these books contain techniques that enable the self to escape the fleshy conditions of life and gain a spiritual salvation. In other words, the type of beliefs typical of gnosticism.

Its relevance here is that gnostics were highly individualistic and experiential as they based knowledge of God and salvation on what lies within, and escapist in their beliefs about the world, flesh, and matter in general. And it's these tendencies—as many scholars have pointed out—that define much of modern religion, and especially popular Christianity as it was influenced by the frontier revivalists and the pattern of worship they made fashionable. Though not sufficiently understood, these parallels merit attention. As Lathrop highlights, some unintended consequences have followed from the modern *ordo*:

> The danger of this influential pattern should now be clear, however. It's characteristics—only a little scripture, and that mostly verses with

---

[52] Jaroslav Pelikan, *The Christian Tradition: A History of the Development of Doctrine*, Vol. 1, 86–7.

[53] Gordon Lathrop, *Holy Ground*, 129ff.

an accent on techniques for self-realization; the importance of the individual; preaching as concrete help; then, no prayers for the world; no meal; little sense of assembly; no sending to the poor—place this pattern far closer to the "discourse gospels," . . . than to the way of assemblies marked by the pattern of the four Gospels of the New Testament. The frontier *ordo*, in all its permutations, can easily support individualism and the gnostic tendency of American religion, doing so without reorientation or transformation.[54]

One of the problems, he points out, is that this pattern tends to give divine sanction to the idea that the self, with its personal self-realization, is central. Parishioners go to church as easily as to a shopping mall and primarily to get assistance in their search for "happiness," "fulfillment," or their "family's well-being." Worthy as these are, from an historic Christian standpoint they're always secondary and in need of challenge and enlargement. But that enlargement can come only by the dethronement of our self-centeredness and desire to flee the material world; the very things on which modern worship tends to focus and which Lathrop rightly remarks do "not offer us a harmless, value-free medium for the communication of the Christian idea, as is sometimes proposed. Rather, it carries within itself values that . . . were anciently called 'gnostic.'"[55] The modern *ordo*, the medium in Neil Postman's sense, has become the message of self-focus and world-renunciation.

Bottom line is that not all worship patterns are created equal. As Lathrop has noted, we're not free to substitute a new medium or center the meeting on our own ideas or techniques without damaging the faith.[56] Nor should we, in consumer fashion, put the matter of music or style at the center of worship and our choice between them as too important. Leaders need to avoid deceiving themselves that their practice conforms to the biblical pattern when the real center has been made to be their own self-expression. The challenge for churches is to recover a biblical *ordo* as the central form of

---

[54] Gordon Lathrop, *Holy Ground*, 140.
[55] Gordon Lathrop, *Holy Ground*, 141–3.
[56] Gordon Lathrop, *Holy Ground*, 147.

the Sunday meeting, as it's only this that can continually challenge our cultural malformations and reorient our worldviews. It's only an *ordo* with scripture and Christ's eucharistic presence at its center that can set us firmly in the here and now, in space and time. Christianity never was, and can never be, a world-renouncing religion with a set of techniques for getting out of here. Understood biblically, it will always insert the assembly into concrete history and orient it to those outside its walls.[57] Similarly, it can never be an inward-looking religion that focuses our attention and hope on that which lies within. As we've seen throughout this book, we're not equipped with either the answers or the ability to scale to the heavens. On the contrary, the only thing we're equipped with is sin and death (detailed in our ending Postscript), which can only be dealt with by being reoriented in God's word and receiving the forgiveness of sins in the eucharist.

This is what the biblical *ordo* offers; and it doesn't merely offer, but performs what it promises in its ritual enactment.[58] By keeping us focused outward on Jesus' death and resurrection, on the reception of the forgiveness of sins concretely offered in the here and now in the eucharist, it restrains our sin and idolatrous nature. It's perhaps notable that the *Apostolic Tradition* insists that the teachings of the apostles are given concrete expression in the liturgy. As both admonition and warning, the document advises:

> And so if these things are received with thankfulness and true faith, they provide upbuilding in the church and eternal life for those who believe. I advise that these things should be guarded by all those who are truly wise. For if all of you hear the apostolic tradition and follow it and keep it, no heretic or anyone at all can deceive you. For in this way many heresies have grown up, because the pre-eminent ones were unwilling to learn the purpose of the apostles but, following their own desires, did as they wished and not what was fitting.[59]

---

[57] Alexander Schmemann, *Introduction to Liturgical Theology*, 72–3.

[58] For the function of the performative use of language, see J. L. Austin, *How To Do Things With Words* (Cambridge, 1975), 1–8, 13.

[59] Hippolytus, *On the Apostolic Tradition*, 212–3.

Does this mean that the liturgy is a panacea for the church's failure to understand the true meaning of the gospel? Certainly not, and any suggestions along these lines are doomed. To give it sole guardianship is too much to ask. As the Reformation debates so aptly illustrate, rightly dividing the word is a matter that also requires the church's scripturally based confession. But it would be a serious mistake to disregard the biblical pattern of worship, of word and table, that the church for two millennia has been duty bound to follow. Alongside a scriptural confession, the liturgy provides the only proper framework for the assembly to continue to understand that salvation doesn't lie within, but only outside of us in the God that was crucified outside of the city gates in a desolate place called Golgotha.

CHAPTER 7

Clothed in the "Word of Christ"

Up to this point we've looked at a broad range of evidence that shows the unexpected results of default human behavior. One of the things we saw was how we anchor on superficial information and then draw flimsy conclusions with only a surface connection to reality. Perhaps worse, being especially swayed by the sensational, we treat our theories as prized possessions[1] which then makes it difficult to graft in new information that contradicts our early opinions—even if the information is obviously more accurate. Nassim Taleb points out that two mechanisms are at work here: the confirmation bias (the preference for data that supports existing ideas) and belief perseverance (the tendency not to reverse opinions we already have).

Given our penchant for the superficial, this chapter will explore how the apostles institutionalized depth by placing firm boarders around the doctrines that defined the early Christian movement. Understanding better than anyone how radical their message was, the apostles recognized that Christianity exists on a delicate equilibrium of ideas in tension, and that guardrails are necessary. Ideas that, at first glance, might appear opposed to one other: of God becoming man, of law and Gospel, of eternal life in the here and now and the anticipation of the not yet. As history shows, it doesn't take much to turn any of these concepts into something monstrous. But the apostles' approach is as applicable today as it was then, combating not

---

[1] Nassim Nicholas Taleb, *The Black Swan: The Impact of the Highly Improbable* (New York, 2010), 144.

just our love of the superficial but also our proclivity to chase idols. Recall that particularly in the spiritual realm, our sin and lack of understanding leave us woefully unprepared to stand alone, apart from the clothing and protection of God's word—apart from a biblically pregnant framework that properly anchors our thoughts and actions.

Yet for over a century much of Christianity has been biased against formal structure. Recall that at the same time frontier revivalists were jettisoning the historic liturgy, scholars were pushing a Spirit-fueled theory of how Christianity began. From roughly 1860 to 1914 scholars were making a sharp antithesis between the Spirit-guided, spontaneous New Testament phase and the second century period of formalism and institutionalism.[2] Because of this blatant bias there was no place for the possibility that there were more formalized creeds at the nursery stage of Christianity. Thus the majority of scholars at the time said that creedal structure didn't exist until the middle of the second century—other than the simple baptismal confession "Jesus is Lord," that is.

But the questions we'll ask in this chapter will be as follows: Were the early New Testament witnesses the free-wheeling, creative worshippers so many churches today still believe they were? Were their doctrines and worship the result of a spontaneous Spirit-fueled experience, or was there stricter control over each than often appreciated? If so, was there a detectable standard in the New Testament writings themselves of more formalized structure, both over doctrine and worship?

What we'll find is that, despite the popular bias against it, the New Testament itself betrays a preoccupation with doctrinal and ecclesiastical structure. As J. N. D. Kelly remarks in his detailed study, there's nothing more artificial or improbable than the contrast between the first century church, with its pure creative religion of the Spirit and its complete absence of organization, and the embryonic Catholic Church with all its institutional structure of the late second century. "Had the Christians of the apostolic age not conceived of themselves as possessing a body of distinctive, consciously held

_____

[2] J. N. D. Kelly, *Early Christian Creeds*, third ed. (New York, 1972), 6.

beliefs, they would scarcely have separated themselves from Judaism and undertaken an immense programme of missionary expansion."[3] Like other religious groups they would have been driven to embody life-critical beliefs in their liturgy and institutions. As we'll see, that's in fact what they did as the earliest congregations insisted on worship being governed by the "word of Christ" (Col. 3:16). How this was done will be apparent in various ways, from the formal statements and creeds they developed to the hymns they chanted. What we'll notice underlying each is the presence of a nascent formal structure and how quickly it came to define the early movement.

First, let's look at how the primitive church put a defined structure around its central message.

Transmission of Authoritative Doctrine

As we look at the early church's attitude about controlling its message, we should begin by noting the emphasis found everywhere in the New Testament on the transmission of authoritative teaching. In Jude we read of "the faith which was once for all handed down to the saints" and of "your most holy faith" (3, 20), which the author uses in reference to an accepted body of beliefs. Paul speaks of "the sound doctrine" (2 Tim. 4:3; Titus 1:9), "the deposit," and "the noble deposit" (1 Tim. 6:20; 2 Tim. 1:14), "the faith" in its concrete expression (1 Tim. 1:19; Titus 1:13), and "the splendid teaching" (1 Tim. 4:6). In Hebrews we find frequent allusions to the "confession" to which the author exhorts believers to hold fast whatever the cost (3:1; 4:14; 10:23). And in chapter 6:2, which is mistakenly thought to be about catechesis (instruction leading to baptism), he refers to an elementary education which includes doctrinal instruction around the sacraments and ethics.

Even further, Paul exhorts believers to "hold to the traditions which you were taught" and the "form of teaching" to which you are

---

[3] J. N. D. Kelly, *Early Christian Creeds*, 7–8. See also Aidan Kavanagh, *The Shape of Baptism: The Rite of Christian Initiation* (Collegeville, 1978), 24, and Alexander Schmemann, trans. Ashleigh E. Moorehouse, *Introduction to Liturgical Theology* (Crestwood, 1966), 53–7.

committed (2 Thess. 2:15; Rom. 6:17). Paul also frequently uses the generally descriptive term "the faith." Thus, he admonishes his readers to be "established in your faith, just as you were instructed" and clinches his argument about the unity of the body by saying there is "one Lord, one faith, one baptism" (Col. 2:7; Eph. 4:5). Peter reminds his readers of "the word which was preached to you" (1 Pet. 1:25) which would have formed the basis of their baptismal instruction. As Kelly notes, "Examples could easily be multiplied, and the conclusion is inescapable that . . . the documents themselves testify to the existence of a corpus of distinctively Christian teaching. In this sense at any rate it is legitimate to speak of the creed [a formal statement of belief] of the primitive Church."[4] Given this it's easier to understand Irenaeus' remark—who was a student of Polycarp (martyred in 156), who in turn had been a disciple of the apostle John himself—that the "rule of faith" would have been sufficient for the transmission of Christian doctrine even if the church had been left without the apostles' writings.

Thus we can see clear traces of the apostolic preoccupation with a more formalized transmission of Christianity's central doctrines. While this might surprise some, historically it's the only thing that makes sense given the context of the primitive church. On the one hand, its Jewish roots would have primed it for a formal "passing on" of tradition (of which we'll see evidence below); and on the other, its placement within a Roman pagan environment would have necessitated careful formulation of beliefs to distinguish truth from error.

Early Liturgical Formulae

Even before the first New Testament writings appear, we can detect clear signs of doctrinal structure in the liturgy of the earliest congregations, particularly around Jesus' divine status and his equality with the Father. We know these liturgical formulae predate the first Christian writings because the apostles simply quote them and make no attempt to justify what would otherwise have been explosive ideas.

---

[4] J. N. D. Kelly, *Early Christian Creeds*, 8–11. Geoffrey Wainwright, *Doxology: The Praise of God in Worship, Doctrine, and Life* (New York, 1980), 185.

In other words, they've already become crystallized in the liturgy of the first congregations by the time our earliest documents appear.

Let's look at a few examples, starting with Rom. 1:8 in which Paul thanks God "through Jesus Christ." For a monotheistic Jew, the phrase signified the important place Jesus occupied in the prayers of the early churches. What's interesting is that Paul makes no attempt to explain why he includes Jesus in the prayer: he simply assumes the Christians in Rome are already familiar with the liturgy he's citing, meaning that it's been used in worship for quite some time before he wrote the letter.

Reinforcing this are the numerous passages reflecting the liturgical prayers of the early churches, in which God and Jesus were addressed and invoked together.[5] In 1 Thess. 3:11–13, for instance, Paul recites the following prayer:

> Now may our God and Father Himself and Jesus our Lord direct our way to you; and may the Lord cause you to increase and abound in love for one another, and for all people, just as we also do for you; so that He may establish your hearts without blame in holiness before our God and Father at the coming of our Lord Jesus with all His saints.

Notice the inseparable connection between Jesus and God. Jesus is to bring believers successfully to God's final appearance with his holy ones. Paul's characteristic "grace and peace" greetings perform the same function of linking God and Jesus. For instance: "The God of peace will soon crush Satan under your feet. The grace of our Lord Jesus be with you." Important to include as well is Rom. 10:9–13, "that if you confess with your mouth Jesus as Lord."

In addition, 1 Cor. 16:22 preserves an important practice of the earliest Christians still used in the eucharistic liturgy. It comes in the form of the *maranatha*, which roughly means "Our Lord, come!" An appeal for Jesus to be present in the liturgical worship of the church, it simultaneously beseeches him to wrap up history

---

[5] Larry W. Hurtado, *Lord Jesus Christ: Devotion to Jesus in Earliest Christianity* (Grand Rapids, 2003), p. 139–142.

and make his final appearance. Since only YHWH can consummate history, it demonstrates that all power has been given to the crucified one. All of this shows that liturgical invocation of Jesus was widely known and accepted by the earliest believers, so much so that by the 50s when Paul's letter was written it was already commonplace even among the Gentile churches (which were geographically farther dispersed than the first congregations). That demonstrates an incredibly rapid and widespread unity of formalized confession for both Jewish-Christian and Gentile-Christian believers. An unbelievable pace from any historical standpoint, which points to their origin in the earliest Christian communities, beginning with the Aramaic speaking disciples in Jerusalem.

We should also note that practically every one of Paul's letters (and others) show evidence of liturgical phrases already hardened into a common formula by the time the epistles were written (e.g., Rom. 15:6; 2 Cor. 1:3; 11:31; Eph. 1:3; 1 Pet. 1:3; 1 Tim. 1:2; 2 Tim. 1:2; Titus 1:4). For instance, virtually every letter opens with the conventional greeting mentioned above, "Grace and peace be to you from God the Father and the Lord Jesus Christ." In 2 John 1:3 we find the parallel, "grace, mercy, and peace . . . from God the Father and from Jesus Christ, the Son of the Father."

What's important to recognize is that scholars widely accept these as liturgical formulae already in use—at the very latest— by the 50s, and that it was uncontroversial to link Jesus with God as the source of the blessings invoked in worship. But judging from Rom. 15:6 ("so that with one accord you may with one voice glorify the God and Father of our Lord Jesus Christ"), we have every reason to believe they were there from the earliest moments of the Christian movement.[6] In his impressive six hundred plus page study, Larry Hurtado reports that we know of no analogy in Roman-era Jewish groups for what was the instant and common practice of linking Jesus with God in the liturgy and prayer life of the early church.

---

[6] J. N. D. Kelly, *Early Christian Creeds*, 21.

Formal Tradition

In addition to what we've seen, there's evidence in Paul's letters that early Christians practiced a "formal" transmission of tradition, which was authoritative doctrine that would have been used for catechetical purposes.[7] By formal we mean that there were specific methods to ensure tradition was faithfully handed on from a qualified authority. The evidence is found in Paul's use of the technical terms for handing on (*paradiddomi*, 1 Cor. 11:2, 23, corresponding to the Hebrew *masar*) and receiving tradition (*paralambano*, 1 Cor. 15:1, 3; Gal. 1:9; Col. 2:6; 1 Thess. 2:13; 4:1; 2 Thess. 3:6, corresponding to the Hebrew *qibbel*). Pregnant with technical meaning, these terms were used for the formal transmission of tradition and would have been familiar to Paul's readers. We know this is what Paul intended because he was educated in the pharasaic school of Judaism and it's obvious he took the technical terminology from his training.

Here's why it matters. To "hand on" tradition isn't just to tell it or speak it, and to "receive" a tradition isn't just to hear it. Rather, handing on tradition "means that one hands over something to somebody so that the latter possesses it," while receiving tradition "means that one receives something so that one possesses it." While this sometimes meant verbatim memorization, it always entailed some process of teaching and learning so that what was communicated was accurately retained. It's certainly one reason why teachers played such a prominent role within the earliest Christian communities—they were even the first regularly paid ministry.[8] In 1 Cor. 15:3, Paul says he received the tradition from competent authorities and thereby places himself in a chain of transmission. In so doing he provides us with the earliest evidence of how traditions were transmitted, and it shows that a considerable degree of precise memorization was involved.

One of the more significant sections from Paul involves his *handing on* of the resurrection appearances. For context, here's the passage:

---

[7] Richard Bauckham, *Jesus and the Eyewitnesses: The Gospels as Eyewitness Testimony* (Grand Rapids, 2006), pp. 264ff. J. N. D. Kelly, *Early Christian Creeds*, 17.

[8] James D. G. Dunn, *Jesus Remembered* (Grand Rapids, 2003), 176–177.

For I delivered to you as of first importance what I also received, that Christ died for our sins according to the scriptures, and that He was buried, and that He was raised on the third day according to the scriptures, and that He appeared to Cephas, then to the twelve. After that He appeared to more than five hundred brethren at one time, most of whom remain until now, but some have fallen asleep; then He appeared to James, then to all the apostles (1 Cor. 15:3–7).

What's interesting is that it's a textbook case of a pre-existing formula Paul hands on to his Corinthian audience. Scholars agree that the tradition probably reaches back into the first five years after Jesus' crucifixion. Here are the reasons.[9] First, the words Paul uses to introduce verses 3–7 correspond to the technical rabbinical terms used to transmit tradition (1 Cor. 11:23) referenced above. Second, the verses contain many non-Pauline traits, meaning that the style and syntax isn't consistent with the rest of Paul's writings. In other words, it's obvious he didn't write them. Third, what's cited as evidence for Jesus' resurrection way exceeds what was necessary in the context of the letter. Paul simply hands on a set tradition he probably received when he first became a Christian one to three years after the crucifixion. Further, it's an example of an early formalized creed and would have been used for catechesis and preaching as it gives the gist of the Christian message in a concentrated form.[10]

The tradition's origin is also significant. First Corinthians 15:11 states that the apostles preached the same tradition, which points to Jerusalem as the place of origin for the resurrection formula. Since the church began in Jerusalem, the Twelve, which included Peter, would have acted as guarantors of the tradition. We know Paul probably received the formula in Damascus immediately after his conversion. We also know from Gal. 2 that Paul personally met with Peter and James in Jerusalem three years after his conversion. He spent two weeks with Peter in particular. Since Paul had been educated a Pharisee, his natural inclination would have been to seek out

---

[9] William Lane Craig, *Assessing the New Testament Evidence for the Historicity of the Resurrection of Jesus* (New York, 1989), 15–20.

[10] J. N. D. Kelly, *Early Christian Creeds*, third ed. (New York, 1972), 17.

doctrinal authorities able to transmit authentic tradition, which is what Jewish teachers and students did. Thus we can have no doubt why Paul went to Jerusalem: to gather and validate the tradition he'd already received.

But here's what's significant about the timing of his visit: it was only six years after Jesus' crucifixion, and given the incredibly short period between the appearances and when Paul received it, we can see how important formalized statements were to the early church (as well as showing how unlikely it was that the list of eyewitnesses was legendary). So given its early date and Jerusalem origin, it likely goes back to the apostles themselves.[11]

We have many other examples of formal transmission, but an interesting one involves independent material both Paul and Luke report and its early date makes it worthwhile to highlight. It concerns the ancient tradition of the Lord's Supper. In 1 Cor. 11:23–25, Paul "hands on" the words of institution he no doubt received directly from Peter during his two week visit to Jerusalem shortly after his conversion. Beyond the fact that it's extremely early, here's what's interesting. Luke and Paul each report the tradition, and although they're completely independent of one another the verbal similarity between the two accounts is striking (1 Cor. 11:23–25 and Luke 22:19–20). Clearly an instance of formal transmission (here almost word-for-word similarity), the two accounts can't be explained any other way because they couldn't have been aware of the other's text. Luke's Gospel—which was written later than Paul's letter—couldn't have been available to Paul. And Luke shows no familiarity with Paul's letters. Only strictly memorized oral tradition explains the high degree of verbal resemblance.

The Last Supper, which forms the basis of the Lord's Supper in Paul's letter, is on similar ground. It appears in multiple texts (Matt. 26:26–29; Mark 14:22–25; Luke 22:17–20), yet we know it was an earlier formalized oral tradition. Evidence shows that the eucharistic language in these accounts was already embedded in the church's

---

[11] Birger Gerhardsson, *Memory and Manuscript: Oral Tradition and Written Transmission in Rabbinic Judaism and Early Christianity with Tradition and Transmission in Early Christianity* (Grand Rapids, 1998), 297–298.

liturgy long before the Gospels or Paul's letters were written, meaning we know they were disseminated through the formal handing
on of tradition very early. The Lord's Prayer is in the same position. As Dunn remarks, "it was a matter of fundamental tradition,
the sort of tradition which Paul took care to pass on to his newly
formed churches (1 Cor. 11:23), the sort of tradition which gave
these churches their identity . . . It was tradition remembered as
begun by Jesus himself, and remembered thus from as early as we
can tell."[12]

   One other quick point before moving on. Much of what Paul
says in his letters implies that his hearers already know what he's
talking about. He assumes they know the traditions of Jesus' death
and resurrection, as well as liturgical practices and how Christians
should live their lives.[13] Parallel to what we observed above, given
that he wrote his letters in the 50s, believers must have received
the traditions much earlier (especially because many of them were
already part of the liturgy). Thus we can surmise that the passing on
of tradition was part of the founding of churches from the very first.
And Paul was careful to refer his churches back to those foundational traditions, which included things pertaining to Jesus' identity
and resurrection from the dead (2 Tim. 2:8; Rom. 1:3–4), community tradition (1 Cor. 11:2, 23) and how new converts should live
(Phil. 4:9; 1 Thess. 4:1; 2 Thess. 3:6), among others.

Early Creedal Formulae

Beyond the crystallization of liturgical phrases and the formal transmission of tradition, scholars have pointed out that are many early
creedal statements (of which 1 Cor. 15:3–7, mentioned above, should
be included) within the New Testament. For instance:

> Concerning His Son, who was born of a descendant of David accord-
> ing to the flesh, who was declared the Son of God with power by the
> resurrection from the dead, according to the Spirit of holiness, Jesus

---

[12] James D. G. Dunn, *Jesus Remembered*, 226–231.
[13] James D. G. Dunn, *Jesus Remembered*, 176–179.

Christ our Lord, through whom we have received grace . . . (Rom. 1:3–5)

Christ Jesus is He who died, yes, rather who was raised, who is at the right hand of God, who also intercedes for us . . . (Rom. 8:34)

Remember Jesus Christ, risen from the dead, descendant of David . . . (2 Tim. 2:8)

Kelly highlights other echoes of catechetical formulae, such as "Jesus Christ, who gave Himself for our sins" (Gal. 1:3–4); "If we believe that Jesus died and rose again" (1 Thess. 4:14); and ". . . through our Lord Jesus Christ, who died for us" (1 Thess. 5:9–10). A lengthier passage is found in 1 Pet. 3:18ff.:

For Christ also died for our sins once for all, the just for the unjust, so that He might bring us to God, having been put to death in the flesh, but made alive in the spirit; in which also He went and made proclamation to the spirits now in prison . . . through the resurrection of Jesus Christ, who is at the right hand of God, having gone into heaven, after angels and authorities and powers had been subjected to Him.

As the passage reads like a blend between a paraphrase and quotation of an instructional manual in preparation to baptism, we can better understand the insertion of the meaning of the sacrament in verses 20ff.[14] Paralleling this is Paul's contrast between the "many gods and many lords" of paganism and the one Christian God, ". . . yet for us there is but one God, the Father, from whom are all things and we exist for Him; and one Lord, Jesus Christ, by whom are all things, and we exist through Him" (1 Cor. 8:6). The formulary nature of this passage is unmistakable.

Closely related is Paul's formula in 1 Tim. 2:5–6: "For there is one God, and one mediator also between God and men, the man Christ Jesus, who gave Himself as a ransom for all . . ." Another

---

[14] J. N. D. Kelly, *Early Christian Creeds*, 18–9, 21.

1 Timothy creed-like confession reads as follows: "I charge you in the presence of God, who gives life to all things, and of Christ Jesus, who testified the good confession before Pontius Pilate, that you keep the commandment without stain or reproach until the appearing of our Lord Jesus Christ" (1 Tim. 6:13–14). Again, this seems to be a paraphrase of a formal confession that was used in preparation for baptism. Many other examples of creedal formulae can be cited (e.g., 2 Tim. 4:1; Rom. 4:24, 8:11; 2 Cor. 4:14; Gal. 1:1; 1 Thess. 1:10; Col. 2:12; Eph. 1:20; 1 Pet. 1:21), but this should be sufficient to show that they're scattered throughout our earliest material. What the evidence shows is that the second century belief in a "rule of faith" that Christians had inherited from the apostles themselves, was true to the extent that it was foreshadowed in the "pattern of teaching" found in the confessions and early credal summaries contained in the New Testament documents themselves.[15]

Baptismal Use of Creeds

As we've alluded, it's widely agreed that creeds were originally connected to the liturgy of baptism and that we can already see traces of it within the New Testament, which would explain its universal practice in the following centuries. In Acts 16:14–15, Lydia "and her household" were baptized after hearing Paul's preaching. Her statement, "If you have judged me to be faithful to the Lord" implies that she'd given some token of Paul's instruction before being baptized.

Beyond the passing references in Acts, it's likely that Paul's remark, "if you confess with your mouth Jesus as Lord, and believe in your heart that God raised Him from the dead" (Rom. 10:9), refers to baptism. The actual confession seems to be specifically mentioned in 1 Tim. 6:12: "Take hold of the eternal life to which you were called, and you made the good confession in the presence of many witnesses." Hebrews implies the same when insisting, "let us hold fast our confession" (4:14). In reference to some type of creedal confession at baptism, Kelly comments that it has "been conjectured that a declaration of belief must have been forthcoming corresponding

---

[15] J. N. D. Kelly, *Early Christian Creeds*, 29.

to this formulary, and the conjecture is abundantly borne out by the Church's practice in regard to the formulary in succeeding generations."[16] These early creedal confessions could have been in declaratory form—in the form of the first person, "I believe in God, the Father Almighty . . ."—or as an interrogatory creed which consisted of assent to questions addressed to the baptismal candidate (which seems to have been more common), to which the person being baptized assented "I believe."

The *Apostolic Tradition* (one of our most ancient church-order documents) provides an excellent example of the latter:

> When the one being baptized goes down into the waters the one who baptizes, placing a hand on him, should say thus: "Do you believe in God the Father Almighty?"
> And he who is being baptized should reply: "I believe."
> Let him baptize him once immediately, having his hand placed upon his head. And after this he should say: "Do you believe in Christ Jesus, the son of God, who was born of the Holy Spirit and Mary the virgin and was crucified under Pontius Pilate and was dead and buried and rose on the third day alive from the dead and ascended in the heavens and sits at the right hand of the Father and will come to judge the living and the dead?"
> And when he has said, "I believe," he is baptized again.
> And again he should say: "Do you believe in the Holy Spirit and the holy church and the resurrection of the flesh?"
> And he who is being baptized should say: "I believe." And so he should be baptized a third time.[17]

Given the evidence, we can conclude that early credal formulae were first used in catechetical instruction for the person wanting to be baptized, which is why the church's central message quickly hardened into formulaic patterns. Kelly notes that the process was in full swing in the second century, with the "rule of faith" dominating

---

[16] J. N. D. Kelly, *Early Christian Creeds*, 40–2.

[17] Hippolytus, *On the Apostolic Tradition*, second edition (New York, 2015), 134. Geoffrey Wainwright, *Doxology: The Praise of God in Worship, Doctrine, and Life* (New York, 1980), 183–4.

discussions of the period. Declaratory creeds were intended as an end to popular instruction. "When the bishop has 'handed out' the creed in the later weeks of Lent, he proceeds to comment on it clause by clause, while the catechumens are required to learn it by heart as a convenient synopsis of what they are in duty bound to believe. Similarly they are expected to 'give it back' on the eve of their baptism, their ability to recite it being a demonstration that they are now sufficiently grounded in the faith."[18] Notice here the clear "passing on" and "receiving" of the apostles' teaching. Bottom line is that declaratory creeds were a by-product of the church's fully developed catechetical system leading to the sacrament. Thus the content of the later declaratory creeds were largely borrowed from the already existent baptismal interrogations.

Why Creeds At All?

In wrapping up our comments on primitive formulae and creeds, we should note that they served the historic church in three ways. First, from the very beginning creeds provided a guardrail to keep believers safely within the bounds of Christian doctrines that needed only a slight touch to turn them into something blasphemous. While much of modern Christianity degrades them as overly "formal," creeds were put into formulae by early believers to protect central ideas from morphing into heresy. Exclusion of error was paramount, which was·(and still is) a real threat to spiritual health. Primitive creeds, followed by the declaratory creeds that were based on them, certified that the faith was the same as that proclaimed by the apostles—in contradistinction to the heretical sects of the time.

Second, as creeds became more engrained in regular worship, the believer's baptismal faith was continually recapitulated. The act of confessing one's faith, and most importantly *what* that faith is *in*, and remembering his or her salvation through baptism is why St. Augustine took the extra step of recommending the creed for private practice. "Say the creed daily," he said, "When you rise, when

---

[18] J. N. D. Kelly, *Early Christian Creeds*, 50–2, 206.

you compose yourself to sleep, repeat your creed, render it to the Lord, remind yourself of it, be not irked to say it over."[19] In commending it for regular private use, Augustine implicitly recognized the concerns we began with about man's wayward mind and its need for structure. In providing the necessary mental furniture, the creed becomes "the daily clothing of your mind," as he put it. It was an important insight, but further bolstered by the fact that creeds are necessary given man's linguistic nature—meaning we must express ideas in language and that language itself is part of what constitutes man *as* human—and from the Christian insistence that God revealed himself as Word.

Lastly, Christians have never existed in a vacuum. Not only do we exist in a synchronistic culture in which Christianity is just one of many religious options, but the church owes its existence to a rich store of thought that came before. When confessing our baptismal faith in creeds pregnant with biblical language, we're again initiated into a fellowship of people across time and space that has an historical identity in the Christ who is the "same yesterday, today and forever." As long as believers continue to recapitulate this historic confession, they're assured of their own identity in the identity of the universal church. "The liturgical use of the traditional creeds is a sign that it is indeed the Church of Jesus Christ to which the believer belongs . . ."[20]

"Word of Christ" in Early Hymns

We've noted in previous chapters that a sizable number of today's churches have removed the traditional reading of scripture and communion liturgy and replaced them with the singing of songs as a central component of the worship service. Considering the profound influence of the American revivalist movement with its focus on creativity and the shedding of a traditional framework, it's easy to see why the musical development of the twentieth century took the trajectory it did. As the entertainment culture solidified, it was all

---

[19] Geoffrey Wainwright, *Doxology*, 187–9.

[20] Geoffrey Wainwright, *Doxology*, 190–1.

but a forgone conclusion that musical content would be reduced to the least common denominator and centered on emotion. Because it's now so prevalent and taken for granted, it's important we take a serious look at what we know of the earliest Christian hymns in order to benchmark current practices. Two questions will occupy our attention as we close this chapter: First, is there evidence that the earliest Christian music had the same sort of doctrinal control that we see with those early formulae, and second, more generally what do we know of the hymnic content? In other words, did the early Christians insist on any particular *content* in worship music, and if so, what was it?

To begin, we know that the singing of hymns was a basic part of the earliest Christian worship and that it was intended to reinforce the church's doctrinal deposit. In essence hymns were a sung confession of faith, meaning that they resembled creeds and had a similar aim.[21] What's interesting is that scholars have shown that many passages in the New Testament were originally hymns used within the early congregations before they were quoted in the written text.[22] Because it's agreed that the setting for these was undoubtedly for worship, it makes them excellent examples of the crystallization of liturgical material.[23]

Particularly important for the apostles were the messianic psalms (for instance, Pss. 2; 8; 110; 118), with 118 likely being the last psalm Jesus sang with the disciples before his passion and which would have prophetically pointed to his impending fate ("The stone which the builders rejected has become the chief corner stone," v. 22). That the liturgical use of Ps. 118 must go back to the earliest believers is attested by the fact that the hosanna, "Blessed is the one who comes in the name of the Lord," appears in all four Gospels as Jesus entered Jerusalem, in the eucharistic liturgy of the Didache (10:6), and in Hegesippus' account of James' martyrdom.[24] These

---

[21] Geoffrey Wainwright, *Doxology*, 183, 214.

[22] Larry W. Hurtado, *Lord Jesus Christ*, 147–148, 606–608.

[23] J. N. D. Kelly, *Early Christian Creeds*, 18.

[24] Martin Hengel, *Between Jesus and Paul: Studies in the Earliest History of Christianity* (Eugene, OR, 2003), 92.

hymns, which were adapted from the Old Testament psalms and made into psalms of Christ, have identifying marks that betray their hymnic qualities. As a whole, they're formulated in the third person and talk about the identity of Jesus and his death and resurrection. As such they were particular in their content, proclaiming Jesus' pre-existence, his mediation of creation, his incarnation and death on the cross, the salvation that death achieved, and his resurrection and exaltation.[25]

With that said let's take a closer look at the early evidence, starting with Col. 3:16–17, which states: "Let the word of Christ richly dwell within you, with all wisdom teaching and admonishing one another with psalms and hymns and spiritual songs, singing with thankfulness in your hearts to God. Whatever you do in word or deed, do all in the name of the Lord Jesus, giving thanks through Him to God the Father." All in the context of worship, Paul insists that the "word of Christ" is to govern everything when the community meets for worship. His word is to be present and found in abundance within the Christian congregation.[26] While he uses three terms, "psalms and hymns and spiritual songs," he's not referring to three different types of music but uses the most important terms the Greek Old Testament used for religious singing. They all refer to the same type of song, which was the psalm singing typical of the Jewish tradition that was chanted by the congregation and, in Christian circles, interpreted christologically.

The "word of Christ" which produces the song in the heart through the Spirit is aimed at the praise of God. By making the word of Christ dwell in its midst through the singing of psalms to Christ, the early church gave glory to God the Father; thus intimately linking YHWH to Christ in the act of worship and confessing that God has disclosed his final salvation only through his Son. Remarkable is the fact that we actually have more evidence of hymns to Christ than to God in the New Testament. As to their original setting, the

---

[25] Martin Hengel, *Studies in Early Christology* (London, 2004), 286. Martin Hengel, *Between Jesus and Paul*, 88.

[26] Martin Hengel, *Between Jesus and Paul*, 79–81, 93–4. Larry W. Hurtado, *Lord Jesus Christ*, 508.

142 IN DEFENSE OF CHRISTIAN RITUAL

hymn to Christ was centered around the joy of the Lord's Supper (Acts 2:46) which was understood as an anticipation of the expected return of the Son of Man. Though he sits at the right hand of God, Jesus is nevertheless actively among earthly believers in the Spirit, and concretely at the table.

Thus the word of Christ takes form in worship through the songs which served both the teaching and edification of the early Christian community. It was recognized that it's only his word that can move man's heart and lips, just as the psalmist confessed, "O Lord, open my lips, that my mouth may declare Your praise" (Ps. 51:15). Martin Hengel remarks that the "aim and the perfecting of the 'word of Christ' which produces the song in the heart through the spirit for the edification of the community, is the praise of God. In that the community makes the word of Christ 'dwell' in its midst by singing psalms to Christ, in order to instruct and admonish itself by the hymnic narration of the saving action of Christ, it gives glory to God, the Father of Jesus Christ. So it is a matter of inner consistency that the hymn to Christ in Philippians ends with the phrase 'to the glory of God the Father' (2:11)."[27]

As for typical content, the hymn in Col. 1:15–20 illustrates nicely the earliest Christian "psalms, hymns and spiritual songs."[28] It reads as follows:

> He is the image of the invisible God, the firstborn of all creation. For by Him all things were created, both in the heavens and on earth, visible and invisible, whether thrones or dominions or rulers or authorities—all things have been created through Him and for Him. He is before all things, and in Him all things hold together. He is also head of the body, the church; and He is the beginning, the firstborn from the dead, so that He Himself will come to have first place in everything. For it was the Father's good pleasure for all the fullness to dwell in Him, and through Him to reconcile all things to Himself, having made peace through the blood of His cross; through Him . . . whether things on earth or things in heaven.

---

[27] Martin Hengel, *Between Jesus and Paul*, 80.

[28] Larry W. Hurtado, *Lord Jesus Christ*, 508–9. Martin Hengel, *Studies in Early Christology*, 113.

We should note that its hymnic nature is betrayed by its cadences, the fact that it's a self-contained passage, has compact phrasing, and is specific in its content. It lyrically proclaims Christ as the agent of creation who then also reconciled all things to himself through his death on the cross. "In the Greek, the repeated use of the third-person pronouns ('he/him') has the effect of making his centrality emphatic at every point."[29] What the Colossians passage illustrates is that hymns provided believers content about Christ's unique person and work as creator and redeemer, and thus played a key role in promoting christological teaching among the earliest believers.

Paul makes this further evident in Colossians by exhorting his readers to have knowledge and "spiritual wisdom" so that they "walk in a manner worthy of the Lord" (1:9–10). He urges believers who have "received Christ Jesus the Lord" to live their lives "in Him," "having been firmly rooted and now being built up in Him and established in your faith" (2:6–7)—and warns against being ensnared by "philosophy and empty deception" that isn't "according to Christ," in whom "all the fullness of Deity dwells in bodily form" (2:8–9). Christians therefore shouldn't allow themselves to be condemned by others for not observing strict dietary rules (2:16), or be deceived by those who, based on supposed visions, promote the "worship of the angels." These falsely detract from Christ "from whom the entire body, being supplied and held together . . . grows with a growth which is from God" (2:18–19).

In this Paul explicitly recognizes what we've seen in previous chapters: that man tends to lose his footing in delusionary speculations. The "word of Christ" is to guide both our minds and our actions. As in other cases we've seen, we should point out that the hymn has to be extremely old because Paul makes no attempt to justify the extraordinary notion that not only is Jesus the pre-existent Son of God, but that by his death on a cross he reconciled all things to himself.

---

[29] Larry W. Hurtado, *Lord Jesus Christ*, 505–7, 610.

Additional Early Material

Before concluding this chapter, we should mention a few other significant examples of early hymns. The first comes from Philippians, which reads as follows:

> . . . who [referring to Christ Jesus], although He existed in the form of God, did not regard equality with God a thing to be grasped, but emptied Himself, taking the form of a bond-servant, and being made in the likeness of men. Being found in appearance as a man, He humbled Himself by becoming obedient to the point of death, even death on a cross. For this reason also, God highly exalted Him, and bestowed on Him the name which is above every name, so that at the name of Jesus every knee will bow, of those who are in heaven and on earth and under the earth, and that every tongue will confess that Jesus Christ is Lord, to the glory of God the Father.

Scholars agree that the hymn wasn't written by Paul and probably has an ancient Palestinian origin. It speaks specifically of Jesus' divine nature, being "in the form of God" along with his surrender even to the point of crucifixion; and then proclaims that God exalted Jesus to an equal status which entitles him to universal reverence. The passage (and others like it) shows that singing/chanting in the worship of Jesus was a characteristic feature of the Christian service from the beginning. Again, the dates must be early because they show up in our earliest records, but already by the time of Paul's writing were imbedded in the worship service. It's instructive to recall the report of the Roman administrator Pliny, which was the first report on early Christian worship from an outsider which he derived from interrogating apostates and by torturing two deaconesses.[30] In his letter to Trajan, Pliny summarizes their regular worship by saying that they chant a hymn "to Christ as to a god."

Perhaps our most detailed description of an early Christian worship service comes from St. John in Revelation chapters 4–5. While depicting heavenly worship before the throne of God, it's likely that John is echoing the liturgical practices of his own community.

---

[30] Larry W. Hurtado, *Lord Jesus Christ*, 606.

Chapter five begins the scene's climax with the appearance of Christ, the "Lamb who has been slain." He alone is worthy to receive the book of judgment from God. Signifying Jesus' authority over all things, the four creatures and the twenty-four elders fall down and worship Christ by singing a new song:

> Worthy are You to take the book and to break its seals; for You were slain, and purchased for God with Your blood men from every tribe and tongue and people and nation. You have made them to be a kingdom and priests to our God; and they will reign upon the earth (vv. 9–10).

Following this dramatic scene, the choir of all the heavenly beings sing the hymnic narrative of the saving action of Christ, giving the "Lamb once slain" the absolute worship which is given only to God himself. The climax of the heavenly liturgy—which lies at the root of all earthly liturgy[31]—occurs in the final doxology (a word coming from the Greek word *doxa*, meaning glory), and now all creatures "in heaven and on earth and under the earth and in the sea and all that is in them" praise God and Christ as one choir: "'To Him who sits on the throne, and to the Lamb, be blessing and honor and glory and dominion forever and ever.' And the four living creatures kept saying, 'Amen.' And the elders fell down and worshipped" (vv. 13–14). Unambiguously, the liturgy makes clear that from the earliest times Christians understood Christ to be YHWH himself and worthy of absolute allegiance and worship.

In a similar way and drawing on several hymns (including from the Old Testament), Heb. 1:3ff. explicitly references Jesus' unique status as divine over against all heavenly and earthly creatures: "And He is the radiance of His glory and the exact representation of His nature, and upholds all things by the word of His power. When He had made purification of sins, He sat down at the right hand of the Majesty on high, having become as much better than the angels, as He has inherited a more excellent name than they." Given the fact that it draws on other (and therefore older) hymns, we know that

---

[31] Martin Hengel, *Studies in Early Christology*, 236.

they were already in use within the Christian liturgy and, like the others, extremely early. The other notable point about Heb. 1–2 is how the author uses and interprets various Old Testament psalms as hymns to Christ (for example, Ps. 8:5–7)—which brings this particular psalm quotation close to the "prologue in heaven" of Rev. 5 and Phil. 2:9–11.

Before summarizing, let's make a final observation on the influence of Pss. 8 and 110 on the early hymns. Of the passages we've noted, Hengel remarks that Rom. 8:34 may be the most fascinating. The formula Paul uses, "who is at the right hand of God," occurs in the same words in 1 Pet. 3:22, and again in the context of a hymn. What's striking is that already by the time Romans is penned the formula has taken on a stereotyped liturgical form, bearing witness to a longer development of that tradition. The same holds true for the immediately following phrase "who also intercedes for us" in which the eternal high priesthood of Christ is explained with reference to Ps. 110:4. The intriguing thing about this is that Rom. 8:34 is akin to Heb. 7:25b, even down to its formulation, and it's therefore likely that the high priestly service of the exalted Christ in both already existed as a hymn fragment which was then used by Paul. It was through this Lord who sits at the right hand of God that the earliest believers had access to the heavenly sanctuary in worship, with its prayers and hymns that we saw in Rev. 5. His sitting at the right hand of God meant that there was constant symmetry between worship before the divine throne and the earthly community under persecution. It further expressed the close connection in the present between the disciples and their Lord who'd been exalted to God's throne. We should note in closing that there are other hymns and hymn fragments, which include Phil. 2:6–11; John 1:1–18; 1 Cor. 8:6; Eph. 5:14; 1 Tim. 3:16; 1 Pet. 3:18–22; Eph. 1:20–22; and Rom. 8:34.[32]

We'll end with Hengel's summary, who was one of the foremost experts on the subject.[33] He points out that the hymns to Christ grew

---

[32] Martin Hengel, *Between Jesus and Paul*, 86–8. Geoffrey Wainwright, *Doxology*, 49–50.

[33] Martin Hengel, *Between Jesus and Paul*, 85, 93–4.

out of the liturgy of the earliest Christian community after the Easter event, and are therefore as old as the community itself. In addition to their function as praise, they were meant to instruct believers by highlighting Jesus' passion, glorification, and subjection of all things. An immediate reaction to the resurrection which took the disciples by surprise, hymns were a spontaneous formulation of the new reality with which they were confronted. While in their form they took the character of Jewish psalmody, hymns were part of the community's praise of God, and in their content they presented the work, nature, and destiny of the crucified and exalted Lord—and therefore took on a narrative character about Jesus. And while the focal point may differ, the majority of them had one thing in common: the contrast as well as the connection between Jesus' death and his exaltation as they're depicted in the visionary "prologue in heaven" in Rev. 5.

Conclusion

We've now seen compelling evidence that the Christian movement had a rather structured approach to doctrine and worship, which manifested itself in creedal formulae and narrative hymns from the earliest moments. So early in fact that they were already crystallized into liturgical summaries before the first New Testament documents were published (and in which they're quoted). Given what we know of the first century this shouldn't surprise us. Not only would a for- malized structure have been natural in the disciples' Jewish environ- ment, but even more it would have been considered necessary to distinguish truth from error. Early believers understood better than anyone that, as Chesterton said in the twentieth century, the core Christian ideas "need but a touch to turn them into something blas- phemous or ferocious." And the entire history of Christianity has indeed been a fight against these small touches. As Chesterton put it:

> Here it is enough to notice that if some small mistake were made in doctrine, huge blunders might be made in human happiness. A sentence phrased wrong about the nature of symbolism would have broken all the statues in Europe. A slip in the definitions might stop all the dances; might wither all the Christmas trees or break all the

Easter eggs. Doctrines had to be defined within strict limits, even in order that man might enjoy general human liberties. The Church had to be careful, if only that the world might be careless.[34]

He goes on to say that Christian doctrine was a balancing act that forbade the church from swerving even a hair's breadth on either side if it was to be kept from turning into something monstrous. The moment you let some idea become less powerful some other idea becomes too powerful, which is due to the fact that Christianity exists in a delicate balance between ideas in tension; of God becoming man, of God crucified as an outcast, of law and gospel, of the reception of salvation in the here and now and the anticipation of the not yet. If we're to maintain that equilibrium and not give in to the latest fads, then doctrines must be maintained in all purity and within a proper framework. Chesterton was right to say that it's easy to be a heretic. "It is always easy to let the age have its head; the difficult thing is to keep one's own." It's all too natural to fall for every cultural fashion, such as the current demand for entertainment. What's not natural is to remain steadfast in the faith which was "once for all handed down" (Jude 3) by the apostles and "received" by the church. In the end, it's by this faithful reception that the "word of Christ" remains among us, and by which God gives us himself and promotes the interiorization of our faith.[35]

As we now move to the final chapter, let's discuss the idea we've referenced on several occasions that Christianity exists in a delicate balance between ideas in tension.

---

[34] G. K. Chesterton, *Orthodoxy* (San Francisco, 1908), 106–7.

[35] Geoffrey Wainwright, *Doxology*, 217.

CHAPTER 8
Safeguarding the Tensions

F. Scott Fitzgerald once said that "the test of a first-rate intelligence is the ability to hold two opposed ideas in the mind at the same time, and still retain the ability to function."[1] By the time Fitzgerald made the observation his life was a shadow of its former glory, and it's been suggested that he may have said it as a reproach to himself. Nevertheless, because of its simple and evident truth his statement has been immortalized. It's true that too often we're fooled into thinking in binary terms—that we have to choose one thing over another or hold one truth at the expense of another. If modernity has accomplished anything, it's been to create a superficial way of thinking that flattens out the world into something that's always easy to grasp. We've been conditioned to think like Procrustes (the in-keeper in Greek mythology) who, in order to make the travelers fit his bed, cut the limbs of those who were too tall and stretched those who were too short—thus fitting the bed to visitors with total perfection.[2] The trouble is that reality is more complex and resists being forced into artificial categories, even though we may wish it to be otherwise. Because we naturally prefer ideas that create the most cognitive ease and involve the least

---

[1] F. Scott Fitzgerald, "The Crack-Up," https://www.esquire.com/lifestyle/a4310/the-crack-up/. See also Philip E. Tetlock and Dan Gardner, *Superforecasting: The Art and Science of Prediction* (New York, 2015), 229–30.

[2] Nassim Nicholas Taleb, *Antifragile: Things That Gain From Disorder* (New York, 2014), 81.

tensions, it's not hard to see why our news sources, social media posts, and even our churches have flattened tensions requiring more effortful thinking.

In his insightful treatment of strategy and the history of war, John Gaddis provides a helpful illustration of our modern either/ or thinking. It comes from the hedgehog or fox distinction made famous by Isaiah Berlin. Hedgehogs, Berlin suggested, know one thing and have a stubborn sense of direction or a goal they're determined to achieve, while foxes constantly zig zag this way and that as they adapt to their environment. As the distinction was later popularized it was thought that people fall into one or the other category. Either you charge through life toward a grand goal without adapting to your changing environment, or you lack a grand idea and go from one thing to another without a true north. Business books have proliferated on the topic and often argue why it's best to be one or the other, which no doubt is fueled by our tendency to think in binary terms: people are either hedgehogs or foxes, optimists or pessimists, republicans or democrats.

Gaddis provides various examples of this either/or thinking and shows how it prevented many leaders from appreciating the world's inherent complexities, with the result that they were often driven down disastrous paths. By way of illustration, he highlights a scene in Steven Spielberg's film, *Lincoln*, in which Daniel Day-Lewis (who plays Abraham Lincoln) has been arguing the case that all men are created equal—a cause that would delight any hedgehog. To abolish slavery, however, Lincoln has to move the Thirteenth Amendment through a divided House of Representatives, at which point the movie shows him becoming as wily as a fox. He makes deals, offers bribes, flatters, and even does some arm-twisting in smoke-filled rooms. When Thaddeus Stevens (played by Tommy Lee Jones) asks him how he can reconcile a noble aim like abolishing slavery with such less than noble maneuvering, Lincoln responds as follows: "[A] compass . . . [will] point you true north from where you're standing, but it's got no advice about the swamps and deserts and chasms that you'll encounter along the way. If in pursuit of your destination, you plunge ahead, heedless of obstacles, and achieve nothing more than to sink in a swamp . . . [then] what's the use of knowing true north?"[3]

As far as we know, the historic Lincoln never uttered these exact words, but the record shows that he implicitly understood he couldn't afford to be either a hedgehog or a fox. He had to be both, and he had to know when to be one or the other. He was a hedgehog insofar as he kept the long-term goal of abolishing slavery as a true north, and a fox insofar as he continuously adapted to immediate necessities; both of which were in his mind at the same time. Constantly connecting big and small things, the film shows a president who understood that the vote in the House—and the future of slavery in America—may depend on who gets to be postmaster in some small village. In this Lincoln stands out from other world leaders. Napoleon lost his empire by confusing his long-term goals with his present capabilities—Lincoln saved his country by not doing so.[4] He was able to hold, as Fitzgerald said, opposites in his mind and still retain the ability to function. He recognized and respected contradictions. That was his greatness. His good judgment enabled him to rethink assumptions while preserving his existing worldview.

But our modern culture has taught us to avoid what feels like contradictions, the tensions that make thinking an effortful activity. As recently as the twentieth century, we've seen governments show what happens when contradictions are suppressed, when the topography of ideas and society are flattened out to conform to some plastic ideal. In these instances people were offered freedom from the need to make choices by giving them over to a higher authority, whether that was a collective, state, or even a theory. It was a liberty that flattened competing truths and led to tyranny and the murder of millions of innocent people. The brilliance of the American

---

[3] John Lewis Gaddis, *On Grand Strategy* (New York, 2018), 14–17. Carl Von Clausewitz noted a similar duality with war when he famously stated that it's a continuation of political activity by other means. "The political object is the goal, war is the means of reaching it, and means can never be considered in isolation from their purpose." See *On War* (Princeton, 1976), 87.

[4] John Lewis Gaddis, *On Grand Strategy*, 309–11.

Founders is that they not only kept, but leveraged, inconsistencies. They respected reality with its topographies and crafted choices within them.

It's this increasingly rare ability that we'll explore here, particularly as it bears on our examination of ritual. What we'll see is that, in contrast to popular culture, Christian liturgy delivers a framework within which we're compelled to keep seemingly opposite ideas in our minds at the same time. We'll show that anytime in church history the tensions were flattened out, particularly around the person of Jesus, heresy was the inevitable result. Next we'll explore the important distinction, and necessity, of law and Gospel, followed by some comments around the biblical pattern of prayer in the Christian assembly. All in all, it will be evident that retaining the tensions between apparent contradictions within the biblical materials is crucial for rightly understanding the Christian faith.

First, though, a quick recap of how we've gotten to where we are.

Modern Information Delivery

To put this chapter in context, let's do a quick recap of some earlier observations. Recall that the form in which ideas are expressed affects what those ideas will be, with the consequence that the medium becomes the message. This was shown particularly in the rise of television in the twentieth century, which has had a profound influence on how people develop intellectually and socially. Setting the precedent for a new and pervasive medium, it quickly determined not just the content we learn, but more significantly the benchmark for *how* we come to know anything at all.[5] As with any communication medium, it defines how truth is derived, which is one reason so many of our conversations have been reduced to silliness. Because of the way it directs us to organize our minds and integrate our experience of the world, a cascade of consequences have followed for how we process ideas of truth and falsehood.

---

[5] Neil Postman, *Amusing Ourselves to Death: Public Discourse in the Age of Show Business* (New York, 1985), 16–18, 24, 27, 84.

As to how, it does so by requiring that messages be compressed into short and simple bites that are easily digested without effort. Drama, or storytelling, is preferred over exposition; being sold a solution is better than being confronted with questions and problems. As Philip Tetlock observes, we want yes or no answers, which explains why the media bursts with large personalities full of assurances that they can predict what's coming no matter how bad their forecasting records may be.[6] Confidence, no matter how inaccurate, is rewarded because we correlate it with competence. This makes sense in an environment where perplexity is a fast-track to low ratings, meaning that there shouldn't be anything that has to be remembered, studied, or endured. What's evident in TV and all such related media—including, perhaps especially, social media—is that contentment, not the growth of the learner is paramount.[7]

We also pointed out that because this newer media is speed-of-light, it's necessarily present-centered and permits no access to the past. In the age of show business, not only is ideological and theological content absent, but historical context is as well. It's not that we refuse to remember or keep things in proper context, it's that we're being rendered unfit to remember. As we've shown, this is only made worse by the fact that humans tend to see only what's in front of them at present. Recall that Kahneman refers to this tendency as "what you see is all there is."[8] Information that isn't there might as well not exist, so if we've become accustomed to a media that consistently reinforces our natural state by its present-centered format then it's no wonder why our ability to reach deep has been compromised. This is becoming worse the easier it gets to access whatever tidbits we want with a simple search or Twitter feed. Bottom line is that our most popular media present information in a simplistic, non-substantive, non-historical, and non-contextual form. So rather than delivering information of real value, the new media focuses on shallow data packaged as entertainment, and the wave has engulfed not only our

6 Philip E. Tetlock and Dan Gardner, *Superforecasting*, 138.

7 Neil Postman, *Amusing Ourselves to Death: Public Discourse in the Age of Show Business* (New York, 1985), 127–132, 147–148, 154, 156.

8 Daniel Kahneman, *Thinking, Fast and Slow* (New York, 2011), 86.

24-hour news cycle but our churches as well.[9] Neil Postman's comments deserve repeating:

> It [TV] does not accommodate complex language or stringent demands. As a consequence, what is preached on television is not anything like the Sermon on the Mount. Religious programs are filled with good cheer. They celebrate affluence. Their featured players become celebrities. Though their messages are trivial, the shows have high ratings, or rather, *because* their messages are trivial, the shows have high ratings . . . I believe I am not mistaken in saying that Christianity is a demanding and serious religion. When it is delivered as easy and amusing, it is another kind of religion altogether.[10]

In his classic, *The Closing of the American Mind*, Allan Bloom adds that educated men used to be harangued on Sunday morning about death and eternity in a way that caused deeper reflection. However, preferring not to deal with hard things we've become proficient at forgetting, which is now one of our primary modes of problem-solving. Without the tough questions in view, our problems are then easily solved in vacuous abstractions. "We are learning to 'feel comfortable' with God, love and even death," says Bloom.[11] And with a gray net of abstraction, we're able to simplify and explain the world in a pleasing way. Artificial though it is, the net has become the world in our eyes with the result that at almost every level we've slipped into an indefensible relativism. Bloom's comments deserve attention:

> We are like ignorant shepherds living on a site where great civilizations once flourished. The shepherds play with the fragments that pop up to the surface, having no notion of the beautiful structures of which they were once a part. All that is necessary is a careful excavation to provide them with life-enhancing models. We need history,

---

[9] Neil Postman, *Amusing Ourselves to Death*, 136–137, 141.

[10] Neil Postman, *Amusing Ourselves to Death*, 121–123.

[11] Allan Bloom, *The Closing of the American Mind* (New York, 1987), 230, 238.

not to tell us what happened, or to explain the past, but to make the past alive so that it can explain us and make a future possible.[12]

What is common to all this is our innate and modern desire to flatten out reality and eliminate its apparent contradictions. Yet it's this, we'll argue, that ritual prevents us from doing as it frames experience within the tensions. Why is it important, though, beyond mere academic banter? The ever-insightful G. K. Chesterton provides two reasons. First, grappling with the world's complexity has always created and sustained sanity and health:

> He [the sane man] has always cared more for truth than for consistency. If he saw two truths that seemed to contradict each other, he would take the two truths and the contradiction along with them. His spiritual sight is stereoscopic, like his physical sight: he sees two different pictures at once and yet sees all the better for that. Thus he has always believed that there was such a thing as fate, but such a thing as free will also. Thus he believed that children were indeed the kingdom of Heaven, but nevertheless ought to be obedient to the kingdom of earth. He admired youth because it was young and age because it was not. It is exactly this balance of apparent contradictions that has been the whole buoyancy of the healthy man.[13]

Second, and more importantly, the idea of this combination is central to Christianity. Of its chief figure, Jesus Christ, the church insisted that he wasn't "a being apart from God and man, like an elf, nor yet a being half human and half not, like a centaur, but both things at once and both things thoroughly, very man and very God."[14] As we proceed, we'll show how the church's ritual sought to maintain the idea of the incarnation with all its tensions. To do so, let's first introduce the idea of biblical juxtapositions, the setting of one thing next to another.

---

[12] Allan Bloom, *The Closing of the American Mind*, 239–40.

[13] G. K. Chesterton, *Orthodoxy* (San Francisco, 1908), 33.

[14] G. K. Chesterton, *Orthodoxy*, 98.

Biblical Juxtapositions

Gordon Lathrop points out that, in accordance with scripture itself, Christian liturgy uses juxtapositions—the setting of one thing next to another—as its basic tool of meaning.[15] Word is set next to table; the Hebrew scriptures are set next to the New Testament, creating a juxtaposition begging for interpretation in the sermon. As the ancient scriptures are set next to preaching the assembly is prompted to pray for the world. Then as the meal is set next to texts, our understanding deepens and the meanings of those ancient words are found to have surprising new referents. Every deliverance story is made to speak of the central Christian event: Israel delivered from slavery, Sara from the demon, Jonah from the sea, the three children from the furnace. As old texts are set next to new, and as they're both set next to the meal, the assembly hears of the God who raised Jesus and who will also raise us.

> Here is the manna, the lamb, the temple meals, the feast for all nations upon the mountains. And, besides these meal stories, all the other stories of the scriptures resonate here, in the meal of Christ, as well. Here is the survival from the flood, the assembly of the people of God, the dwelling place of God, the beginning of the wiping away of years. Then the meal is tangible and visible word, an eating of the meaning of the scriptures, as if we were eating the scroll given to Ezekiel (Ezek. 2:8–3:3).[16]

By setting one liturgical thing next to another, the deep structure of biblical language is replicated and evoked.[17] We pray with angels, and though we do we're kept from trying to occupy the heavenly sphere as we pray for the lost, the lonely, and the dejected here on earth—which counteracts our hyper-spiritual desire to flee the material world with a necessary anti-spirituality. It's through this

---

[15] Gordon Lathrop, *Holy Ground: A Liturgical Cosmology* (Minneapolis, 2003), 65–6, 70, 127.

[16] Gordon Lathrop, *Holy Things: A Liturgical Theology* (Minneapolis, 1998), 50–3, 79–80, 89.

[17] Gordon Lathrop, *Holy Things*, 33, 44.

word/table framework that our cardinal direction is found; or more pointedly it's through this triangulation, through liturgical pairs reconciled in the body and blood of the crucified one that meaning is discovered.

What's crucial is that any loss of these juxtapositions diminishes the clarity and depth of the faith. Even further, they're necessary to speak faithfully about God incarnate in Christ: human and divine, letter and spirit, now and not yet, hidden and revealed, immanent and transcendent, law and Gospel. And as they're maintained they secure the counterintuitive truth that the spiritual is intimately tied to the material—as God became man—making the truth about God inseparable from the ordinary, as inseparable as God was from humanity in Jesus.

Two Natures

The doctrine of Christ is the chief article of the Christian faith and serves as the foundation of every other doctrine, including the trinity. Because Christ is so central, it's critical that we understand who he is and what was, and continues to be, his work on our behalf. As history shows, the slightest push too far to one side or the other has thrust countless people into heresy and caused them to misrepresent the faith. This is because navigating the seemingly contradictory passages affirming that Jesus is both God and man has proved daunting, spawning particular errors that resulted in condemnation by the church. In fact, the errors here account for some of the more significant christological heresies, and ones that continue to vex even well-meaning Christians today.

As should become clear, a primary cause of the heresies we'll see comes from the human tendency to flatten reality, but we have an added challenge in our cultural demand for entertainment; with the two together creating a recipe for disaster, especially as it relates to the doctrine of Christ which demands affirming two opposing ideas at the same time, such that neither can be minimized without destroying the foundation on which the faith stands. Before exploring the errors, though, let's first lay out what scripture says about Jesus so that we have a proper benchmark.

While it's no doubt a mystery and difficult to understand, scripture insists that Christ is true God with all his divine attributes, yet also true man with all the attributes common to all men.[18] Or more simply, the New Testament insists that Christ is true God and true man, or the God-man.[19] That he's true God and coeternal with the Father is attested in passages such as John 1:1, "In the beginning was the Word, and the Word was with God, and the Word was God," and John 10:30, "I and the Father are one." scripture is also clear in ascribing the divine attributes to Jesus: eternity (John 1:1; 8:58; 17:5; Phil. 2:6); omniscience (John 21:17); omnipresence (John 1:48–50); and omnipotence (Mark 4:38–41; John 2:11; 5:21; 10:28–30). It also makes clear Jesus' divine role in creation: "For by Him all things were created, both in the heavens and on earth, visible and invisible, whether thrones or dominions or rulers or authorities—all things have been created through Him and for Him. He is before all things, and in Him all things hold together" (Col. 1:16–17; John 1:3; Heb. 1:2). Further, Jesus is worshipped, which is something reserved for God alone (John 5:23; 20:28; Phil. 2:9).

That he's also true man is made explicit as the scripture ascribes to him: human flesh and blood like other men (Matt. 26:38; Luke 23:46, 22:42, 24:39; John 2:21; Heb. 2:14); while born without sin (Is. 53:9; John 8:46) a human descent (Matt. 1:1ff.; Luke 3:23ff.; Rom. 9:5); a human, though miraculous, conception in the womb of Mary (Luke 1:42); human emotions (Mark 3:5; 14:34; John 11:35); human physical needs (Matt. 4:2; Luke 8:23; John 19:28); and finally, human suffering and death (Matt. 27:46; John 19:30). Christ had to be both divine and human to fulfill the divine law in man's place (Gal. 4:4–5) and redeem us from sin (Is. 53:7–11). Any denial of either his divine or human nature is a denial of his

---

[18] Martin Chemnitz, *The Two Natures in Christ*, trans. J. A. O. Preus (St. Louis, 1971), 37–65.

[19] John Theodore Mueller, *Christian Dogmatics: A Handbook of Doctrinal Theology for Pastors, Teachers, and Laymen* (St. Louis, 1955), 256–61, 63. For the Reformed position see Charles Hodge, *Systematic Theology*, Vol. 2 (Grand Rapids, 1986), 378ff.

vicarious atonement and his mediatorial work as our great High Priest (John 1:1–14; Heb. 2:14).

It's also important to point out that though Christ had two natures he didn't consist of two persons. scripture makes it clear that Jesus consists of one indivisible person, as the eternal logos—the second person of the trinity—assumed a human nature, not a distinct (separate) human person.[20] In other words, the human nature was received into the person of the logos (John 1:14; Gal. 4:4–5; Heb. 2:14) with the result that Christ was one undivided person, not two that consisted of one human and one divine. Theologians call this the personal union, which occurred when in his incarnation the logos assumed human nature into his divine person, with the result that in the incarnate Christ God and man are forever one undivided person. Is this difficult to understand? Absolutely, and it's why St. Paul referred to it as the "mystery of godliness" (1 Tim. 3:16) and "God's mystery" (Col. 2:2–3). But it's important to maintain both truths for the mystery to stand as is—and it's the basis on which Luther rightly insisted that there can be no valid relationship with God which isn't found in the union of the God-man.[21] Firmly on biblical ground, Luther insisted that apart from Christ there is no God[22] as "in Him all the fullness of Deity dwells in bodily form" (Col. 2:9). To know God is to know him as he's found dying on a criminal's cross. No other knowledge is saving knowledge.

All this being said, humans will be human. Even without the relentless modern demand for entertainment, we naturally flatten out truths and avoid the complexity that makes thinking effortful. This is true of all generations, which is why the idea of Christ being both God and man was also difficult for the ancients. Well before modern errors surfaced, the ancients had already set major heretical precedents as they leaned too far in one direction or the other, which was the reason the church convened councils to arbitrate controversies. Among them was a the council convened at Nicea in

---

[20] Martin Chemnitz, *The Two Nature's in Christ*, 87–102.

[21] Marc Lienhard, *Luther: Witness to Jesus Christ* (Minneapolis, 1982), 341–343.

[22] WA XXVI 332.18–21.

325 A.D., out of which came one of the most important Christian creeds because of its pronouncements—grounded in scripture and earlier creeds—about Jesus' divine and human natures and the doctrine of the trinity. But to understand the Nicene creed we need to take a look at the heresies that precipitated it.

Early Christological Heresies

While there have been many heresies over the centuries the christological ones stand out as most important. One of the earliest involved a movement known as monarchianism, which sought to uphold the idea that God is one, the sole monarch of the universe.[23] While there are two varieties of monarchianism (adoptionism and modalism) they each have in common the belief in the fundamental unity and oneness of God, which doesn't permit a second person to share the title of deity—thereby denying the Christian doctrine of the trinity. So what did they do with Jesus, whom the scriptures declare to be both man and God?

The adoptionists flattened out scriptural tensions by holding that Jesus is a mere man endowed with a special power from God and adopted as God's Son; the modalists by viewing the persons of the trinity as simply different modes of the one God, meaning that they're not distinct persons. For the adoptionist, Christ isn't really God but an adopted man; for the modalist, he's not only God, he's the Father himself (simply in a different mode). God reveals himself, the modalist claimed, under different modes in different ages: as the Father in creation and giving of the law, as the Son in Jesus, and as the Holy Spirit after Christ's ascension. We should also note that modalism was docetic (another heresy), teaching that Christ was human in appearance only, but not really. Unfortunately, both errors are more common in today's churches than we'd like to think.

Why do either matter, though, aside from their plain opposition to the scriptural notion of Christ's two natures? What, in other words, are the practical implications of the two heresies? Simply and

---

[23] Harold O. J. Brown, *Heresies: The Image of Christ in the Mirror of Heresy and Orthodoxy from the Apostles to the Present* (Grand Rapids, 1984), 95–6, 99.

importantly this: they both deny in their own way Jesus' vicarious atonement for sin. If Jesus was a mere man (even with special powers), he couldn't be the perfect and sinless sacrifice for our sin, and couldn't have overcome sin and death on his own behalf, let alone ours. As Luther commented, "whoever is redeemed by the humanity only, is certainly not yet redeemed, nor will he ever be redeemed."[24] Sin and death had to be overcome, which required a direct divine act. If Jesus is not true man the same problem follows, as the idea of atonement implies what theologians refer to as substitutionary satisfaction for sin. Jesus, as the perfect and sinless man, had to fulfill the demands of the law on our behalf, as man. But only as Jesus is both God and man could he make satisfaction for the law's demands and conquer sin and death.

Against this background, Arius seems to have offered a position that—on the surface—sounded like a viable alternative; however, it turned out to be just as heretical as previous errors. Arius accepted Jesus as a supernatural being (and even preexistent) but believed him to be lower than the Father. As such Jesus is a semi-divine being that was created, not eternally begotten, by the Father and had an origin in time. But so long as Jesus is subordinate (ontologically, or in his very essence) to the Father he can't be of the same substance or nature as the Father. As Arius stated, "there was when he [the Logos] was not,"[25] meaning that Christ didn't possess deity by nature but developed it by virtue of his growing unity with God. Thus he can be our savior only insofar as he gives us the example of commitment to the good, necessarily implying that our hope is in attaining perfection ourselves as Christ did. It was anti-biblical moralism through and through.

What's critical about the Arian controversy is that it precipitated the now infamous council at Nicea in which the church developed the Nicene Creed. Convened by the emperor Constantine in 325 A.D., the creed aimed to settle the dispute by explicitly including the biblical doctrine that Christ is "the Word of God, God of God, light of light, life of life, the only begotten Son." As you can see below in the creed's deliberate wording, the controversy clarified as much about the trinity as it did Christ's two natures:

---

[24] *Luther's Works*, Vol. 37, ed. Robert H. Fischer (St. Louis, 1961), 231.
[25] Harold O. J. Brown, *Heresies*, 105–17.

I believe in one God,
the Father Almighty,
maker of heaven and earth
and of all things visible and invisible.

And in on Lord Jesus Christ,
the only-begotten Son of God,
begotten of his Father before all worlds,
God of God, Light of Light,
very God of very God,
begotten, not made,
being of one substance with the Father,
by whom all things were made;
who for us men and for our salvation
came down from heaven
and was incarnate by the Holy Spirit of the virgin Mary
and was made man;
and was crucified also for us under Pontius Pilate.
He suffered and was buried.
And the third day he rose again
according to the scriptures
and ascended into heaven
and sits at the right hand of the Father.
And he will come again with glory to judge
both the living and the dead,
whose kingdom will have no end.

And I believe in the Holy Spirit,
the Lord and giver of life,
who proceeds from the Father and the Son,
who with the Father and the Son together
is worshipped and glorified,
who spoke by the prophets.
And I believe in one holy catholic Church,
I acknowledge one Baptism for the remission of sins,
and I look for the resurrection of the dead
and the life of the world to come. Amen

Nicea turned out to be a watershed moment for the church, not simply because it settled a dangerous controversy, but because it formulated a brief confession of faith that was so clear, scriptural, and concise that even a child could memorize it with ease. Not only was the doctrine of Christ made explicit, but the doctrine of the trinity which it necessarily implied was framed in simple language. Countless Christians have since learned the basics of the faith through its use in catechetical instruction as well as its repetition in the weekly service. Its impact has thus been profound, so much so that any church that denies it should be considered outside the bounds of the historic faith.

A Name with Contradictions

Elsewhere I've noted the inherent contradiction that the disciples would have seen in Jesus' claim that his Messiahship is not of this world, and the extreme difficultly they had in accepting the notion of a crucified God.[26] Absurd would have been the only word to describe such a suggestion. From an early age, their hope was for an earthly king, a Messiah who'd finally put an end to Jewish subservience to foreign rule and punish the wicked. The idea of God crucified as a blasphemer and outsider required a radical upending of their very idea of God, holiness, and their own sinful condition. After Golgotha, the name Jesus Christ could only serve as a constant reforming criticism of their (and our) natural desire for a God of glory—a God perched above it all, disentangled from our wicked world.

Thus Lathrop's insight that "Jesus Christ" is far from a simple name is spot on, as it professes profound, double-sided meaning that reinterprets daily life. Widely regarded as originating from a liturgical formula of confession and praise, the name carries the whole Old Testament tradition of kingship and messianic hope. Yet in juxtaposition to that tradition, it refers to a crucified messianic pretender who is no king or messiah of any first century expectation. This messiah, this king, rules not from an earthly throne but from a cross outside

---

[26] David Andersen, *Faithless to Fearless: The Event That Changed the World* (Irvine, 2019), 82–87.

the gates of Jerusalem. As the name Jesus Christ is next to its historical connotations, we're reoriented in our confession of being reigned over by one who serves us, saved by one who dies, and embraced by one made to be nothing in the eyes of earthly rulers. "If we may hear the surprise of this title, we may begin to hear what new things, what new understandings of our world and ourselves, are being brought from the old texts and rites."[27] It carries with it not only the liturgical community but also the world's outsiders. Walking in the world as Christians we're surrounded by all the dualities this name holds together, including insiders and outsiders, us and them, disorder and order, life and death.

The name also carries the ancient longing for the perfect king, the perfect bringer of public justice on earth, but with it the tension-laden duality that it's the same crucified Jesus who is confessed to be this king. While true king he doesn't reign, has no crown, no court, and no anointing except "beforehand for . . . burial" (Mark 14:8). "He has been killed, executed in a manner that left him not only exposed and powerless but also ritually unclean, a pollution on the land. Yet, faith says, in this cross are life and health for all things, more than any king's reign would ever bring. In this cross, God has come so deeply into our wretchedness that henceforth all falling into wretchedness is falling into God and God's mercy, not away from God."[28] And yet this crucified one is resurrected, still present and continually giving himself away. This presence is his reign, and extends far beyond that of any other kingdom and is now found in the humble means of word, table, and water.

As the liturgical assembly confesses this "profound contradictoriness"—that, as Luther correctly said, "apart from this man there is no God"[29]—it reaffirms that this human being is God. In Christ, the finite contains the infinite; this bread is the body of Christ; this cup is the blood of Christ; this water immerses us into Christ's death. In this liturgical duality, we're invited to treasure the goodness of the earth and our bodies and to maintain solidarity with those who suffer and are outside our walls. The name Jesus Christ also bars us

[27] Gordon Lathrop, *Holy Things*, 31.

[28] Gordon Lathrop, *Holy Ground*, 74–6.

[29] *Luther's Works*, ed. Robert H. Fischer, Vol. 37, 218.

from drawing a sharp line between "us" and "them," between those in and those outside. Because if we do, it reminds us that Jesus will always be on the other side of the line; it reminds us that it was the historic Jesus who eats with sinners and outsiders, who is made a curse and sin itself, who justifies the wicked, who himself is the hole in our self-exalting ideologies.

> The one around whom we gather when we actually use the build-ing, the one who is present for us in the hearing of the scriptures and the celebration of the sacraments, is himself always also away from here, identified with those who are outside our circles, disas-sembled. In him, the Spirit blows where it will. In him, every place, even and especially the most god-forsaken, is before God.[30]

And as we confess in the creed one baptism for the remission of sins, we're reminded that the washing of which we speak isn't simply about "purification," but also a participation in the cross of Christ and an identification with the weakness of others. Thus the church that was created by baptism carries its own tension: a centered peo-ple oriented to the open door. But as Chesterton so well articulates, the church's tension was one created in the cross itself:

> In a garden, Satan tempted man: and in a garden, God tempted God. He passed, in some superhuman manner, through our human hor-ror of pessimism. When the world shook and the sun was wiped out of Heaven, it was not at the crucifixion, but at the cry from the cross: the cry which confessed that God was forsaken of God. And now let the revolutionists choose a creed from all the creeds and a god from all the gods of the world, carefully weighing all the gods of inevitable recurrence and of unalterable power. They will not find another god who has himself been in revolt. Nay, (the matter grows too difficult for human speech,) but let the atheists themselves choose a god. They will find only one divinity who ever uttered their isolation; only one religion in which God seemed for an instant to be an atheist.[31]

---

[30] Gordon Lathrop, *Holy Ground*, 64–5.

[31] G. K. Chesterton, *Orthodoxy*, 145.

Law and Gospel

Earlier we noted that at the heart of scripture lies the concept of God's holiness and man's sin. In order for God to give his people safe access to him, it was necessary to establish the sacrificial ritual enactments that consume the bulk of Leviticus. Recall how central it was throughout the Old Testament that human beings are unclean and in need of constant purification, which is why the congregation of Israel with its priests and high priest needed to be purified before entering the sanctuary and sharing in God's holiness. It was only through his decrees that they were made holy and clean, which occurred in the daily service. Because of the vital role the daily service played, we pointed out that Israel's faith can't be understood apart from how it was ritually enacted. What's important here is that something similar occurs in the New Testament as it continues to underscore God's holiness and man's sin, with it too being best understood within the ritual enactment of word and table.

This shouldn't be surprising of a movement steeped in Old Testament language and practice, which is why the early church continued to be concerned about dealing with man's sin. That it continued to enact its central beliefs in ritual is shown in the fact that, from early on, the assembly began with a corporate confession of sin as a way of acknowledging human dependence on God's mercy, now realized in Christ's death. Word was set next to table, the Hebrew scriptures were set next to the New Testament, which begged for interpretation. As the ancient scriptures were set next to preaching the assembly was prompted to pray for the world. Then as the meal was set next to texts, it was made clear that man can only bring his sin in exchange for God's holiness in Christ. And like its Old Testament counterpart, the church confessed that holiness was wholly dependent on God, most saliently at the table where believer ate Christ's body and blood for the forgiveness of sin.

Underlying its ritual enactments were two important truths that the New Testament refers to as law and Gospel. As it makes clear, particularly in Paul's letters, the law has a specific function in that it only makes demands and tells us what we're to do, and then justly condemns us for being sinful. It can only say "Thou shalt" and make conditional if/then promises: *if* you do this, *then*. Its promises are predicated on the condition that we fulfill the law perfectly and completely; in other words, it makes its demands not just on our action but on our nature, thoughts, words, and works.[32] Consider, for example, how Jesus reveals the law with all its consequences in the Sermon on the Mount:

> For I say to you that unless your righteousness surpasses that of the scribes and Pharisees, you will not enter the kingdom of heaven. You have heard that the ancients were told, "You shall not commit murder" and "Whoever commits murder shall be liable to the court." But I say to you that everyone who is angry with his brother shall be guilty before the court; and whoever says to his brother, "You good-for-nothing," shall be guilty before the supreme court; and whoever says, "You fool," shall be guilty enough to go into the fiery hell . . . You have heard that it was said, "You shall not commit adultery;" but I say to you that everyone who looks at a woman with lust for her has already committed adultery with her in his heart.

As we can see from the passage, Jesus presses the law to its logical conclusion: that it's not just what a man does that makes him guilty of sinning against the law, but what he is and thinks. "For out of the heart come evil thoughts, murders, adulteries, fornications, thefts, false witness, slanders" (Matt. 15:19). Thus the function of the law is to reprove sin, "for I would not have come to know sin," says Paul, "except through the Law" (Rom. 7:7), demand perfect obedience (Gal. 3:12), pronounces a curse on all transgressors (Gal. 3:10), render all the world guilty before God (Rom. 3:19), and mediate knowledge of sin (Rom. 3:20).[33]

In stark contrast, as the law speaks only to our action, the Gospel speaks only to God's and makes no demands. It simply offers forgiveness to those condemned by the law's punishing demands. As such it offers grace, peace, and salvation to sinners (Rom. 1:16–17; 10:15;

---

[32] C. F. W. Walther, *The Proper Distinction Between Law and Gospel* (St. Louis, 1986), 9–10.

[33] John Theodore Mueller, *Christian Dogmatics*, 471–2.

Acts 20:24). "But God, being rich in mercy, because of His great love with which He loved us, even when we were dead in our transgressions, made us alive together with Christ (by grace you have been saved)" (Eph. 2:1–9). Thus while the law demands perfect obedience in every way and condemns all who are disobedient, the Gospel demands nothing, freely offering to sinners grace, life, and salvation for Christ's sake. "The same sinners whom the Law consigns to everlasting damnation the Gospel, for Jesus' sake, assigns to everlasting glory in heaven, Rom. 5, 18–21. The Law requires works, Luke 10, 28; the Gospel declares that the sinner 'is justified by faith, without the deeds of the Law,' Rom. 3, 28."[34] As the law's promises are conditional on perfection (Gal. 3:10–11), the Gospel promises are pure grace. Or to put it another way, the law promises life to the sinner provided he obeys it perfectly, but the Gospel promises life and salvation without the works of the law and by grace to he who "believes in Him who justifies the ungodly" (Rom. 4:5).

Though scripture makes the distinction between the two clear, it's important to understand that both law and Gospel are essential and the divinely inspired word of God. Their function is simply different: the law drives sinners to the cross and the Gospel offers forgiveness in Christ. Because all men have sinned and stand under the curse of the law, Paul insists that "by the works of the Law no flesh will be justified in His sight" (Rom. 3:9–20). "Therefore," says Paul, "the Law has become our tutor to lead us to Christ, so that we may be justified by faith" (Gal. 3:24). This means that both law and Gospel pertain to all people and must be taught side by side until the end of time (including for Christians). And they must each be taught at the top of their energy, with all of the law's brutal consequences as well as the Gospel's reckless grace.

Due to our penchant for leveling the doctrinal topography, this point merits repeating: Any weakening of either law or Gospel results in a dilution of both. If one weakens the law's terror then man will continue in his delusion that he can earn God's favor through his self-justifying works. The exact same thing occurs if the Gospel's consequences are diminished. Recall our Procrustean tendency to

---

[34] John Theodore Mueller, *Christian Dogmatics*, 473.

flatten out reality and force it to fit within our constricted worldview. One way we make it fit the Procrustean bed is to either weaken the law or undermine the radicalness of the Gospel. In contrast, scripture keeps them both furious such that, on the one hand, sin has to be named for what it is regardless of our cultural desire to remold clear biblical definitions. On the other, since all sins are an affront to God's law, there is no sin more debased than any other. Meaning that in the first case man isn't free to carve out certain sins and call them natural or good, and in the second he can't claim some sins are more evil than others. This is important since human beings, especially in modernity, are selective in their application of outrage and permissiveness.

No doubt the tendency partly explains why we so quickly elevate or diminish one sin at the expense of the bigger picture. How often is Paul's list in Gal. 5:19–21 and 1 Cor. 6:9–10 used in exactly this way in opposition to its intent? A list that spans sins such as adultery, immorality, and idolatry, all the way to strife, jealousy, disputes, and envy. Given the context of his letters with their clear law/ Gospel distinction, Paul is saying that they're all equally sinful and condemned by the law, yet we can't help but to call out drunkenness while making exceptions for outbursts of anger. Without law and Gospel each at the top of their energy man only misuses the little he knows.

Thus you can see why maintaining both with all of their uncomfortable ramifications is difficult, but necessary if we're to protect the scriptural idea that Christ died for the lost, for the outsider and the outcast. Because it's only by keeping them both, furiously and with all their radical consequences, that we understand that we're all outcasts. And it's only in this way that we can keep our sight stereoscopic and focused on the radical implications of the cross. The point here is that the tensions pregnant in the church's ritual serve as a guardrail for keeping these seemingly opposed ideas at the forefront. They also provide an important bulwark against man's desire to justify himself by keeping the brutal consequences of sin front and center.

Thanksgiving and Beseeching

This chapter wouldn't be complete without mentioning that fact that each phase of the liturgy is marked by both praise and lament, thanksgiving and beseeching. Evident throughout the ritual, the assembly conforms to the biblical pattern of prayer as it first praises God by recounting and acknowledging his mighty deeds, which is the ground on which the people beseech his faithfulness and beg him to remember his promises.[35] "It is because of what the LORD did for me when I came out of Egypt" (Ex. 13:8) was the confession generation after generation and a constant feature in both Testaments. When scripture was read in the "great synagogue"—the gathering in Jerusalem that was the heart of book of Nehemiah and taken as a pattern of all synagogues—the people stood up, and as led by Ezra, blessed God in a prayer that recounted his deeds of creation and redemption (Neh. 9:3–37). Afterwards the present needs of the people were juxtaposed to this praise.

This same biblical pattern has been followed by Christians for millennia, and can be seen in the frequent formula found in Paul's letters—a formula that includes thanksgiving "through Jesus Christ" (Rom. 1:8; Phil. 1:3–6) and beseeching for the lives grounded in Christ (Rom. 1:9–10; Phil. 1:9; Col. 1:9). In the assembly, the proclamation of scripture's promises are followed by enunciating the needs of the world in the intercessions; the thanksgiving prayer at the table cries out for the hunger of the world; the Lord's Prayer cries out for the reign of God, "thy kingdom come, thy will be done," before also confidently asking for what the community already has, bread and forgiveness as the presence of that reign. Lathrop notes that "Christian prayer 'may be the angry protestation before God that the world is nothing like it was supposed to be', yet it will also be 'the wondering expression of gratitude for the paradoxical beauty of things.'"[36]

As thanksgiving turns to beseeching, Lathrop adds that we're made to understand that the miraculous meal of which we partake isn't large enough. Outside of those within our walls is a hungry world in need of God's mercy. Were we to be content with just

---

[35] Gordon Lathrop, *Holy Things*, 56.

[36] Gordon Lathrop, *Holy Ground*, 79.

thanksgiving it would be as if we were saying that God approves of the fact that those others don't have such food; as if God were glad to be praised for this arrangement, as if praise were a way to bribe him to keep the arrangement. Thanksgiving by itself could thus be taken as uncritical support for the status quo. But the encounter with the triune God always creates a hole in any status quo. Christ may gather us into this prayer at this table, but he also eats and drinks with tax collectors and prostitutes and identifies with those outside our closed circle.

> The beseeching that expresses faith in such a God is not intended as a salve to our wounded conscience, a sop in the general direction of the truth, but as a genuine prayer to a God who acts, as a hole in our thanksgiving, an intentional diminishment of our joy when our joy is for ourselves alone, and as a line into the world that we ourselves may follow.[37]

Around these paradoxes a liturgical spirituality follows a life of thanksgiving, and it also follows beseeching. As long as we don't cut off the juxtapositions then the faith that responds to the reading set next to preaching, the meal set next to prayer and sending, can't help but pray for the whole needy world beyond our circle; prayers for justice, national and local leaders; prayers for the hungry, the sick, and the dying. These tensions in other words lead us to prayer for others, not just ourselves. They constantly reorient us and how we see ourselves and others in a broken world in need of redemption.

Bottom line is that this biblical juxtaposition of prayer is used to carry the heart of the Christian faith. Just as the word and table speak of the meaning of Jesus Christ, so praise and beseeching are summed up in him. The principal deed we remember in our assembly is the death and resurrection of the Son of God, which means that the grounds of our thanksgiving is found in a crucified man. All our sufferings have been gathered up into Christ. He was, and is, among the wretched and God-forsaken. Thus while on the basis of his mighty self-giving act we praise him, he's also the ground of our

---

[37] Gordon Lathrop, *Holy Ground*, 81, 142–3.

beseeching—and yet our beseeching gives way to praise. The wiping away of tears has already begun, in the here and now, in the midst of the outsiders and wretched. "While thanksgiving and beseeching," Lathrop notes, "are marks of biblical and Jewish prayer, in Christian use they form us in the meaning of the death and resurrection of Christ."[38]

Conclusion

In his best-selling book, *Good to Great*, Jim Collins relates an interview he conducted with Admiral Jim Stockdale—the highest ranking U.S. military officer in the "Hanoi Hilton" prisoner-of-war camp during the height of the Vietnam War.[39] Tortured over twenty times during his eight-year imprisonment, Stockdale lived out the war without any prisoner's rights, no set release date, and uncertain whether he'd ever see his family again. What's interesting about the interview are Stockdale's comments about those who did and didn't make it out, as follows:

"I never lost faith in the end of the story," he [Stockdale] said, when I asked him. "I never doubted not only that I would get out, but also that I would prevail in the end and turn the experience into the defining event of my life, which, in retrospect, I would not trade."

I didn't say anything for many minutes, and we continued the slow walk toward the faculty club, Stockdale limping and arc-swinging his stiff leg that had never fully recovered from repeated torture. Finally, after about a hundred meters of silence, I asked, "Who didn't make it out?"

"Oh, that's easy," he said. "The optimists."

"The optimists? I don't understand," I said, now completely confused, given what he'd said a hundred meters earlier.

"The optimists. Oh, they were the ones who said, 'We're going to be out by Christmas.' And Christmas would come, and Christmas would go. Then they'd say, 'We're going to be out by Easter.' And

---

[38] Gordon Lathrop, *Holy Things*, 58.

[39] Jim Collins, *Good to Great: Why Some Companies Make the Leap . . . and Others Don't* (New York: 2001), 85.

Easter would come, and Easter would go. And then Thanksgiving, and then it would be Christmas again. And they died of a broken heart."

Another long pause, and more walking. Then he turned to me and said, "This is a very important lesson. You must never confuse faith that you will prevail in the end—which you can never afford to lose—with the discipline to confront the most brutal facts of your current reality, whatever they might be."

From the interview it's evident that Stockdale understood that, for survival, two seemingly opposed ideas had to be maintained at the same time. Not only did the prisoners have to understand the brutal facts of their reality, which were many, but they had to simultaneously maintain an unwavering faith that they'd be released at some point. They needed to be pessimists, as Chesterton once said, able to acknowledge the world's evil without acquiescing to it, yet also be optimists who refuse to whitewash it and defend the indefensible.[40]

Through unthinkable hardships, Stockdale illustrates precisely what we've seen throughout this chapter: the necessity of holding apparently opposed ideas in our minds at the same time and still being able to move forward. Reality, with all its topographies, has to be respected. Given modernity's love for leveling the terrain, we've shown how Christian ritual as expressed in its historic liturgy keeps those difficult realities front and center. Christ's two natures, without which we'd still be in our sins; law and Gospel, a distinction without which we'd believe our salvation depends on our own works; and the tensions found throughout the liturgy, without which we'd be content to live in our own constricted worlds.

---

[40] G. K. Chesterton, *Orthodoxy*, 74–75, 77.

Conclusion

For generations, Americans have been conditioned by a medium of communication that's made discourse more and more shriveled and absurd. As we've pointed out throughout this book, the form in which ideas are expressed affects what those ideas will be. Television, and now social media, have created a medium that determines not only the content we learn but the benchmark for how we come to know anything at all. The result has been a new orientation for thought that increasingly depletes the attention span and centers people on the ephemeral present, making the "new" the only criteria for what deserves our focus.

As Neil Postman observed, knowing facts has morphed into a person no longer understanding implications, background, or connections. Intelligence now means knowing *of* lots of things, not knowing *about* them. Our current use of language and ideas denies interconnections, proceeds without context, argues the irrelevance of history, and offers fascination in place of complexity and coherence. In other words, modern communication is more suited to amuse than to inform—and as such has ushered in a world in which a new event pops into view for a moment, then vanishes again. It's entirely self-contained, with no context and endlessly entertaining. As substance has been muted, we've been conditioned to think that anything worth learning should take the form of entertainment.

Parallel to the development that Postman documents was the emerging conflict between tradition and progress. Pushed especially by the cultural intellectuals, all things "traditional" were mocked as an impediment to "progress," a progress that was interpreted in a

particular moral, religious, and scientific way. Spreading like wild-
fire, these attacks became the rallying cry for throwing off conven-
tion wherever it could be found. Because of this it was commonplace
for intellectuals to applaud what one prominent historian said, that
"Tradition is almost by definition reprehensible, something to be
mocked and deplored."[1] Never mind that such ideas were, and still
are, equivalent to sawing off the branch on which we sit—as tradition consists of those silent forces that brought us to where we
are now, most notably in the remarkable success of the sciences
themselves, but also all the other achievements of man. Still, it's
striking that the most prevalent peddlers of these ideas were teachers, journalists, and the media, i.e., those who viewed themselves as
the intellectual guardians of society. F. A. Hayek's comments merit
attention:

> Those who have really done most to spread these ideas, . . . having
> absorbed rumours in the corridors of science, appoint themselves as
> representatives of modern thought, as persons superior in knowledge
> and moral virtue to any who retain a high regard for traditional values,
> as persons whose very duty it is to offer new ideas to the public—and
> who must, in order to make their wares seem novel, deride whatever
> is conventional. For such people, due to the positions in which they
> find themselves, 'newness', or 'news', and not truth, becomes the main
> value, although that is hardly their intention—and although what
> they offer is often no more new than it is true.[2]

Bottom line is that the convergence of these forces was unstop-
pable, impacting everyone in society from the intellectual class on
down. No one has been immune. With Kahneman's research showing how humans naturally take the easiest route and then quickly
jump to conclusions, it's evident that we have a toxic recipe for
the most egregious superficiality. But perhaps most tragically, the
Christian church has become a pawn of the de-contextualization of

---

[1] F. A. Hayek, *The Fatal Conceit: The Errors of Socialism*, ed. W. W. Bartley III
(Chicago, 1989), 52–4.

[2] F. A. Hayek, *The Fatal Conceit*, 55.

the modern mind—evidencing little regard for the rich context out of which Christianity emerged, with religious bits of information peddled as commodities that are easily separable from the whole. Entertainment of parishoners has seemed as much a requirement as anywhere else in society. It has been unavoidable, then, that our religious expectations have been shaped by the times in which we live. And it's those expectations, the mindsets we've been conditioned to accept as the default, that need to be challenged and reoriented if we want to take more seriously the confession of the apostles and early believers.

Yet the power of our expectations over how we experience things are just now being explored in a critical way. Given the new research on the topic, let's take a quick look at just how powerful they've been shown to be, and suggest a way forward.

Expectations and Their Effects

Columbia University psychologist, Alia Crum, recruited housekeepers at seven hotels across the U.S. for a study of how beliefs affect health and weight. As reported by Stanford psychologist, Kelly McGonigal, housekeeping is strenuous work that burns over 300 calories an hour, which puts it on par with weight lifting and walking 3.5 miles per hour.[3] Despite that, two-thirds of the housekeepers believed they weren't exercising regularly, and one-third said they got no exercise at all. And their bodies reflected the perception. On average, the housekeepers' blood pressure, waist-to-hip ratio, and body weight was what we'd expect of someone who is truly sedentary.

For the study, Crum designed a poster describing how housekeeping qualifies as exercise, along with the calories burned while doing each activity. She also added that, given the facts, housekeepers were meeting or exceeding the surgeon general's recommendations for physical exercise. Because of this they should expect to see the health benefits of being active. She communicated the information in a fifteen-minute presentation at four of the seven hotels, while the

[3] Kelly McGonigal, *The Upside of Stress: Why Stress is Good For You, and How to Get Good At It* (New York, 2015), 4ff.

housekeepers at the other three were a control group; which simply got information about how important exercise is for health, but weren't told that their work qualified as such.

Four weeks later Crum checked the results. Those who'd been told their work was exercise had lost weight and body fat, their blood pressure was lower, and they liked their jobs more. And the only thing that had changed was their perception of themselves as exercisers. None of the housekeepers in the control group showed any improvement. As we might imagine, the result made headlines but some caveats had to be made clear about the data. While it showed the rather profound impact of expectations on the activity's effects, it didn't mean that a couch potato can simply tell himself he's exercising while eating chips and receive the benefits. What Crum told the housekeepers was actually true. The difference was that now they saw their work as exercise, and that made the difference. Her hypothesis was that when two outcomes are possible, one's expectations influence which outcome is more likely: the effect you expect is the effect you get.

To expand her findings, she devised another experiment dubbed the "Shake Tasting Study." For this she invited hungry participants to the lab at eight in the morning after an overnight fast on two separate occasions. On the first, participants were given a milkshake labeled "Indulgence: Decadence You Deserve," with a nutritional label showing 620 calories and 30 grams of fat. On the second they drank a milkshake labeled "Sensi-Shake: Guilt-Free Satisfaction," with 140 calories and zero grams of fat. As they drank they were hooked up to an intravenous catheter that drew blood samples, which Crum used to measure changes in blood level of ghrelin (known as the hunger hormone). As blood levels of ghrelin go down we feel full, and as they go up we look for a snack. When eating something high in fat or calories, ghrelin levels drop dramatically, with less filling food having less impact. This means that drinking the Sensi-Shake should lead to a small decline in ghrelin while the Indulgence should produce a much bigger drop—as in fact occurs on normal occasions.

But this isn't what happened in the experiments because the labels were a sham. Both times, the participants were given the same 380-calorie milkshake—meaning there should have been no difference in how their digestive tracts responded. Yet when they believed the shake was an indulgent treat, their ghrelin levels dropped three times as much as when they thought it was a diet drink. Once again, expectations determined the outcome. "Crum's study showed," McGonigal remarks, "that expectations could alter something as concrete as how much of a hormone the cells of your gastrointestinal tract secrete."[4]

What about Stress?

Having now uncovered some counter-intuitive results, Crum began to ask if similar effects could be measured in relation to stress. Specifically, could someone's mindset about the benefits or harm of stress impact how their bodies experienced it? To explore this she devised an experiment that manipulated the participants' view of stress and then watched how their bodies responded to a stressful situation.[5]

In the study, subjects were told that they'd face a mock interview and that the object was to get them better at it, which the interviewers would do by giving live feedback. However to make it extra stressful, the interviewers had been trained to give negative feedback no matter what the participant said or did. To prime them, participants were randomly assigned to watch one of two videos on stress before the interview. One talked about how stress can actually be enhancing while the other focused on its negative effects—each of which was designed to activate a specific perception of stress. In addition to a saliva test that was done to analyze stress hormones, participants had a blood pressure cuff, electrodes measuring blood flow and sweating, a thermometer to track body temperature, and were hooked up to an impedance cardiology machine that monitored heart activity.

What Crum wanted to see was if changing a person's perception of stress can modify the growth index (the ratio of DHEA to cortisol) of a stress response. The results were clear. Participants who watched the stress-is-enhancing video before the interview released more DHEA and had a higher growth index—which is a predictor

---

[4] Kelly McGonigal, *The Upside of Stress*, 6–7.

[5] Kelly McGonigal, *The Upside of Stress*, 8–10, 16, 92.

of thriving under stress, academic persistence, and even recovery after child abuse—than those who watched the stress-is-debilitating video. Viewing stress as enhancing made it so; and not in a subjective, self-reported way, but in the ratio of stress hormones produced by the adrenal glands. Crum's research also showed that people who believe stress is enhancing are less depressed and more satisfied with their lives than those who believe it's harmful. They have more energy and fewer health problems. Bottom line is that they think differently about stress, viewing it as normal and not believing it's either possible or desirable to have an entirely comfortable, safe life. They see it rather as an opportunity to grow.

As McGonigal notes, researchers refer to this as a "mindset effect," which means that expectations can snowball over time and have an increasing influence and long-term impact; which isn't to be confused with a placebo which tends to have a short-lived impact on a highly specific outcome. Transcending preferences and opinions, mindsets are core beliefs reflecting one's philosophy of life and are usually based on a theory of how the world works. Further, they don't just affect present experiences but influence the future, and thus have the potential to shape how we interpret experiences and make decisions.[6] "When a mindset gets activated—by a memory, a situation you find yourself in, or a remark someone makes—it sets off a cascade of thoughts, emotions, and goals that shape how you respond to life. This, in turn, can influence long-term outcomes, including health, happiness, and even longevity."[7] The effect has been shown in various areas, including longitudinal studies on aging where those with the most positive views of aging had an 80 percent lower risk of heart attack (along with other risks).

Our Expectations of Church

From this, it's not unreasonable to conclude that our expectations of the idea of church profoundly impact what we get out of the

---

[6] Carol S. Dweck, *Mindset: The New Psychology of Success* (New York, 2006), 10.

[7] Kelly McGonigal, *The Upside of Stress*, 11–12, 14.

experience. If we believe, even unconsciously, that church shouldn't be "boring" (whatever that means) and that it should have as one of its goals to keep us entertained, then we're necessarily narrow-framing what Christianity can mean in our modern world. Yet in so believing we run the risk of skirting along the edge of the gnostic heresies that seem so common in today's hyper-spiritualistic, world-renouncing environment. In spite of our modern biases, however, early Christians didn't believe that the point of going to church was to feel affirmed or to hear soothing words of encouragement. It was never primarily to feel emotional stimulation or to hear sermons on the five steps to a better marriage. It was aimed rather at the truth—the truth about our most pressing and urgent problem, our sin and idolatrous unbelief. It was aimed at proclaiming the death of the only-begotten Son of God for the sins of the world, and to provide that ritual space within which we meet God on his terms and receive the forgiveness of sins through his sacraments.

As we change our mindset and our expectations of what church means—that it's God's merciful service to a sinful and dying world—we're bound to start seeing it as a treasured opportunity to hear scripture, receive forgiveness, and grow in faith. This is central because we so rarely think about the fact that what we want is often not what we need. As in so many other things, our answers don't lie within, which is why the word/table framework functions to keep our memory and mind focused on that which lies outside of us and in the crucified and risen Jesus. Doing so it keeps our minds centered on that happy exchange (as Luther put it) wherein Christ gives us what is his—forgiveness, life, and salvation—in exchange for what is ours—sin and death.

But its benefits extend beyond even this. As we've now seen, the liturgical framework best provides us with a common language and set of beliefs—for example in the creeds—and constrains our tendency to act based on whether things feel or don't feel right. It places a check on our impulsiveness by reinforcing the language and grammar of scripture, and instilling the mental furniture with which we can face moments of crisis and uncertainty. Further, since losing the forest for the trees is all too human, Christian ritual uniquely forces a zooming out of our present-centered myopia which causes Narcissus to think of nothing but himself. Providing a necessary

realty check on our thoughts, which so often fly off in fits of imagination, the word/table structure pulls our feet back to the ground;
to the world of our bodies, of flesh and blood, and to the needs of
others. As in other human endeavors, the liturgical framework challenges our mental maps and forces a realignment to reality, to those
words "Given and shed for you for the forgiveness of your sins."

As we end, it deserves repeating that the apostolic teaching
embodied in the church's liturgy was never intended to be outdated
or rendered irrelevant in light of current fads. It was never meant
to be a relic of the ancient past, but a structured way of bringing
the "memoirs of the apostles" to the people, of bringing the message
and actualization of Jesus' death for sinners to the here and now. It
was a way of safeguarding the truth, with all the tensions intact, for
believers of every generation. Does that make it a panacea? Certainly
not. It would be a mistake to force it to do too much. Scriptural
teaching around the central biblical ideas is necessary for a proper
understanding of the liturgy. And all of the church's institutions and
beliefs need to constantly, as the Reformers insisted, stand under the
reforming criticism of the cross, of Christ sacrificed for outcasts and
outsiders. Yet it would be an equal mistake to fail to recognize that
the liturgical life of the church informs believers and shapes them in
their faith—that it's the place in which we meet God *for us* and the
framework within which he forgives our sins. It's a both/and, not an
either/or.

Postscript

Ritual and Man's True Problem

On Sunday, June 12, 2016 Omar Mateen walked into an Orlando nightclub and ruthlessly killed forty-nine people and wounded fifty-three others, making it the deadliest attack on U.S. soil since the terrorist attacks on 9/11. During the trial of Mateen's wife as an accomplice (which she was acquitted of), federal investigators revealed that they believed Disney World had been Mateen's primary target. Robert Iger, Disney's CEO, relates that CCTV footage shows Mateen walking back and forth in front of the entrance near Disney's House of Blues.[1] Due to a heavy metal concert that night there was extra security (five armed police officers)—and after casing the area for a few minutes, Mateen could be seen walking back to his car.

Security cameras picked up two weapons in his possession—a semiautomatic rifle and a semiautomatic pistol—that were hidden inside a child's stroller, along with a baby blanket that was still in the package. Investigators suspected that he planned on covering up the weapons with the blanket and wheeling them up to the entrance before pulling them out. The evidence from Mateen's phone, which was found at the scene of the shooting, showed that he got back into his car and searched for nightclubs in Orlando. He drove to the first club that came up but there was construction in front of the entrance and the traffic was backed up. Pulse was the second result, where he ended up committing the massacre.

---

[1] Robert Iger, *The Ride of a Lifetime: Lessons Learned From 15 Years as CEO of the Walt Disney Company* (New York, 2019), x–xii.

Tragedies like this remind us that evil is all too real. It's hard to imagine what could drive someone to inflict such violence on innocent people and upend the lives of entire families. It seems senseless, as if the acts are committed for the sake of suffering itself. While we feel sadness and empathy, we also know that—thankfully—things like this are the exception rather than the rule and are therefore remote. But because they are, we can easily be led to believe that evil is a marginal phenomenon in the world;[2] and this can lead us to believe that it can be eliminated by singling out the perpetrators one at a time. Attempting to do so, however, brings on the realization that the more we try to eliminate evil, the more it pops up in other areas—even in what's supposed to be good, including the social structures designed to repress it. Still, we tend to think of it as remote, so when it does strike us personally we usually deflect and place blame on others—on those closest to us, on our friends, family, co-workers, and even the social structures of society. Rarely do we pause to consider what really lies within.

Here, we'll attempt to do precisely that and consider the biblical view of evil, which is starkly different than what's fashionable today. In contrast to the idea that it's primarily to be found in others, Christianity finds its root in the individual, in each one of us. What we'll see is that not only are we sinful from the inside out, but that religiously we're always looking for the next thing that can tantalize and facilitate our relentless drive for self-aggrandization. Because of this, sin is our primary problem and has to be dealt with head-on and continuously. But how? We'll argue that a ritual framework is best suited for forcing us to confront what ails us; that it provides the mental and spiritual space necessary for us to recognize our true situation, while opening us up to be newly receptive to Christ's redemptive work on the cross.

Before diving into the biblical details, however, let's begin by taking a look at the big picture.

---

[2] Wolfhart Pannenberg, *Systematic Theology*, Vol. 2, trans. by Geoffrey W. Bromiley (Grand Rapids, 1994), 237.

What Man Can Do

In his recent best-seller, Jordan Peterson notes that as human beings
we have a unique understanding of our vulnerabilities. We know
exactly how and where we can be hurt, and why; what makes us suffer; how dread and pain can be inflicted on us, and how we can be
exploited. But this means we know how we can consciously terrify
others; how we can hurt and humiliate them for faults we know only
too well; how we can torture them, slowly and terribly, and exploit
them. "Only man," says Peterson, "could conceive of the rack, the
iron maiden and the thumbscrew. Only man will inflict suffering for
the sake of suffering. That is the best definition of evil I have been
able to formulate. Animals can't imagine that, but humans, with
their excruciating, semi-divine capacities, most certainly can. And
with this realization we have well-nigh full legitimization of the idea,
very unpopular in modern intellectual circles, of Original Sin."[3]

Simply put, human beings have a tremendous capacity for
wrongdoing. We can and do voluntarily make things worse with full
knowledge of what we're doing. As Peterson asks, who among us can
deny the sense of guilt—that sense of inherent corruption and capacity for wrongdoing—that pervades human experience? And who can
avoid noting that without that guilt man is only one step away from
psychopathy? One look at the totalitarian horrors of the twentieth
century, with its concentration camps, forced labor, and murderous
ideologies should be enough to convince even the most hardened
skeptic of man's innate capacity for evil. At Auschwitz, guards who
were as human as the rest of us, would force an inmate to carry a
hundred-pound sack of wet salt from one side of the large com-
pound to the other—and then back again. All for senseless torment.
All for the mere making an art of pain and suffering.

Communists of the Soviet Union killed millions of their own
people as well. Aleksandr Solzhenitsyn wrote of the horrors when
tens of millions were stripped of employment, family, identity, and
life. All to dehumanize a fellow being, to reduce him or her to the
status of a parasite, to torture and slaughter with no consideration of

---

[3] Jordan B. Peterson, *12 Rules for Life: An Antidote to Chaos* (Canada, 2018),
54–55.

innocence or guilt.[4] In the 1930s, Stalinists sent two million kulaks (the richest peasants) to Siberia. From the communist perspective, kulaks had gained wealth by plundering those around them and deserved their fate. Wealth signified oppression and private property was considered theft. More than thirty thousand kulaks were shot on the spot. Many more died at the hands of their unproductive neighbors who used the communist ideals as a mask for their murderous intent.

The kulaks were driven naked into the streets, beaten and forced to dig their own graves. The women were raped and their belongings "expropriated," meaning of course that everything was stolen. Kulaks sent to Siberia faced the most horrid conditions and many died, including children, from typhoid, measles, and scarlet fever. These "parasitical" kulaks were, however, the most skillful and hardworking farmers; and as you might expect, with their elimination agricultural output crashed. Six million people died of starvation in the Ukraine. Closer to home, soldiers who develop post-traumatic stress often do so not because of what they saw, but because of something they did. Now and then, Peterson points out, something possesses a naive farm-boy from Iowa, and he turns monstrous.[5] He massacres infants of My Lai and rapes and kills women—all as he watches himself do it and with some dark part of him enjoying it.

Lest we think we can wall off evil from the outside and create boundaries that will keep us free, we need to realize that it would appear within. We're the problem, not just them. Solzhenitsyn perceptively insisted, the line between good and evil cuts through the heart of every human being.[6] As Peterson points out, the human mind has an enormous capacity to deceive, scheme, manipulate, falsify, and mislead. A big part of this is that human rationality is flawed and subject to the single worst temptation: to raise what it knows now (or thinks it knows) to the status of an absolute. This means that reason falls in love with itself and its own productions. Further, it elevates and worships them as absolutes: "To say it again: it is the

[4] Jordan B. Peterson, *12 Rules for Life*, 196–197, 308–310.

[5] Jordan B. Peterson, *12 Rules for Life*, 180–181.

[6] Jordan B. Peterson, *12 Rules for Life*, 47.

greatest temptation of the rational faculty to glorify its own capacity and its own productions and to claim that in the face of its theories nothing transcendent or outside its domain need exist. That means that all important facts have been discovered. This means that nothing important remains unknown."[7]

Scripture: Man and Sin

Peterson's willingness to highlight the idea of original sin is somewhat unique with today's intellectual elite, who see man as basically good and evil as something that happens—out there—but can be ultimately stamped out. It's become fashionable to belittle, despite overwhelming evidence to the contrary, the biblical view that sin and evil spring from the individual. And Peterson deserves credit for bringing this prejudice to the surface and showing it for what it is.

Scripture, however, is even more pointed in its analysis. From its perspective, everything man does that departs from God's law is sin; that is, everything we do that's not pleasing and acceptable to God. St. John defines sin as "lawlessness" (1 John 3:4), with the law being summed up in the Ten Commandments (Ex. 20:1–17) and given its fullest expression in the New Testament (Rom. 13:8–10). Not only does man fail to conform to the law, but he also actively opposes it; meaning that he's destitute of righteousness and in active rebellion against it. So it's not just that man permits himself to be seduced by the devil, but that he also runs after evil in order to possess it (Gen. 3:16–17; John 8:44).

While some may argue, as did the Pharisees, that sin is only in the doing, Jesus says otherwise in the Sermon on the Mount. Yes, sin manifests itself in our actions, but it's out of the human heart that evil flows (Matt. 15:19). "You have heard that the ancients were told," says Jesus in this pointed sermon, "'You shall not commit murder' . . . But I say to you that everyone who is angry with his brother shall be guilty before the court; and whoever says to his brother, 'You good-for-nothing,' shall be guilty before the supreme court; and whoever says, 'You fool,' shall be guilty enough to go into the fiery hell." And again

---

[7] Jordan B. Peterson, *12 Rules for Life*, 217–218.

he continues: "You have heard that it was said, 'You shall not commit adultery'; but I say to you that everyone who looks at a woman with lust for her has already committed adultery with her in his heart" (Matt. 5:21–22, 27–28). While it manifests itself in our actions, such as murder, theft, or adultery, sin originates in the heart. "'That which proceeds out of the man, that is what defiles the man. For from within, out of the heart of men, proceed evil thoughts, fornications, thefts, murders, adulteries, deeds of coveting and wickedness, as well as deceit, sensuality, envy, slander, pride and foolishness. All these evil things proceed from within and defile the man'" (Mark 7:20–23). "You desire truth in the innermost being," David once said (Ps. 51:6), but since the fountain has been polluted in fallen man the waters flowing from it are unclean.[8]

Though guilty before God through sin (Gen. 2:17; Gal. 3:10; Rom. 6:23), man willingly suppresses the harsh truth about himself and is incapable of seeing himself objectively. Because of this Paul says (Rom. 1:18ff.) that the wrath of God is revealed against all mankind, which willingly suppresses the truth in unrighteousness, because that which is known about God is evident to them. "For since the creation of the world His invisible attributes, His eternal power and divine nature, have been clearly seen, being understood through what has been made, so that they are without excuse." Even though people know God, they refuse to honor him and become fools who glory in their own speculations. Their hearts are darkened, and they exchange the glory of God for an image of themselves; they become their own unhappy and pathetic gods. Paul continues (Rom. 1:28–32):

> And just as they did not see fit to acknowledge God any longer, God gave them over to a depraved mind, to do those things which are not proper, being filled with all unrighteousness, wickedness, greed, evil; full of envy, murder, strife, deceit, malice; they are gossips, slanderers, haters of God, insolent, arrogant, boastful, inventors of evil, disobedient to parents, without understanding, untrustworthy, unloving,

---

[8] John Theodore Mueller, *Christian Dogmatics: A Handbook of Doctrinal Theology for Pastors, Teachers, and Laymen* (St. Louis, 1955), 224.

unmerciful; and although they know the ordinance of God, that those who practice such things are worthy of death, they not only do the same, but also give hearty approval to those who practice them.

Elsewhere Paul presses the point even further, saying we're all dead in trespasses and sin and by nature children of wrath (Col. 2:13; Eph. 2:1–3). Jew and Gentile alike are all under the curse of sin: "There is none righteous, not even one; there is none who understands, there is none who seeks for God" (Rom. 3:9ff.). And in one of scripture's most poignant and vulnerable passages (Rom. 7:14–25), Paul explicitly confesses:

> For what I am doing, I do not understand; for I am not practicing what I would like to do, but I am doing the very thing I hate. But if I do the very thing I do not want to do, I agree with the Law, confessing that the Law is good. So now, no longer am I the one doing it, but sin which dwells in me. For I know that nothing good dwells in me, that is, in my flesh; for the willing is present in me, but the doing of the good is not. For the good that I want, I do not do, but I practice the very evil that I do not want. But if I am doing the very thing I do not want, I am no longer the one doing it, but sin which dwells in me. . . . Wretched man that I am!

We, with Paul, practice the very evil we don't want to because sin causes rash and false judgments about spiritual things and we harden ourselves against God (Acts 7:51; 17:18).[9] Man is a slave to sin, scripture tells us (Rom. 6:17, 20; Heb. 2:15), and the mind set on it is "hostile toward God; for it does not subject itself to the law of God, for it is not even able to do so" (Rom. 8:7). Making things worse is that man is so blinded he regards the Gospel as foolishness (1 Cor. 1:23; 2:14) and seeks hope in the very law which condemns him (Gal. 3:1ff.; Eph. 4:17–18). Even man's good deeds are ego-centric and don't flow from a true love of God but from a love of self, ever aiming to get praise and credit from the world (Matt. 23:25–28).[10]

---

[9] John Theodore Mueller, *Christian Dogmatics*, 219–221.

[10] Wolfhart Pannenberg, *Systematic Theology*, Vol. 2, 238, 244, 256, 263.

With all this in mind, let's bring it together by noting three primary effects of sin. First, by nature we're spiritually dead (Rom. 5:12) inasmuch as we've lost the divine image and have become alienated from God and corrupt in the entirety of our nature (Gen. 5:3).[11] Second, we'll experience temporal death with all the misery and disease that come with it (Gen. 3:16–19). Third, we face eternal death in light of our condemnation by the law (2 Thess. 1:9; Rom. 3:19–23). While stark, these realities have to be emphasized since man in his depravity refuses to acknowledge what the law teaches about sin and its consequences, even though his conscience accuses and condemns him (Rom. 1:32; 2:15).

Where the Rubber Meets the Road

If this all sounds a bit theoretical, consider this. Evidence suggests that we're predisposed to engage in unwarranted judgment of others, with many studies showing that we instantaneously make what Robert Sapolsky refers to as Us/Them distinctions. He points out that the brain groups faces by race, gender, or social status within a few hundred milliseconds—all based on minimal cues.[12] We're more prosocial with those we think are part of our in-group, even with people who share the most meaningless traits with us. In one study, subjects talked with a researcher who, unbeknownst to them, did or didn't mimic their movements (for instance, leg crossing). Mimicry is pleasing and activates mesolimbic dopamine, which made the subjects more willing to help with things like picking up a dropped pen. This was an unconscious Us-ness that was born from someone slouching in a chair like you.

Further, we have a propensity for generating biased Us/Thems from arbitrary differences. This occurs when we assign an arbitrary marker such as dress, ornamentation, or regional accent to a particular culture's values and beliefs. That they are arbitrary is shown in the fact that there is nothing intrinsic to clothes and accents that

---

[11] John Theodore Mueller, *Christian Dogmatics*, 215.

[12] Robert M. Sapolsky, *Behave: The Biology of Humans at our Best and Worst* (New York, 2017), 388–390.

necessarily links them with values and beliefs;[13] those are associations we apply and then substitute in our judgment of Thems. And the Us/Them distinction arises early as shown by its emergence in the very young. Already by three or four years of age, kids group people by race and gender, have more negative views of Them, and perceive other-race faces as being angrier than same-race faces. Infants even learn same-race faces better than other-race.

Sapolksy notes that Us/Them-ing usually involves inflating the merits of Us concerning core values—we're more correct, moral, wise, worthy and knowledgeable about what God (or the gods) want, about the economy, and raising kids. We also inflate the merits of our arbitrary markers, which as you might imagine can force twisted logic. Further, it's been shown in economic games that players are more trusting, generous, and cooperative with in-group than with out-group members—even when players know that the groupings were arbitrary. Sports fans are more likely to come to the aid of an injured spectator if he's wearing a home-team insignia. And people will more readily forgive an Us than a Them, which is often rationalized with "we screw up because of special circumstances; They screw up because that's how They are."[14]

At its core Us-Them-ing is emotional and automatic, with our thoughts being post-hoc justifications for feelings and intuitions we use to convince ourselves we've come to our conclusions rationally. In other words, our thoughts run to catch up with our emotional selves, searching for a plausible fabrication that explains why we're critical of Them. And it's even worse with groups, which tend to be more competitive and aggressive than individual interactions between Us-es and Thems—meaning, groups tend to amplify rather than moderate extremes in individuals.

At the heart of Us/Them-ing probably lies man's tendency toward moralism, which manifests itself in an inability to accept solidarity with those who become entangled in sin's destructive power. Jesus refers to this in the parable of the Pharisee and tax collector (Luke 18:9–14). In the parable, the Pharisee thanks God that he's not

---

[13] Robert M. Sapolsky, *Behave*, 391–395.
[14] Robert M. Sapolsky, *Behave*, 395, 400, 404.

like other sinners while the tax collector beats his breast and says, "God, be merciful to me, the sinner!" "I tell you," says Jesus, "this man [tax collector] went to his house justified rather than the other; for everyone who exalts himself will be humbled, but he who humbles himself will be exalted."

What Jesus makes clear, as with the Sermon on the Mount, is that sin's universality forbids moralistic hypocrisy. The fact of original sin demands that we preserve solidarity with evildoers, in whose conduct the sin that's at work in all of us finds expression.[15] Central to this is the biblical insistence that sin precedes all individual acts, such that we're each alienated from God, and any attempt to weaken that fact opens the door to the moralism that seeks evil in others and produces self-destructive guilt. Our voluntary committing of sin is enough to make us each guilty before God. At no point can we separate ourselves from sin, and we have to recognize that the evil of sin is our own. Thus, man's moralism is unjustified and only produces a false sense of superiority over others, with whom in reality he stands on equal sinful ground.

Sin's Allure

How does sin actually deceive us? Summing up the law's commandments with, "You shall not covet" (Rom. 7:7–8), Paul provides insight into its real power over us and perverted nature—namely, its manifestation in evil desire. Sin expresses itself in desires that are against the commands of God, and therefore against God.[16] Taking its opportunity through the law, which tells us God's will, sin produces opposite desires; so that what was latent sin becomes blatant sin in our desires that are contrary to God's commands. With this Paul shows that desires, even though they haven't produced any action, are still sin. This doesn't mean that desire is bad in itself. What's bad is when our will identifies itself with desire instead of raising itself above mere self-seeking.

But why is desiring the law's opposite so tantalizing? Because sin through our desire promises us a fuller and richer life.[17] For "sin,

---

[15] Wolfhart Pannenberg, *Systematic Theology*, Vol. 2, 238.

[16] Wolfhart Pannenberg, *Systematic Theology*, Vol. 2, 240, 247.

[17] Wolfhart Pannenberg, *Systematic Theology*, Vol. 2, 265.

taking an opportunity," says Paul, "through the commandment, deceived me and through it killed me" (Rom. 7:11). Sin uses the law as a means through which it stirs up the rebellion and aggression against God and his commandments that live in our hearts. Our desire, which is oriented to what's forbidden, deceives us into thinking we have a better idea of what will promote life (Gen. 3:6). It seduces us to think that God's commands are inimical to life, as though faithfully observing his will would hold us back and force us to renounce life's riches. This is exactly the picture we see as Adam and Eve take the forbidden fruit in the Garden.

What Paul is saying is that the law becomes a means by which sin achieves dominion, as it actively turns away from God and embraces all that the law forbids. It does so by setting reason and the traditional moral order aside. Under its pressure we come into collision with both the law, which we believe hampers our true happiness, and our own reason—which agrees with God's law but is also a slave to the blind drive for self-fulfillment. "For I joyfully concur with the law of God in the inner man, but I see a different law in the members of my body, waging war against the law of my mind and making me a prisoner of the law of sin which is in my members" (Rom. 7:22–23). Pannenberg's comments are instructive:

> Even after two thousand years this description is still so true to life that commentary is hardly needed. The different forms of frenzied conduct offer impressive examples of the way in which the drive for self-fulfillment leads to a frenzy that will finally spoil life, narrow the actual field of freedom of decision, and not infrequently end in death. In spite of some obvious differences . . . all of us according to Paul have ultimately fallen victim in some way to a greediness for life that in all cases ends in death. "The wages of sin is death" (Rom. 6:23; cf. 7:11).[18]

We should take special note of Paul's link between sin and death. He recognizes that sin as separation from God already implies death as its consequence. Since God alone is the source of life, and

---

[18] Wolfhart Pannenberg, *Systematic Theology*, Vol. 2, 265–266, 270–271.

sin is alienation from him, death is the natural result. Further, being in opposition to our creator, we're also in opposition to other human beings, animals, and the earth (Gen. 3:14–19). Despite this, God in his mercy intervenes by limiting the radical consequences that sin unleashes, even though in sin we fail to appreciate it. In his patience with sinners we see God's continued creative activity in his government of the world, which over and over brings good out of evil. "Important in this regard is the fact that by the continued creative activity of his Spirit, God constantly rescues his creatures from the entanglement of self-centeredness that comes as a result of their anxieties and desires."[19]

Man's Speculative Addiction

We'll conclude our examination of sin by returning to an observation mentioned earlier by Jordan Peterson, in which he points out the fact that man tends to fall in love with his own ideas—and in doing so he then worships them as absolutes. Aside from his refreshingly honest appraisal, what's interesting is how much it parallels the position of the sixteenth century Reformer, Martin Luther, who had similar concerns on purely scriptural grounds. Because Luther explores this aspect of man's behavior so deeply, his thinking will be especially relevant as we flesh out the consequences for corporate worship.

To begin, Luther observes that a consequence of sin is that man's mind naturally gets lost in ungrounded speculations. Never idle, it constantly "imagines" sinful thoughts. "For it is always opposed to God's Law; it lies in sin; it is under the wrath of God; and it cannot be freed of this evil by its own powers . . ."[20] If you want a true picture of man, he says, then recognize that he's a rational animal with a heart that imagines evil against God's law and against his neighbor. "Holy scripture ascribes to man a reason that is not idle but is always imagining something. But it calls this imagination evil, ungodly, and execrable." Luther's point is that the very formation of man's thinking is evil.

---

[19] Wolfhart Pannenberg, *Systematic Theology*, Vol. 2, 274–275.

[20] *Luther's Works*, Vol. 2, ed. Jaroslav Pelikan (Saint Louis, 1960), 122–123.

To be more specific, the mind is caught up in an unrelenting inquisitiveness, which lies at the heart of original sin itself; which is why man feels compelled to get to God through his speculation.[21] Luther points out—based on Gen. 3—that in man's fall from paradise, his reason wasn't satisfied and wanted to rise higher and know God in a different manner than provided in his Word. In other words, Adam and Eve were not content to stay with what God had said but wanted something more. The consequences of their rebellion against God then followed as a matter of course. Once they disregarded God's Word they turned to their own thoughts, from which they could only form false ideas about God, salvation, and themselves.

Like Adam and Eve, we are alienated from God through sin, and we all lack true knowledge of not just God, but also of ourselves and our dire condition. But this is where Luther's insight becomes poignant. Because we can't be without worship of something, we invent our own god as we either lack or disregard God's word. And though some knowledge of God is available through creation, we misuse it in the interest of self-exaltation.[22] Just as we use good works to justify ourselves and conceal our anxiety about sin, so we misuse the knowledge of God to puff up our already over-blown egos. Yet this only furthers our illusions about our true situation. Speculation, Luther argues, then becomes a terrible decease with only one cure: to know God in the crucified Christ.

To capture Luther's thinking, it's helpful to understand a distinction he made between the "hidden" and "revealed" God. Because by nature God is invisible and we can't know him as such (the hidden God), he's condescended to our level and taken our flesh in the person of Jesus (the revealed God). That means that outside of Jesus's physical body we have no saving knowledge of God. We can't rise to heaven and know the "absolute" God any more than Moses could

---

[21] *Luther's Works*, Vol. 5, ed. Jaroslav Pelikan (Saint Louis, 1968), 44–45. David R. Andersen, *Martin Luther—The Problem of Faith and Reason: A Reexamination in Light of the Epistemological and Christological Issues* (Eugene, OR, 2012), 90ff.

[22] Jürgen Moltmann, *The Crucified God: The Cross of Christ as the Foundation and Criticism of Christian Theology* (Minneapolis, 1993), 211.

see God face to face on the mountain (Moses only saw God's "back" as he passed by, Ex. 33:23). We'd be crushed by his majesty just like Moses. For this reason, he reveals himself in a way that speaks to our sin and weakness: in an infant child and most fully in a cross built for slaves, outcasts, and criminals.

If Luther is right—and all the evidence says he is—that human nature is such that it can't be without the worship of something (even if it's the self), then we must take our thoughts captive to God as he reveals himself in the crucified Jesus. Paul says in 1 Tim. 6:16 that God dwells in unapproachable light. It's because of this that he's spoken to us in these last days "in His Son, whom He appointed heir of all things, through whom also He made the world" (Heb. 1:2). This is why Luther insists that those who adhere to Christ understand God, while those who boast of visions, revelations, and enlighten-ments are overwhelmed by God's majesty and remain in ignorance. "The incarnate Son of God is, therefore, the covering in which the Divine Majesty presents Himself to us with all His gifts, and does so in such a manner that there is no sinner too wretched to be able to approach Him with the firm assurance of obtaining pardon."[23] Beyond this, there's the additional problem that Satan transforms himself into an angel of light to deceive even Christians into false practices (2 Cor. 11:14), making the only safe path that which was revealed by Jesus and his word.[24] Luther once warned that if you see someone ascending to heaven and putting one foot there, pull him back; for if he puts both feet there, he'll find that he's not in heaven, but in hell. Stark, but as true today as then.

Thus, we should restrain our speculation and remain within the bounds placed before us by God. He wanted us to walk on the earth, not the clouds—to follow his word and command and not inquire, as did Adam and Eve, about the reasons for his command. In doing so they put themselves in the place of God, and in effect wished to be gods. We too want to be our own gods, which we have to bring captive our entire Christian lives by knowing "nothing . . . except Jesus Christ and Him crucified" (1 Cor. 2:2). It was, and still is, Satan's primary

---

[23] *Luther's Works*, Vol. 2, 46, 49.

[24] *Luther's Works*, Vol. 3, ed. Jaroslav Pelikan (Saint Louis, 1961), 108, 139.

goal to lead us to disregard God's promises and commands through subjective religious ecstasy. David Steinmetz sums this aspect of Luther's thinking up nicely:

> Because God is hidden outside his revelation, Luther is adamantly opposed to any attempt to uncover the naked being of God through speculative reason or religious ecstasy. The dazzling glory of the being of the hidden God would blind and terrify us if we could uncover it. God must hide his glory in his revelation; he must accommodate himself to our finitude and sin. The gospel is the good news that we are not required to ascend to God through prayer, self-denial, and the discipline of reason and desire. God has descended to us as a child on its mother's lap. He has met us at the bottom rung of the ladder, on our level rather than on his. Holiness may alarm and terrify us, but no one is frightened of a child.[25]

Luther often referred to Jacob's dream in which he saw a ladder that was set on earth with its top reaching heaven—and on which the angels of God were ascending and descending (Gen. 28:12). Jesus refers to this when he tells Nathanael (John 1:51), "Truly, truly, I say to you, you will see the heavens opened and the angels of God ascending and descending on the Son of Man." Pointing to the mystery of the incarnation (God becoming man in Jesus), the ladder signifies that in one and the same person there is true God and man—and upon which the angels of God ascend and descend. Perhaps more pointedly than anyone else in church history, Luther insists that Jesus is the connecting link between heaven and earth, and the angels descend worshiping him as though there were no God up in heaven. In reference to Hebrews where we read, "Let all God's angels worship Him," Luther says this: "They adore Him as He now lies in the manger at His mother's breasts. Indeed, they adore Him on the cross, when He descends into hell, when He has been subjected to sin and hell, when He bears all the sins of the whole world. And they submit themselves forever to this lowest One."[26] Because

---

[25] David C. Steinmetz, *Luther in Context* (Grand Rapids, 1995) 25.

[26] *Luther's Works*, Vol. 5, 220.

God revealed himself in suffering to the point of death on a criminal's cross, all of our speculations about him are reduced to ashes.[27] We can know God only where he's promised to be found: the flesh of Jesus, which is offered for us only in his word and sacraments.[28]

Jürgen Moltmann adds that in revealing himself in the crucified Christ, God contradicts our god-complex and shatters our arrogance; he kills our gods and brings us back to our despised and abandoned humanness. He makes us face our true condition. Man in his corruption is in reality inhuman in the sense that he's not as God intended; and that's because he's under the compulsion of self-justification and deification. He exalts himself because he can't ensure himself the way he is, and he can't quell his constant anxiety without putting himself in the place of God. Unable to let God be God, he makes himself the unhappy god of his own self.[29] All of this only gives his inhumanity more fuel. But God reveals himself in the contradiction of Christ's suffering, which is against all that we regard as exalted, beautiful, and religious; it's against all that dehumanized man seeks for himself and therefore perverts.

This is all to say that we know God, not in his glory, but only in his suffering on the cross where we see his true heart and will. "The 'ascent of knowledge of God' takes place in the 'decent of self-knowledge', and the two come together in the knowledge of Christ."[30] Carl Jung once said that "No tree can grow to Heaven unless its roots reach down to Hell," meaning that upward movement isn't possible without a corresponding move down. But "Who is willing to do that?" Peterson asks, "Do you really want to meet who's in charge, at the very bottom of the most wicked thoughts?" The brutal truth lying in each of us, he argues, is why enlightenment is so rare. Avoiding what's beneath is like trying to cure a disease by merely treating its symptoms.[31]

---

[27] Marc Lienhard, Luther: Witness to Jesus Christ (Minneapolis, 1982), 341–343

[28] Marc Lienhard, Luther, 233.

[29] Jürgen Moltmann, The Crucified God, 69–72, 211–212.

[30] Jürgen Moltmann, The Crucified God, 212.

[31] Jordan B. Peterson, 12 Rules for Life, 180.

In spite of this, in humbling himself and becoming flesh Jesus takes up suffering, anxious man into his situation and takes it seriously. "In becoming weak, impotent, vulnerable and mortal, he frees man from the quest for powerful idols and protective compulsions and makes him ready to accept his humanity, his freedom and his mortality."[32] If man sees and believes God in the suffering and dying Jesus, he is set free from the concern to be his own god. The cross then liberates dehumanized man from his fatal obsession with being a god himself. "It sets him free from his inhuman hubris, to restore his true human nature. It makes the *homo incurvatus in se* [the man turned in on himself] once again open to God and his neighbor, and gives Narcissus the power to love someone else."[33]

In the suffering Jesus, God brings us back to himself by meeting us at the bottom rung of the ladder and keeps us on earth as we face who we truly are: sinners lost in our hubris and wrapped in self-centered concern. Because in Adam we tried to scale the heavens and be equal with God, he descended to us to bring us back to knowledge of himself. This is the significance of his becoming man. The person who knows God in the lowly, weak, and dying Christ, knows him in the humanity he himself has rejected and despised. And that brings to ashes his illusory equality with God, which has dehumanized him, and restores to him his humanity.[34]

Conclusion

If anything is clear, it's that sin is our primary problem and it must be confronted. Turned-in-on-ourselves we all struggle with Narcissus, naturally defaulting to a love of self that alienates us from both God and neighbor. On that scripture is direct, despite our tendency to deny or suppress it. Sin is deeper and more far-reaching than any of us realize, even in our most vulnerable moments. Not only that, but our minds are active in forming baseless speculations about God, the world, and ourselves; and all in a way that bolsters our ego and

---

[32] Jürgen Moltmann, *The Crucified God*, 303.

[33] Jürgen Moltmann, *The Crucified God*, 72.

[34] Jürgen Moltmann, *The Crucified God*, 212–213.

feeds the notion that we're our own god. Any attempt to lessen sin's impact is bound to falsely infuse the law with a moralistic overtone and dilute the true meaning of the Gospel. Because of that, any worship claiming to have the crucified Lord at its center must deal with the harsh reality of sin; and not superficially as is so common today, but explicitly and deliberately.

As we've seen throughout this book, this is something that ritual does especially well. As Mary Douglas comments, ritual focuses attention by framing, which it does by refreshing the memory and linking the present with the past; and as a result, it adds to our perception of things. Or it might be truer to say that it changes perception because it changes what we're paying attention to. It focuses us on details we lose sight of in our frantic world and forces us back to basics that, left to ourselves, we'd try to ignore. "So it is not enough to say that ritual helps us to experience more vividly what we would have experienced anyway. It is not merely like the visual aid which illustrates the verbal instructions for opening cans and cases. If it were just a kind of dramatic map or diagram of what is known it would always follow experience. But in fact, ritual does not play this secondary role. It can come first in formulating experience. It can permit knowledge of what would otherwise not be known at all."[35] In this way, ritual brings our destructive self-centered and speculative impulses captive.

By setting the gravity of our sin and its consequences within a ritual context, it's guaranteed we face it in a way not possible otherwise. The liturgical act of corporate confession changes our perception by changing what we focus on, which in that moment draws our minds to the reality of our sin and death, making us newly receptive to the words of absolution. Moltmann was right to say that the ascent of knowledge of God can take place only in the decent of self-knowledge, which makes that ritual space all the more critical—especially in a culture which does everything it can to deny the reality of sin.

---

[35] Mary Douglas, *Purity and Danger: An Analysis of the Concepts of Pollution and Taboo* (London, 1979), 64.

Bibliography

Andersen, David R. *Faithless to Fearless: The Event That Changed the World*. Irvine, CA: 1517 Publishing, 2019.

———. *Martin Luther—The Problem of Faith and Reason: A Reexamination in Light of the Epistemological and Christological Issues*. Eugene, OR: Wipf and Stock, 2012.

Ante-Nicene Fathers. 10 Vols., eds. Alexander Roberts and James Donaldson. Peabody, MA: Hendrickson Publishers, 2012.

Arndt, William F. and F. Wilbur Gingrich. *A Greek-English Lexicon of the New Testament and Other Early Christian Literature*, Second Edition. Chicago: The University of Chicago Press, 1979.

Ashton, Kevin. *How To Fly A Horse*. New York: Doubleday, 2015.

Bauckham, Richard. *Jesus and the Eyewitnesses: The Gospels as Eyewitness Testimony*. Grand Rapids, MI: William B. Eerdmans Publishing Company, 2006.

Bloom, Allan. *The Closing of the American Mind*. New York: Simon and Schuster, 1987.

Brewer, William F. "What is Autobiographical Memory?" in *Autobiographical Memory*, ed. David C. Rubin. Cambridge, UK: Cambridge University Press, 1986.

Brown, Brené. *Rising Strong: How the Ability to Reset Transforms the Way We Live, Love, Parent, and Lead*. New York: Random House, 2017.

Brown, Harold O. J. *Heresies: The Image of Christ in the Mirror of Heresy and Orthodoxy from the Apostles to the Present*. Grand Rapids, MI: Baker Book House, 1984.

Brown, Tim. "Design Thinking" in *Harvard Business Review*, June, 2008.

Burridge, Richard A. *What Are the Gospels? A Comparison with Graeco-Roman Biography*. Grand Rapids, MI: William B. Eerdmans Publishing Company, 2004.

Burton, Robert A. *On Being Certain: Believing You Are Right Even When You're Not*. New York: St. Martin's Griffin, 2008.

Catmull, Ed with Amy Wallace. *Creativity Inc.: Overcoming the Unseen Forces That Stand in the Way of True Inspiration*. New York: Random House, 2014.

Chemnitz, Martin. *The Two Nature's in Christ*, trans. J. A. O. Preus. St. Louis, MO: Concordia Publishing House, 1971.

Chesterton, G. K. *Orthodoxy*. San Francisco: Ignatius Press, 1908.

Clear, James. *Atomic Habits: An Easy & Proven Way to Build Good habits & Break Bad Ones*. New York: Avery, 2018.

Cohen, Geoffrey L. "Party Over Policy: The Dominating Impact of Group Influence on Political Beliefs" in *Journal of Personality and Social Psychology*, 2003, Vol. 85, No. 5, p. 808–822.

Collier, Andrew. *Critical Realism: An Introduction to Roy Bhaskar's Philosophy*. New York: Verso, 1994.

Collins, Jim. *Good To Great: Why Some Companies Make the Leap . . . and Others Don't*. New York: Harper Business, 2001.

Craig, William Lane. *Assessing the New Testament Evidence for the Historicity of the Resurrection of Jesus*. New York: Edwin Mellen Press, 1989.

Dalio, Ray. *Principles*. New York: Simon & Schuster, 2017.

Damasio, Antonio. *Descartes' Error: Emotion, Reason, and the Human Brain*. New York: Penguin Books, 1994.

Deming, W. Edwards. *The Essential Deming: Leadership Principles from the Father of Quality* ed. Joyce Nilsson Orsini. New York: McGraw Hill, 2013.

Deutscher, Guy. *Through the Language Glass: Why the World Looks Different in Other Languages*. New York: Picador, 2010.

Douglas, Mary. *Purity and Danger: An Analysis of the Concepts of Pollution and Taboo*. London: Routledge & Kegan Paul, 1979.

Duhigg, Charles. *The Power of Habit: Why We Do What We Do in Life and Business*. New York: Random House Trade Paperbacks, 2014.

Duke, Annie. *Thinking in Bets: Making Smarter Decisions When You Don't Have All the Facts*. New York: Portfolio/Penguin, 2018.

Dunn, James D. G. *Jesus Remembered*. Grand Rapids, MI: William B. Eerdmans Publishing Company, 2003.

Dweck, Carol S. *Mindset: The New Psychology of Success*. New York: Ballantine Books, 2006.

Dyer, Jeff, Hal Gregersen, and Clayton M. Christensen. *The Innovator's DNA: Mastering the Five Skills of Disruptive Innovators*. Boston: Harvard Business Review Press, 2011.

Elster, Jon. *Alchemies of the Mind: Rationality and the Emotions*. Cambridge: Cambridge University Press, 1999.

Ericsson, Anders and Robert Pool. *Peak: Secrets From the New Science of Expertise*. Boston: Eamon Dolan, 2016.

Fitzgerald, F. Scott. "The Crack-Up," https://www.esquire.com/lifestyle/a4310/the-crack-up/.

Furr, Nathan and Jeff Dyer. *The Innovator's Method: Bringing the Lean Startup Into Your Organization*. Boston: Harvard Business Review Press, 2014.

Gaddis, John Lewis. *On Grand Strategy*. New York: Penguin Press, 2018.

Gawande, Atul. *The Checklist Manifesto: How To Get Things Right*. New York: Picador, 2009.

Gerhardsson, Birger. *Memory and Manuscript: Oral Tradition and Written Transmission in Rabbinic Judaism and Early Christianity with Tradition and Transmission in Early Christianity*. Grand Rapids, MI: William B. Eerdmans Publishing Company, 1998.

Gino, Francesca and Michael I. Norton, "Why Rituals Work," https://www.scientificamerican.com/article/why-rituals-work/.

Gladwell, Malcolm. *Blink: The Power of Thinking Without Thinking*. New York: Back Bay Books, 2005.

———. *Outliers: The Story of Success*. New York: Little, Brown and Company, 2008.

Gruber, Howard E. *Darwin on Man: A Psychological Study of Scientific Creativity*. Chicago: The University of Chicago Press, 1981.

Hayek, F. A. *The Fatal Conceit: The Errors of Socialism*, ed. W. W. Bartley III. Chicago: University of Chicago Press, 1989.

Heidegger, Martin. *Poetry, Language, Thought*. New York: Harper-Perennial, 1971.

Hengel, Martin. *Between Jesus and Paul: Studies in the Earliest History of Christianity*. Eugene, OR: Wipf and Stock Publishers, 2003.

————. *Studies in Early Christology*. London: T & T Clark International, 2004.

Hippolytus. *On the Apostolic Tradition*, second edition. New York: St. Vladimir's Seminary Press, 2015.

Hodge, Charles, *Systematic Theology*, Vol. 2. Grand Rapids, MI: Wm. B. Eerdmans Publishing Company, 1986.

Holiday, Ryan. *Stillness Is the Key*. New York: Portfolio/Penguin, 2019.

Holmes, Chet. *The Ultimate Sales Machine: Turbocharge Your Business with Relentless Focus on 12 Key Strategies*. New York: Portfolio, 2007.

Horowitz, Ben. *What You Do Is Who You Are: How to Create Your Business Culture*. New York: Harper Business, 2019.

Hsieh, Tony. *Delivering Happiness: A Path to Profits, Passion, and Purpose*. New York: Business Plus, 2010.

Hurtado, Larry W. *Lord Jesus Christ: Devotion to Jesus in Earliest Christianity*. Grand Rapids, MI: William B. Eerdmans Publishing Company, 2003.

Iger, Robert. *The Ride of a Lifetime: Lessons Learned From 15 Years as CEO of the Walt Disney Company*. New York: Random House, 2019.

Jeremias, Joachim. *The Eucharistic Words of Jesus*. London: SCM Press, 1966.

Just Jr., Arthur A. *Luke 1:1–9:50*. Saint Louis, MO: Concordia Publishing House, 1996.

Kahneman, Daniel. *Thinking, Fast and Slow*. New York: Farrar, Straus and Giroux, 2011.

Kahneman, Daniel and Amos Tversky, "Intuitive Prediction: Biases and Corrective Procedures." Technical Report PTR-1042-77-6, Sponsored by Defense Advanced Research Project Agency, June 1977. https://apps.dtic.mil/dtic/tr/fulltext/u2/a047747.pdf

Kavanagh, Aidan. *The Shape of Baptism: The Rite of Christian Initiation*. Collegeville, MN: The Liturgical Press, 1978.

Kelley, Tom and David Kelley. *Creative Confidence: Unleashing the Creative Potential Within Us All*. New York: Crown Business, 2013.

Kelley, Tom and Jonathan Littman. *The Art of Innovation: Lessons in Creativity from IDEO, America's Leading Design Firm*. New York: Doubleday, 2001.

Kelly, J. N. D. *Early Christian Creeds*, third ed. New York: Longman, 1972.

Kleinig, John. *Hebrews*. Saint Louis: Concordia Publishing House, 2017.

———. *Leviticus*. Saint Louis: Concordia Publishing House, 2003.

———. "Witting or Unwitting Ritualists," Lutheran Theological Journal 22/1 (1988), 13–22.

Lathrop, Gordon W. *Holy Ground: A Liturgical Cosmology*. Minneapolis: Fortress Press, 2003.

———. *Holy Things: A Liturgical Theology*. Minneapolis: Fortress Press, 1998.

LeDoux, Joseph. *The Emotional Brain: The Mysterious Underpinnings of Emotional Life*. New York: Simon & Schuster, 1996.

Leetaru, Kalev. "Using Google's Video AI To Estimate The Average Shot Length In Television News." https://www.forbes.com/sites/kalevleetaru/2019/06/03/using-googles-video-ai-to-estimate-the-average-shot-length-in-television-news/#7f1e2de98e3a.

Lewis, C. S. *A Preface to Paradise Lost*. New York: Oxford University Press, 1967.

Lienhard, Marc. *Luther: Witness to Jesus Christ*. Minneapolis: Augsburg Publishing House, 1982.

Lightfoot, J. B. *The Apostolic Fathers*. Grand Rapids, MI: Baker Book House, 1986.

Luther, Martin. D. M. *Luthers Werke*. Kritische Gesamtausgabe. (Weimar, 1883–).

———. *Luther's Works*. 55 Vols., ed. Jaroslav Pelikan. Saint Louis: Concordia Publishing House, 1958-.

McGonigal, Kelly. *The Upside of Stress: Why Stress is Good For You, and How to Get Good At It*. New York: Avery, 2015.

McGrath, Alister E. *A Scientific Theology: Volume 2—Reality*. Grand Rapids, MI: William B. Eerdmans Publishing Company, 2002.

Metzger, Bruce M. *The Text of the New Testament: Its Transmission, Corruption, and Restoration*. 2nd ed. New York: Oxford University Press, 1968.

Moltmann, Jürgen. *The Crucified God: The Cross of Christ as the Foundation and Criticism of Christian Theology*. Minneapolis, MN: Fortress Press, 1993.

Mueller, John Theodore. *Christian Dogmatics: A Handbook of Doctrinal Theology for Pastors, Teachers, and Laymen.* St. Louis, MO: Concordia Publishing House, 1955.

Pannenberg, Wolfhart. *Systematic Theology*, Volume 2, trans. by Geoffrey W. Bromiley. Grand Rapids, MI: William B. Eerdmans Publishing Company, 1994.

Pelikan, Jaroslav. *The Christian Tradition: A History of the Development of Doctrine*, Vol. 1 The Emergence of the Catholic Tradition (100–600). Chicago: The University of Chicago Press, 1971.

Peterson, Jordan B. *12 Rules for Life: An Antidote to Chaos.* Canada: Random House, 2018.

Porter, Michael E. *Competitive Strategy: Techniques for Analyzing Industries and Competitors.* New York: The Free Press, 1980.

Postman, Neil. *Amusing Ourselves to Death: Public Discourse in the Age of Show Business.* New York: Penguin Books, 1985.

Rosenzweig, Phil. *The Halo Effect . . . and the Eight Other Business Delusions That Deceive Managers.* New York: Free Press, 2007.

Rumelt, Richard P. *Good Strategy—Bad Strategy: The Difference and Why It Matters.* New York: Crown Business, 2011.

Sapolsky, Robert M. *Behave: The Biology of Humans at Our Best and Worst.* New York: Penguin Books, 2017.

Satell, Greg. "The Little Known Secret to Pixar's Creative Success." https://www.forbes.com/sites/gregsatell/2015/05/29/the-little-known-secret-to-pixars-creative-success/#7146f6938b28.

Schmemann, Alexander, trans. Ashleigh E. Moorehouse. *Introduction to Liturgical Theology.* Crestwood, NY: St. Vladimir's Seminary Press, 1966.

Seligman, Martin E. P. *Authentic Happiness: Using the New Positive Psychology to Realize Your Potential for Lasting Fulfillment.* New York: Atria Paperback, 2002.

Seneca, *Letters from a Stoic*, trans. Robin Campbell. New York: Penguin Classics, 1969.

Senn, Frank C. *Introduction to Christian Liturgy.* Minneapolis: Fortress Press, 2012.

Steinmetz, David C. *Luther in Context.* Grand Rapids, MI: Baker Books, 1995.

Taleb, Nassim Nicholas. *Antifragile: Things That Gain From Disorder.* New York: Random House Trade Paperbacks, 2014.

————. *The Black Swan: The Impact of the Highly Improbable*. New York: Random House Trade Paperbacks, 2010.

Theological Dictionary of the New Testament, 10 Vols, ed. Gerhard Kittel and trans. Geoffrey W. Bromiley. Grand Rapids, MI: William B. Eerdmans Publishing Company, 1964–1976.

Tetlock, Philip E. and Dan Gardner. *Superforecasting: The Art and Science of Prediction*. New York: Broadway Books, 2015.

Thaler, Richard H. *Misbehaving: The Making of Behavioral Economics*. New York: W. W. Norton & Company, 2015.

Von Clausewitz, Carl. *On War*. Princeton, NJ: Princeton University Press, 1976.

Wainwright, Geoffrey. *Doxology: The Praise of God in Worship, Doctrine, and Life*. New York: Oxford University Press, 1980.

Walther, C. F. W., *The Proper Distinction Between Law and Gospel*. St. Louis: Concordia Publishing House, 1986.